The Enemy of All

The Enemy of All

Piracy and the Law of Nations

Daniel Heller-Roazen

ZONE BOOKS · NEW YORK

2009

© 2009 Daniel Heller-Roazen
ZONE BOOKS
1226 Prospect Avenue
Brooklyn, NY 11218

Printed in the United States of America.

Distributed by The MIT Press,
Cambridge, Massachusetts, and London, England

Library of Congress Cataloging-in-Publication Data

Heller-Roazen, Daniel.
     The enemy of all : piracy and the law of nations /
Daniel Heller-Roazen.
          p. cm.
     Includes bibliographical references (p.   ) and index.
     ISBN 978-1-890951-94-8
     1. Maritime terrorism. 2. Piracy. 3. Hijacking
of ships. I. Title.

HV6431.H418 2009
364.16'4–DC22

                                        2009002085

ὦ ξεῖνοι, τίνες ἐστέ; πόθεν πλεῖθ᾽ ὑγρὰ κέλευθα;

ἦ τι κατὰ πρῆξιν ἦ μαψιδίως ἀλάλησθε

οἷά τε ληϊστῆρες ὑπεὶρ ἅλα, τοί τ᾽ ἀλόωνται

ψυχὰς παρθέμενοι, κακὸν ἀλλοδαποῖσι φέροντες;

Who are you, strangers? From where have you set sail

Along liquid paths? Do you roam for trade

Or for adventure, crossing the seas, like pirates,

Risking their lives and bringing harm to others?

Homer, *Odyssey* 3.71–74; 9.252–55

Contents

Preface

A book on piracy could be many things. It might constitute a history of criminal seafarers of various kinds: ancient pirates, medieval corsairs and privateers, modern sea dogs, filibusters and buccaneers, and doubtless many others too. Historians have often turned their scholarly attention to the depredators of the sea, whose legal and illegal acts have played a crucial role in social, economic, and political developments across the globe. Today the historical research on piracy constitutes a vast body of scholarship, in which much of great interest can be found. Soon, no doubt, there will also be studies of the implications of the use of the concept of piracy for intellectual and ideal property, such as patents, licenses, and copyrights. An examination of piracy might, moreover, with equal justice provide a history not of pirates but of their changing representations. The catalogues of ancient, medieval, and modern literature contain rich material to be employed in pursuit of such a subject. One could add to them a host of other archives, not least those of the law of nations, in which figures of pirates play fascinating, if relatively minor, roles.

This book offers no such account of piracy. Philosophical and genealogical in its aims, this investigation departs from one legal fact in the history of the West: the fact, namely, that the pirate constitutes the original enemy of the human kind. Long before human rights, humanitarian organizations, and the codification of international law in the early modern period, the statesmen of ancient Rome defined the pirate as "the enemy of all." As Cicero once remarked, there are enemies with whom a lawful state may wage wars, sign treaties and, should circumstances permit, put an end to hostilities. Such are the just enemies of war, who, on account of being in principle the equals of their public opponents, may always lay claim to certain rights. But there is also another type of enemy: an unjust antagonist unworthy of such rights. This is the pirate, whom Cicero, for this reason, calls "the common enemy of all." Commenting on the classical authorities, the medieval scholars of the law offered a paraphrase on that ancient Roman title: they named the pirate "the enemy of the human species." Later, the legal and political philosophers of the modern epoch went one step further. They developed a notion that can be traced directly to that of the pirate. This is the idea of the "enemy of humanity," with whom all, today, are familiar.

The pages that follow reconstruct the genealogy of this idea, defining the various legal, political, and philosophical conditions in which it has been possible to conceive of such an exceptional subject as an "enemy of all."

It may seem superfluous to observe that with such a subject, this book can hardly aim to be either comprehensive or exhaustive. It is doubtless more pertinent to note that, while articulated in sixteen chapters, the book's unity lies in one argument. This argument holds that a limited set of traits constitutes the political and legal question of piracy in the tradition that has its origins in classical antiquity and that has led, by various means, to the international law and politics of modern Europe and its erstwhile colonies.

To be precise, four distinctive characteristics define the problem of piracy. When conjoined, the four traits compose a paradigm, whose historical vicissitudes and philosophical consequences this book traces.

The four characteristics may be summarily enumerated as follows:

1. Piracy involves a region in which exceptional legal rules apply, a region of which the high seas and international air space have been until today the dominant examples.

2. Piracy involves an agent who, committing deeds in such an unusual legal space, displays an antagonism that cannot be defined as that of one individual with respect to another or of one political association with respect to another. Such an antagonism may not possess a single object; it may not discriminate in its target. It appears not as particular but as general; it is often represented as "universal." The title "enemy of all" points to the character of this antagonism.

3. As a consequence of the first and second defining characteristics, piracy brings about the confusion and, in the most extreme cases, the collapse of the distinction between criminal and political categories. Acting outside regions of ordinary jurisdiction and conceived as not opponents of one but as "enemies of all," pirates cannot be considered common criminals, whose place may be defined in the terms of a single civil code. But they also cannot be represented as lawful enemies, for by virtue of their enmity with respect to a general collectivity they fail to constitute an association with which there might be peace as well as war.

4. Finally, by virtue of the third defining trait, piracy entails a transformation of the concept of war. Since "enemies of all" are neither criminals nor belligerents in any accepted sense, the operations carried out against them cannot be formally identical to those employed against a lawful enemy. They must involve the measures used in prosecuting both belligerents and criminals: procedures of external relations and of internal security, technologies of politics, as well as of police.

This project has been motivated from its inception by the hypothesis that the piratical paradigm is today a matter of considerable and even extreme significance. How and why the "enemy of all" has now become a crucial contemporary figure will, the author hopes, come gradually to light in the unfolding of the chapters of this book.

CHAPTER ONE

Beyond the Line

Statesman and orator of the classic age of Rome, Cicero studied the books of the philosophers well. He knew the ancient schools and he was familiar with the branches by which past thinkers had articulated the various dimensions of their work: physics and metaphysics, ethics and logic, the doctrine of the soul as well as that of the best régime. But Cicero accorded one of these many fields a title shared by none other, and for a simple reason: this single domain, he held, possessed the most extended terrain of all. "Many weighty and beneficial matters have been discussed accurately and expansively by philosophers," Cicero commented, "but it is their teachings and their advice on the subject of obligations [*de officiis*] that seem to have the widest practical application."[1] Hence the Roman thinker's decision to dedicate a book of considerable amplitude to their theory, which was to be the great political and legal work of his last years: *On Obligations* (*De officiis*), the three-part treatise thought to have been completed in early December 44 BC.[2] In introducing his work, Cicero insisted on the vast domain to which its subject matter by nature pertained. "In no part of life [*pars vitae*], whether public or private, whether in business or in the home, whether one is working on what concerns oneself or dealing with another," he wrote, "can obligations ever be lacking." They are the source of all moral distinctions, for, he added, "on the discharge of such obligations depends all that is right, and on their neglect all that is wrong in life."[3]

In the first book of his treatise on duties, Cicero enumerates and classifies various types of moral obligation, arguing that they are of more than a single "degree" (*gradus*).[4] The tightest link (*arterior colligatio*), he explains, is that which binds the members of a family among themselves. Since the desire to procreate is the "common possession of all living creatures," and since man is no exception to this rule, "the first fellowship," Cicero reasons, must be that which "exists within marriage itself"; the next, that between parents and children.[5] These ties compose the fabric of the home, in which everything is in common. They also constitute the foundation of the city, making of the household "the nursery, as it were, of the city-state" (*quasi seminarium rei publicae*). Next among duties are those that bind siblings to each other and, at a stage of further removal, one finds the responsibilities that link first and second cousins. When a family grows too large to share a single home, Cicero explains, the young naturally leave the household: they "go out into other dwellings, as into colonies." Still, he notes, obligations do not cease. In time, there will be new bonds of marriage, from which more relations will be formed. "Ties of common blood" will hold men fast "through good will and affection," since "it means much," the Roman comments, "to have the same ancestral memorials, to practice the same religious rites, and to share common ancestral tombs."[6]

Outside the walls of the home and the limits of the family, there are also duties that bind a moral agent to the others who share the city-state (*civitas*) with him. "Fellow-citizens," Cicero notes, "have much in common: forum, temples, colonnades and roads, laws and legal rights, law-courts and political elections; and besides these acquaintances and companionship, and the business and commercial transactions that many of them make with others."[7] On account of all they share, citizens owe much to each other. Even those among them who do wrong may rightfully lay claim to that which is due to them. One may not castigate criminals with impunity, because "there is a limit to revenge and to punishment."[8] And at a greater degree of removal from the first nursery of obligation, there lie more distant circles of duty. Past the political unity, a further ring of responsibility unites all those belonging "to a single people, tribe, and tongue.'" Beyond that outer circle lies the last and final set of duties Cicero enumerates: those which hold by virtue of "the immense fellowship of the human species" (*immense societate humani generis*).¹⁰ On account of the first principles that are "reason and speech" (*ratio et oratio*), a necessary connection, the thinker teaches, subsists between human beings as a whole. This is the link that ties all living, speaking beings to each other, ensuring that, "in the processes of teaching, learning, communicating, discussing, and making judgments," men associate with one another and "unite in a kind of natural fellowship."¹¹

The poets, Cicero recalls, knew this point well. They said it more than once: each and every individual has the duty to assist wanderers in finding the paths they seek, helping to set them on their way.¹² Foreigners remain sociable creatures like all others, and they lie squarely within the province of those to whom obligations are due. Even individuals of other peoples who show a clear and forceful animosity toward the home and the fatherland may belong in the orbit of responsibility. It suffices to consider the most extreme example of such cases, namely, enemies. They are hardly an exception, for they too, Cicero asserts, may demand a rightful treatment. In the eyes of the Roman lawyer, this much was, no doubt, in part a matter of tradition. The laws established by the Fetial Code of the Roman people, which defined the rules of proper battle, clearly stipulated that a war might be deemed just only on condition that certain duties be respected. For this reason, Cicero did not omit from his account of responsibilities the old *officia* demanded by the principles of combat. Protection must be given to those who, in battle, lay down their arms; consideration must be shown to the vanquished; and "if any individuals have been constrained by circumstance to promise anything, they are bound to keep their word in such cases."¹³

"In such cases"—but in them alone. This qualification is decisive. The Roman circle of obligation may be extended and even vast, but it is not unlimited. The treatise leaves no doubt that the principles of duty hold for all the individuals united by the ties that bind together "the immense fellowship of the human species." Yet some, it seems, fall outside the borders of this collectivity. They are individuals strikingly unlike all the others: people who, while capable of speech and reason, may not be said to unite in any lawful community; people who, while committing acts that are wrong, may not be defined as criminals; people, finally, who, while often foreign and aggressive, may not be accorded any of the many rights of enemies.

Cicero names such people "pirates," and in the *De officiis* he relegates them to a region beyond the line of duty. In book 3 of his treatise, the Roman author writes:

> There are laws of warfare, and it often happens that fidelity to an oath given to an enemy must be kept. For if an oath has been sworn in such a way that the mind grasps that this ought to be done, it should be kept; if not, then there is no perjury if the thing is not done. For example, if an agreement is made with pirates in return for your life, and you do not pay the price, there is no deceit, not even if you swore to do so and did not. For a pirate is not included in the number of lawful enemies, but is the common enemy of all. With him there ought not to be any pledged word nor any oath mutually binding. (*Nam pirata non est ex perduellium numero definitus, sed communis hostis omnium; cum hoc nec fides debet nec ius iurandum esse commune.*)[14]

Cicero's words must be heard in their full force. That "there ought not to be any pledged word nor any oath mutually binding" with a pirate means no more and no less than this: no obligation should be owed the pirate—not even that to be shown to the rightful antagonist. The pirate escapes not one but all the circles of responsibility drawn in the Roman work. "The common enemy of all" (*communis hostis omnium*), he cannot be considered a criminal, because he does not belong to the city-state; yet he also cannot be counted among the foreign opponents of war, since he cannot be "included in the number of lawful enemies." He moves, as Cicero presents him, in a region in which duties no longer hold. A single consequence follows. If "all that is right depends on the discharge of obligations," even as "all that is wrong in life" depends on their neglect, the pirate, one must infer, stands beyond—or before—both right and wrong.

It would be an error, however, to conclude that the pirate, there-fore, calls the classical order of obligations into question. A contrary claim would be closer to the truth: the "common enemy of all," one may assert, illustrates the set of responsibilities to which he does not belong, exactly as the exception confirms the rule. For Cicero's pirate exposes the one condition which he does not satisfy, and which, by contrast, unites those individuals to whom duties are always owed: the condition, namely, of belonging to the "immense fellowship of the human species."

Admittedly, the Roman thinker offers no clear account of the limits of this society, and one can only wonder as to the crite-rion by which an individual gifted with speech and reason may be included within it or, alternatively, excluded from it. It is possible that the critical fact consists in sedentary life on land. To be within the immense fellowship, according to such a reasoning, would be to belong to a community tied, like the Roman polity, to a clearly delimited territory. But it may also be that the crucial distinction lies in the acceptance or rejection of the principle that, for Cicero, founds legality and justice (*iustitia*) in general: "good faith, that is, constancy and fidelity to what is said and agreed" (*fides, id est dicto-rum conventorumque constantia et veritas*).[15] This would clearly explain why it is that to the lawful enemy a promise must be kept. Even he, while hostile, acts in good faith; despite his aggression, he still seeks to do that which he has sworn to do by the law of duty, thereby ren-dering the "faithful" (*fidem*), according to an etymology proposed by the Stoics, ultimately "factual" (*fiat*).[16] Not so the pirate: nothing ought to be owed to him because he lives without such "good faith."

Cicero shows no signs of doubting the existence of the "common enemy of all," even as he hardly questions that there is, on earth, an "immense fellowship of the human species." Neither assumption, however, can be considered trivial. To the extent to which the classi-cal thinker invokes not one but both terms, in symmetrical relation, he cannot but invite considerable discussion, if not dispute. One might well wish to pause to consider the nature of "this 'immense' fellowship of the human species," such that it allows—whether by chance or by necessity—a figure who, while human, stands so resolutely outside it. It might certainly be argued that, once limited, the "immense fellowship" cannot be said, with any precision, to be "of the human species," precisely because someone, or some ones, cannot be included in its number. A bounded society may be many things, but it is not obviously "of all." At least one common understanding of the nature of totality, in fact, suggests exactly the opposite. One might maintain that if a class of beings considered to be whole admits even of a single exception, it is not genuinely whole; one might assert that, when speaking of "each and every" member in such a case, one invokes an ideal of totality with considerable imprecision. Despite appearances, one would then concede, "all," in truth, is not all.

But a more pressing set of objections can be raised to Cicero and his doctrine of the wide domain of obligation. These rejoinders, too, concern the limit to the law of all counted fellows. But the thornier problems involve less the immense society and its claims to totality than the faithless figures abandoned, by definition, outside it: the illegitimate opponents who "cannot be included in the number of lawful enemies." A moment suffices to register one substantial and perhaps irresolvable difficulty. Some relation must obtain between the large collectivity of dutiful individuals and the antagonists who stand apart from them, even if that relation is one of bare exclusion. But the structure of such a tie—or untying—remains far from evident. To grasp the full intensity of the issue, it is worth reflecting, for a moment, on a question of the simplest logical form: Is the "enemy of all" one, or not one, of "all"?

That query admits of two possible responses, and each leads to perplexity. Cicero suggests one answer when, with every semblance of clarity, he declares that "the pirate is not included in the number of lawful enemies." That statement stipulates, without apparent ambiguity, that the common enemy of all, while human, stands outside the ethical and legal domain of others, more precisely, of all others—all others, namely, who are truly "all." Excepting some from the right to be some of "all," Cicero's claim casts a long shadow over human "society." But even were one to grant the thesis, a further question still could hardly be avoided. Beyond the society of all the speaking, acting beings to whom duties must be owed, where—or what—is then the pirate? Who—or what—is a speaking, acting human being who must, for reasons of moral and legal principle, be excluded from the common domain of obligation that unites the many members of the species?

It is difficult to imagine an answer to that question that would not be thoughtless or iniquitous, or both. One might, however, also choose to respond otherwise to the initial query, proposing a different solution to the problem of deciding whether the "enemy of all" counts as one, or not one, of "all." To save the human fellowship from the prospect of its all too artificial borders, one could revise the exact words of the Roman treatise, choosing to assimilate the exception to the rule. One would then concede that "the common enemy of all," despite hostility, foreignness, and utter unreliability, remains in fact and by right a member of "the fellowship of the human species." Then the pirate might seem to gain a foothold in the society of the dutiful, albeit at its edge. After the many rings of obligation, a further circle would be added, and the least duty-bound of all human beings would appear to acquire a stable, if marginal, place in the wide orbit of obligation. But the appearance would be no more than that, for the consequences of such a decision would be profound and drastic. Once lent such an outer region, the order of obligation could no longer hold, and for a simple reason: the society of the dutiful would include its own foe within itself, since the unlawful enemy would be its lawful member. Such a fellowship, in other words, would be of the faithless as well as of the faithful. It would be a fellowship, more exactly, of the faithful as the faithless and the faithless as the faithful. If one takes the word in its accepted meaning, it would be, therefore, no "fellowship" at all. The principle of collectivity would be a law of strife, which would oppose, in uniting, those who act from duty and those who act without any concern for it. The very trait that defined the order of the whole—that of being a society without a limit—would, in short, define its irreparable disorder. "All," once more, would be not all.

One may decide to set such doubts aside and, if only to understand the Roman writer, choose to admit the twin postulates of an "immense fellowship of the human species" and a "common enemy of all." But in the terms afforded by the *De officiis*, it still remains far from clear how one could ever hope to identify an unlawful antagonist. How to tell with any certainty, on the basis of acts and utterances, that a speaking being has accepted or rejected the very principle of good faith, which founds justice? It will be of little use to ascertain whether an individual has alternatively kept or broken his word, since both such deeds, for Cicero, belong to the domain of duty; only within the sphere of obligations can an oath be binding and a promise made. Action, it would seem, can therefore furnish no criterion for the distinction between those who do, and those who do not, belong to the sphere of responsibility. It goes without saying that speech, taken on its own, can hardly prove any more reliable. Take that simplest of statements: "I am of good faith." A promise of sorts, it holds—or does not hold—on the basis of the distinction between those who swear and those who, by contrast, do not; for this reason, it cannot, on its own, decide it. Still less may one accept the negation of such a sentence. It would be the most contradictory of utterances: "I am not of good faith." For in truth it would mean no more than this: "Faithless, past the purvey of the promise, without the ability to keep and to break my word, I promise you, in good faith, that I am a pirate."

At least one thing, in any case, is certain. In dealing with the common enemy of all, one must act exactly as he does: faithlessly. This much follows from Cicero's assertion that with respect to the pirate, who knows no responsibility, "there ought not to be any pledged word nor any oath" (*cum hoc nec fides debet nec ius iurandum esse commune*). The mode of that proposition, however, calls for some reflection. A commandment to leave the domain of duty, it still remains formulated within the grammar of the injunction, being an imperative, so to speak, to abandon, in certain conditions, the domain of moral and legal imperatives. On formal grounds alone, it cannot but perplex. It suggests a troubling possibility: might there be indeed a word or an oath that would obligate the dutiful to hold their word in all cases, even with respect to those lacking in all duty? The Roman treatise raises the question and forbids it at once. Insisting that nothing be pledged to the pirate, it dictates that the division between those within and those without "the immense fellowship of the human species" be absolute. By that token, it imposes a consequence that is no less unavoidable, in the argument of the treatise, for being nowhere clearly stated as such. In speaking to a pirate, in dealing with a pirate, no matter one's acts, no matter one's word, and no matter one's faith, one cannot fail to don a mask excluded from all the offices of the Roman work: one becomes a pirate oneself.

It is an unexpected development in the punctilious treatise on obligations. Confronted with the "common enemy of all," the dutiful subject finds himself bound, in the name of duty, to renounce his many duties. He must set aside his good faith, not on account of weakness or by accident, but faithfully and on principle, precisely to maintain the formal partition between the many circles of responsibility and that which lies beyond them: the faithlessness of that enemy whose naming suffices to illustrate the order of obligation. The whole set of duties, conceived as a limited class of responsibilities owed to the immense fellowship of the human species, admits and even requires this most paradoxical of all "offices": that there be an obligation to the principle of obligation, which demands that, in some cases, one act without obligation. Of a citizen who deals with a pirate, it may therefore be demanded, by the laws that found every community, not that he obey the principles of his city but that he forsake them altogether; that, in other words, he neither make a pledge nor give his word. It may thus be asked of him that he abandon the terrain of the promise, to step into a region devoid of fidelity and perjury alike: a "part of life" (*pars vitae*) in which obligations can, and indeed must, "be lacking," a part not part of the vast but limited whole set of duties defined and described in the ancient treatise.

This is one domain of words and deeds that Cicero envisaged yet wished not to count. Despite his programmatic claim to present a full treatment of responsibilities in his treatise *On Obligations*, and despite his suggestion that there may be a duty to renounce the very possibility of duty, the Roman author offered no sustained discussion of the obligation, in certain conditions, not to give "any pledged word or any oath." He said little, if not nothing, about the "part of life" in which all those who act and speak, by necessity, must do so — for better or for worse — as the common enemies of all. Perhaps this was because, in the classical lawyer's eyes, such a field without contracts pertained only to the foe who could not be "included among the number of rightful enemies"; perhaps this was because, floating outside the furthest circle of obligation, it could by nature not be annexed to the measured terrain of duty. One can only wonder why the thinker chose to consign this region to the outer edges of his book. But there can be no doubt, in any case, that he did glimpse it. Naming "the common enemy of all" and the complete set of duties which ought not be owed to him, Cicero also unmistakably alluded to the shifting element of irresponsibility in which the pirate moved — even if, for the statesman and the orator, it lay outside the widest expanse of thought, like the open seas beyond the land and shores.

CHAPTER TWO

Rumors of Demise

"Let's shed a tear for the pirate, / For the pirate, for piracy!" (*Versons un pleur sur le pirate, / sur le pirate et sur la piraterie!*).[1] The year was 1936, and Robert Desnos's "Lament for the Pirate" left little room for doubt: from its opening words, it proclaimed the old outlaw to be long gone. Once "filled with drama," the pirate's noble life was definitively past; throughout "the fertile countryside," the castle of his ancestors, like their graves, lay "in ruins."[2] Now came the moment for verse to take the place of the tomb and for the writer's lines to record a disappearance that might otherwise have passed by unseen: such was the poet's pronouncement on the state of sea-marauding in his day. The claim was hardly unreasonable when it was made. Defined in its classic and most general sense as any violent act of depredation committed on the high seas for private gain, piracy seemed to Desnos and his contemporaries a phenomenon of far earlier ages. By the late nineteenth and early twentieth centuries, buccaneers, filibusters, corsairs, and privateers had by all accounts grown scarce. Across the globe, there were ever fewer signs of the exceptional figure the Roman jurists had defined as the "common enemy of all" (*communis hostis omnium*). To be sure, that most nefarious of criminal persons had never altogether vanished from the law of nations and its many books. In modern times, the aged criminal had even acquired a second title, which, although Latin, like the one employed by Cicero, could not be clearly traced to any single ancient source. One could now read in the many languages of modern law that the pirate might be most properly defined as "the enemy of the human species" (*hostis*

23

generis humani).[3] But this frightful figure seemed, by the first half of the twentieth century, if not sooner, almost academic. Civilized humanity believed itself to have safely outlived its archaic foe.

There were several good reasons for such a belief, and they were of more than a single kind. Political considerations played an important role. The end of the nineteenth century constituted a period of relative peace between maritime nations, an epoch in which the role of privateers at sea notably decreased. Technological advances, moreover, altered the nature of ocean travel and reduced its erstwhile risks. The steamship ushered in an age of unprecedented security in the history of seafaring, in which general conditions aboard maritime vessels improved considerably. Events in the law were also of consequence. Above all, a series of prohibitions issued in the course of the nineteenth century announced the imminent end of the most lucrative domain of piratical activities, which had so flourished in the first centuries of the modern age: the slave trade. The outlawing of slaving, to be sure, was gradual and slow, but once underway the process proved irrevocable. When England banned the trade of black Africans in 1807, it was alone among the great powers. But the Americans followed one year later and, in 1815, at the Congress of Vienna, the representatives of Austria, England, France, Prussia, Russia, Sweden, Portugal, and Spain agreed, at least in principle, to put an end to the commerce of people.

Slavery remained legal beyond this time, especially in certain areas of the New World, such as Brazil, the United States, Cuba, and Puerto Rico.[4] But the great business that once sustained European expansion had begun to enter into decline in European waters and several regions beyond them. In 1839, the British parliament approved a bill authorizing English cruisers to capture Portuguese slave ships, wherever they might be, and to judge their sailors for piracy. The United States Congress had made a similar motion in 1820, when it declared any citizen to have participated in the slave trade guilty of piracy and so punishable by death. This rule became practically enforceable by the Americans in 1862, when Abraham Lincoln signed a treaty allowing English ships to search United

States vessels to verify that they were not involved in the forbidden business.[5] Increasing portions of the world's open waters, it seemed, were at last to be subjected to a single body of international legislation, and many predicted that the oceans would soon be cleansed of the outlaws who had so infested them in times of old. By 1924, the *Harvard Law Review* could publish an article by Edwin Dickinson, a distinguished jurist, that bore a title one could hardly have imagined in an earlier age: "Is the Crime of Piracy Obsolete?"[6]

It was true that the second half of the nineteenth century was not altogether lacking in cases of the aged offense. There was the famous trial of Nathaniel Gordon, the American slaver captured and condemned for piracy at the start of the American Civil War. A native of Maine, Gordon had been caught off the coast of West Africa by the American ship, the *Mohican*, as he was practicing the forbidden trade on board his own vessel, the *Eerie*. The criminal captain was brought back to the United States, where he was tried in New York and sentenced, with great notoriety, to death. But Gordon's case had achieved renown precisely because of its rarity, and his much discussed conviction marked the end of an age of trials. Captain Gordon was the last American to go to the gallows for piracy. Shortly before his execution in the Tombs Prison on March 8, 1862, those who sympathized with his cause sought to defend him by recalling the outdated nature of the crime of which he had been accused. Signs posted in New York decried the injustice of the anachronism: "Citizens of New York, Come to the rescue!" they reportedly exclaimed. "Shall a judicial murder be committed in your midst and no protesting voice raised against it? Captain Nathaniel Gordon is to be sentenced to be executed for a crime which has virtually been a dead letter for forty years."[7]

Over half a century later, in 1932, Philip Gosse could conclude his classic *History of Piracy* by suggesting that the period described in the final chapters of his book was also that in which its subject matter had waned and vanished from the earth and its many seas. "The modern age," Gosse wrote in the epilogue to his study, "seems to have done away with piracy [....] What with thirty-five knot cruisers, aeroplanes, wireless and above all the police power of the modern state, there seems very little chance for the enterprising individual to gain a living in this fashion and still less for capital so invested to earn a satisfactory return for the risk involved."[8] Without wanting to pronounce himself with certainty on a thing so indeterminate as the future, Gosse still allowed himself to advance a hypothesis. He wagered that "the passing of the pirate" would be definitive. "It is likely," he concluded, "that the disappearance is permanent. It is hard to conceive that, even if our civilization is overturned and lawlessness again becomes law, the pirate will emerge again. It seems fantastic to think of great powers fighting one another in a Holy Crusade, as did the Turks and the Christians, with outlaws and renegades, or of peaceful steamer lines haunted by buccaneers from little island republics of their own creation whither the fleets of the nations dare not penetrate."[9]

The future, however, turned out to be less than "likely." A dead letter to the people of the mid-nineteenth century, the crime of piracy regained its health within a hundred years. The last decades of the twentieth century witnessed a rise in cases of violent robbery at sea that, however "fantastic to think" it might have seemed a few decades earlier, could hardly be denied. Starting with the end of the Cold War, piracy, it was observed, was "making a comeback."[10] The incentive for gain had dwindled since the golden age of the buccaneers and filibusters, but it had hardly disappeared: with 95 percent of the world's cargo continuing to travel by sea, the profits to be gained by robbery in the territorial and open waters were clear.[11] In the Arabian Sea, off the west and east coasts of Africa, and in southeastern Asia, in particular, piratical incidents began to multiply, growing more numerous with every year. They went largely unreported by the mass media of the age for several reasons. The twentieth-century attacks were moderate in scale, at least with respect to the fabulous depredations of earlier times; they occurred far from the waters of the world's wealthy countries; and they targeted above all ships carrying those relatively inexpensive goods that could be entrusted to the oceans. But the incidents were noticeable nonetheless, the cumulative losses high. In 1984, one observer remarked that "armed attacks on merchant ships and yachts reached epidemic proportions in early 1981 with up to twelve ocean-going merchant ships being reported as under attack each day in the West African area alone."[12] Today that figure, however, no longer seems extreme. In the final years of the twentieth century, the world's seas were to grow still more dangerous.

By 1989, P. W. Birnie concluded that it would be an error to believe that "in an era of population growth, rapid technological developments in enforcement vessels, telecommunications and comprehensive surveillance of the oceans by aircraft, helicopters and satellites," thieves would no longer thrive at sea. "What has happened," he explained, is that piracy "has adapted to modern technical, political, economic and social developments and still exists, albeit in new forms which require new means for suppression."[13] The yearly statistics published by the international entities that monitor insecurity at sea suggest that since the time of that statement, the process of piratical "adaptation" has continued apace. The United Nation's International Maritime Organization (IMO) issues a yearly report, "Acts of Piracy and Armed Robbery against Ships," and its findings are unequivocal. In 1984, the report listed fifty incidents worldwide; in 1997, it documented 250; and by 2000, the yearly total had swelled above 450.[14] The figures contained in the dossier on "Piracy and Armed Robbery Against Ships" released by the International Chamber of Commerce's International Maritime Bureau (IMB) point to a similar conclusion. In the ten years between 1995 and 2005, the number of attacks at sea rose by more than 47 percent. In 2006 alone, fifteen crew members were killed; seventy-five kidnapped; 188 were taken hostage; and at the time of the drafting of the IMB's 2007 report, three members were "still missing." Figures for sea depredations rose in 2007, indicating, as the IMB reported at the end of the year, "an overall increase in the number of attacks as compared to 2006."[15] In 2008, a year of spectacular violence at sea, other reports confirmed that acts of piracy continue to grow in number, regularity, and force.[16]

27

Such a rise in violence at sea would no doubt have startled the nineteenth- and early twentieth-century authors who foresaw the imminent establishment of a lasting maritime order. In itself, however, insecurity at sea can hardly be considered an unprecedented phenomenon. It must be distinguished from a further development of far greater novelty. In the twentieth century, technology was to smile upon piracy, granting the antique crime a new youth beyond the seas. The first instance of the most modern variety of depredation in extra-territorial regions can be dated to the first half of the last century. On February 21, 1931, a group of armed rebel soldiers attempted to seize an aircraft in Arequipa, Peru, and use it for revolutionary purposes. It was in the later decades of the twentieth century, however, that vessels in the air came to be captured and rerouted by private individuals repeatedly and with increasing insistence.[17] The term "hijacker," coined in the 1920s for thieves at sea, now began to admit of two varieties, corresponding to the two terrestrial regions of depredation. The "sea-jacker" would henceforth be distinguished from the "sky-jacker," as the villain of the water could be told apart from the extra-territorial criminal of the air.[18]

The affinities between the two sorts of illegal agents may well be more complex than such a similarity of terms would suggest. What exactly binds the plunderer of the seas of older times to the agents who now threaten travel by air? What precisely links the "enemy of all" of the age of Cicero, for instance, to the so-called "terrorists" of our times? These questions merit consideration, and in its final chapters this study will therefore return to them. But before such issues may be addressed with precision, it is necessary to establish the nature and status of piracy in its classic forms: how, and in what terms, it became possible to conceive of the deeds of pirates as exceptional with respect to criminal and political categories, as either felonies committed in a space beyond the normal jurisdiction of the law or as belligerent acts carried out by agents lacking any legitimate public title to wage a war. Only if it is possible to define the sense in which the law of nations defined pirates as universal foes, in other words, will it be possible to decide whether and to what degree their ancient status holds also for those individuals whom the idioms of our age describe by variations of the old pirate title: "criminals against humanity," "enemies of the human race," "unlawful combatants," and the other non-state agents who may therefore be denied the rights of both criminals and official enemies of state. At this initial point, the questions can be posed; the genealogy alone, once conducted, may contribute the elements from which to draw answers. The least one can assert at this preliminary stage is that it may well be too soon to mourn the demise of the apparently archaic foe. If one sheds "a tear for the pirate, / For the pirate and for piracy" today, one's tears risk falling at the side of a grave that remains to be filled. They may form not a memorial but a veil, which barely conceals from view the image of the "enemy of all," which becomes, with each day, more difficult not to see.

CHAPTER THREE

Along Liquid Paths

The origins of piracy have long been debated. It is certain that they stretch back to the most distant past, for no matter how far one looks, one finds signs of those variously criminal activities King James I memorably defined as "depredations committed on the seas by certaine lewd and ill-disposed persons."[1] Admittedly, material documentation in the strong sense from the oldest periods in the West is lacking. "It is important to establish at an early stage," a classicist has recently recalled, with some severity, "that all evidence of piracy in the Graeco-Roman world is textual."[2] But the written sources are many, and they are both epigraphic and literary. The Homeric corpus, the first in the tradition, already contains several allusions to thievery at sea. Although the epics decline to bestow the title of "pirate" on any of the major individuals involved in the Trojan war and its aftermath, among the Achaeans and their enemies sea robbers are unmistakably present. Eumarios, the hapless swineherd of book 15 of the *Odyssey*, bears witness to their perfidiousness: he recounts how, in the course of a "long voyage to Egypt," his nursemaid was captured "by Taphian pirates" in Phoenicia.[3] The startling truth is that in Homer's universe, even the wiliest of all heroes himself can provoke suspicion. Twice on his voyages, Odysseus and his companions must respond to the same question after landing on unfamiliar shores: "Who are you, strangers? From where have you set sail / Along liquid paths? Do you roam for trade / Or for adventure, crossing the seas, like pirates, / Risking their lives and bringing harm to others?"[4]

Modern scholarly treatments of the beginnings of piracy have tended to turn less to poetry, however, than to history, starting with the famous opening of Thucydides' study of the Peloponnesian war. The so-called *Archaeology* presents thievery at sea as one of the oldest of all Hellenic professions. "The Grecians in old times," Thucydides writes, "and such barbarians as in the continent lived near unto the sea, or else inhabited the islands, after once they began to cross over one to another in ships, became thieves, and went abroad under the conduct of their most puissant men, both to enrich themselves and to fetch in maintenance for the weak; and falling upon towns unfortified and scatteringly inhabited, rifled them, and made this the best means of their living; being a matter at that time nowhere in disgrace, but rather carrying with it something of glory. This is manifest by some that dwell on the continent, amongst whom, so it be performed nobly, it is still esteemed as an ornament. The same also is proved by some of the ancient poets, who introduce men questioning of such as sail by, on all coasts alike, whether they be thieves or not; as a thing neither scorned by such as were asked, nor upbraided by those that were desirous to know. They also robbed one another within the main land. And much of Greece useth that old custom, as the Locrians called *Ozoloe*, the Acarnanians, and those of the continent in that quarter, unto this day. Moreover, the fashion of wearing iron remaineth yet with the people of that continent from their old trade of thieving."[5]

That the earliest people of the sea were robbers is a point often made by modern authors. It can be found as early as in Montesquieu, who, in a passage of the *Spirit of the Laws* that owes much to Thucydides, goes so far as to assert that "the first Greeks were all pirates."[6] The classicists of the late nineteenth and early twentieth centuries expressed this idea more than once. It was for them the basis of a doctrine of the origins of piracy that continues to this day to resonate throughout the considerable scholarly literature on the subject.[7] Jules M. Sestier, the author of the first modern work on classical sea thievery, advanced the claim without hesitation in 1880. Like "all primitive peoples in the Mediterranean," he wrote, the Greeks "practiced piracy in Antiquity."[8] Sestier, and many after him, understood this fact to illustrate a fundamental principle: that of the irreducible conflict pitting civilization against the barbarism that everywhere precedes it. "Throughout its history," Henry A. Ormerod thus explained in *Piracy in the Ancient World*, published in 1924, "the Mediterranean has witnessed a constant struggle between the civilized peoples dwelling on its coasts and the barbarians, between the peaceful trader using its highways and the pirate who infested the routes that he must follow."[9] Time and time again, archaic Greek poetry furnished scholars with the evidence of the admissibility of piracy in primitive times. "In the Homeric age," Coleman Phillipson commented in 1911, referring to sea thievery, "the practice was looked upon as a creditable, indeed glorious, means of enrichment."[10] "In the age Homer was describing," Lionel Casson similarly remarked in 1959, "piracy was a profession that energetic and adventuresome men entered as a respectable way of making a living."[11] Auguste Jardé's classic volume, *La formation du people grec* (*The Formation of the Greek People*), articulated the point in some detail: "In the Homeric poems," the historian wrote, "piracy is common law. It is to be condemned among citizens, yet when it targets foreigners it is, on the contrary, licit and even honorable, as legitimate a means of existence as hunting and fishing."[12]

These scholars all taught that in the history of Hellas such a primitive state of affairs, however, did not last. Immediately after painting his portrait of the ways of the archaic Greeks, Jardé declared: "It is no longer so in the classical age."[13] In that age "piracy is judged as a crime of common law, no less than armed robbery and banditry; and it is only among half-barbarian populations, such as the Aetolians and the Acarnanians, that such activities continue, having become the object of general reprobation."[14] With the emergence of the Greek cities and their constitutions and, still later, with the establishment of the Roman state and its great system of law, piracy, once admissible and even admired, would have naturally diminished, retreating from all the main channels of the seas to "take refuge, so to speak," as Yvon Garlan put it, "at the geographical margins of Greco-Roman legality."[15] The march of progress, the classicists contended, had by then begun. The pirates were early individuals of a world without states; with the rise of the Greek and Roman commonwealths, the sea-faring barbarians had little choice but gradually to fade away. Their disappearance struck more than one modern scholar as announcing a millennial process, which was to reach its final fulfillment only in the age when the order of the modern state began at last to reign over the chaos of the seas. At the close of the preface to his classic monograph, *La piraterie dans l'antiquité* (*Piracy in Antiquity*), Sestier thus conceded that sea plunder did not fully end with the reign of Constantine, the moment in which his own well-documented book came to a close. The scholar admitted that the history of piracy could be continued beyond that time, though he added: "It would present a real interest only starting with the period in which the Saracens and the Muslims appeared in Europe, sprung from a new race, both fanatical and pitiless towards Christians. And this history would end on the day the glorious flag of France was victoriously implanted on the walls of Algiers, that supreme bastion of piracy on the banks of the Mediterranean."[16]

The vision of classical pirates as primitive and barbarian individuals infesting the Mediterranean can be found in countless works on the history of sea banditry. But it invariably runs up against several difficulties. The first of them is philological; it involves a problem of terminology. The ancient Greek authors disposed of several expressions to designate the sea thieves who tended to prey on their ships, among which two, as has often been noted, predominate.[17] The first, *lēistēs* (λῃστής), can be found in works as early as Homer's, who employs it both in the *Odyssey* and in the *Hymn to Apollo*.[18] This word derives from a noun indicating "booty" or "plunder," *lēis* (λῃΐς), which can in turn be traced to the Indo-European root of the same meaning (laϝ).[19] The second term for the ancient outlaw represents the etymological origin of the modern expression "pirate": *peiratēs* (πειρατής). This Greek word appears to have entered the ancient language later than *lēistēs*, its earliest attestation being in an inscription from Rhamnous of the mid-third century BC.[20] Scholars have proposed two accounts of its formation. Most Hellenists hold it to be closely related to the noun *peira* (πεῖρα), "trial" or "attempt," and so to the verb *peiraō* (πειράω): the "pirate" would then be one who "tests," "puts to proof," "contends with," and "makes an attempt."[21] A conceivable, while less likely, analysis also ties the word to the verb *prattō* (πράττω), "to act," "pass through," and "achieve": the pirate, in this sense, would be defined as "one who accomplishes."[22]

Also a people of the sea, the Romans naturally developed their own expressions for the criminals who acted in the waters they considered their own. But in form the Latin vocabulary, despite its material novelty, was "similar in some respects to the Greek," as Philip de Souza has remarked.[23] Among Roman expressions for maritime robbers, two main types of terms may thus be distinguished. The first set refers in its origin, like the Greek *lēistēs*, to the acquisition of wealth by plunder. The principle element in this class is the noun *praedo*, derived from the term *praeda*, "booty." One also encounters the roughly synonymous *latro*, which seems in Plautus to have meant "mercenary" but which gradually acquired the meaning of "bandit" and "pirate," with *latrocinium* functioning, as a result, as an abstract noun for the act of piracy and banditry.[24] The Roman authors also employed the classic term whose more modern forms remain in use today: *pirata*, younger sibling to the Greek *peiratēs*. This was the expression employed by Cicero, for example, when he declared in the *De officiis* that "a pirate [*pirata*] is not included in the number of lawful enemies, but is the common enemy of all."[25]

Among the various ancient terms, one may discern a single common trait: none pertains with any exclusivity to those thieves who act at sea rather than on land. From the archaic age of Greece to later Roman times, the lexicon of early plunderers remains in this sense stable. When the classical authors wished to designate criminal individuals who moved over the waters, in distinction to the land, qualifications were strictly indispensable. Describing the ways of the Bosphoran peoples near Colchis, Strabo thus commented that "they live by plundering *at sea*" (ζῶσι δὲ ὑπο τῶν κατὰ θάλατταν ληστηρίων);[26] and in his *Life of Themistocles*, Cornelius Nepos similarly recounted that the great Athenian statesman rendered the seas safe by "pursuing the *maritime* plunderers" (*maritimos praedones consectando mare tutum reddidit*).[27] Such formulations leave little doubt that the people of antiquity could readily distinguish thievery on sea from robbery on land. But it is striking that the classical authors found no need to forge a special notion for the one criminal practice as distinct from the other. With respect to the ancient world, "to isolate piracy (at sea) from banditry (on land)," Garlan has observed, "is therefore to break the unity of one and the same historical phenomenon — and always to do so according to highly questionable criteria, since these two types of predatory activity were, in actual practice, difficult to separate, ancient piracy being generally carried out along the coasts rather than on the high seas."[28]

The Greek and Latin lexicon, moreover, suggests that the established portrait of pirates as sea-thieves acting for their own gain must be revised on yet another count. Not only do the ancient sources not admit any clear conceptual distinction between the depredators who crossed the seas and those who traveled by land, but, from a modern perspective, the classical authors also fail to distinguish between the isolated agent and the ordered collectivity; for the "pirates" of whom they write are by no means exclusively individuals who act for private interests. When Strabo qualified the Bosphorans as "plunderers," he referred, for example, to an entire people and its way of life, not to the deeds of single persons. Plutarch did no less when, in his *Life of Kimon*, he discussed the erstwhile inhabitants of the island of Skyros, the Dolopians. If we are to believe the ancient author, this people formed a veritable nation of pirates: "not knowing how to cultivate the land," Plutarch explains, "they became pirates across the seas of antiquity. Ultimately, they did not even spare those who disembarked in their country to do business with them; they pillaged the Thessalonians and imprisoned them."[29] Diodorus Siculus and Polybius, by all appearances, spoke the same idiom; neither historian hesitated to judge entire communities "piratical."[30] In this regard again, the Latin usage conforms to the Greek. Thus Livy could repeatedly present the enemies of

Rome as "pirates," while still describing them as organized, no less than other warring peoples, in ships and squadrons; like other foreign antagonists of the Roman state, these fighters were directed by their leader, whom the historian could therefore dub a "pirate chief" (*archipirata*).[31] As Alfred P. Rubin has observed, in such a setting it would be an error to understand the attribute "piratical" as referring to the acts of private individuals. The expression "was not bound to 'piratical' acts on the 'high seas,' but to a conception of 'piratical' villages forming a society [*poleis*] on land which refused to accept Roman supremacy. Relations with the 'pirates' were relations of war, not of policing the internal or imperial Roman law; the results of Roman victory were the normal results of a victorious war at that time and in that place."[32]

As such classical testimonies suggest, piracy and the operations carried out against it were in the ancient world also far from "primitive." Plundering belonged to the classical as well as to the archaic world of Greece and Rome and, with time, depredations assumed forms of ever increasing complexity. A common picture of piracy in antiquity focuses, admittedly, on the earliest stages of recorded history, following Montesquieu and his modern successors in casting the "first" inhabitants of the Mediterranean as "all pirates." Such a vision, however, comprehends little of the ancient reality. Clearly, it cannot account easily for the ample evidence of piracy in the classical and Hellenistic periods; it may accept them only if it can demonstrate that they are no more than remnants of an earlier age. More decisive, however, is that such an account must deprive the ancient vocabulary for the crime of any distinctive value. In an age in which all may be judged looters, the title of pillager means little, if not nothing.

The truth is that the term "pirate" and its various synonyms acquire their full significance when they may be perceptibly distinguished from others. Then the unauthorized plunderer, for example, may be opposed to the merchant and to the warrior; the latter two trade and commit acts of violence on land and sea, yet their names bear witness to a status before the law different from that of the pirate. By such a point, however, the "primitive" epoch of non-distinction is long gone. The differentiated plunderer belongs not to the age before the establishment of order on land and sea but to the time that is, instead, strictly simultaneous with it. A criminal enemy to be apprehended, the classical pirate is a creature of legal authority: more precisely, he is its own presupposition, that against which the civil order must variously strive, and in whose absence it would not be itself.

Under scrutiny, the familiar image, therefore, hardly holds: the pirates known to the ancient authors were by no means exclusively sea-faring, individual, or primitive. It would not be difficult to demonstrate that they were also not "barbarian," if by that term one designates the belonging to a people foreign to the Greeks.[33] Thucydides, in effect, said it all: the famous plunderers of his *Archaeology* were both individuals and whole peoples, such as "the Locrians and the Acarnanians," who practiced robbery "at sea and on main land," "using of customs," the historian noted, which persist "unto this day," among "Grecians and Barbarians."[34] One can only marvel at the insistence by which sea-marauding has been defined by traits of such little historical consistency. But they are revelatory nonetheless. In their impropriety, the purportedly piratical attributes testify above all to the single wish that secretly unites many modern scholars: that the origins of piracy may be containable in a region safely outside the past that the present admits as its own. Such a desire alone explains the good reasons for a set of characteristics that would otherwise be quite perplexing. To be firmly tethered to its supposed beginnings in a world securely situated beyond the borders of the West, the exceptional crime must be assigned, in each respect, to a zone of relative exteriority. There, in a region that remains obscure yet still visibly past the limits of the ancient polity, the pirates may find a home. In space, the criminals are thus to be positioned in the sea, separated from the land and its law; in quantity, they are to be defined as individuals, rather than as groups and peoples; in quality, they are to be largely foreigners, strangers to the civil ways of Greece and Rome; and in time, they are to belong above all to the archaic epoch, before the dawn of the classic age.

Only if one grants such conditions may one set aside a possibility that could otherwise hardly be avoided: the possibility, namely, that in antiquity, piracy did not originate in a region exterior to that of the city and its many laws. The topology of Graeco-Roman piracy may have been a good deal more complex than many modern authors allow. Were it so, to be sure, the positions of the depredators would be difficult to track; the roving robbers might no longer be easily restricted to one segment of the earth. Even within a country protected all along its outer borders by forts and barriers, the nomads, as in Franz Kafka's tale, might one morning suddenly have "been there"; no matter the distance separating their wild homeland in the north from the quiet center of the empire, they might still have "penetrated to the capital," "in a manner incomprehensible" to all those who believed their fatherland well protected by its great wall.[35] Classical history, no less than medieval and modern, contains ample evidence that the early plunderers, when they roamed, respected few limits. Barbaric but not barbarian, their mobile lines crossed the city no less than the sea.

CHAPTER FOUR

Captures

Ancient sources offer several accounts of the relations that may obtain between practices of pillage and the polity. One doctrine finds its roots in the picture painted by Thucydides at the inception of his *Archaeology*. Describing the earliest period in the history of Hellas, the historian recounts how the great Cretan king of old established his empire by suppressing the many plunderers who had until then moved over the Greek waters with impunity. "Minos," Thucydides explains, "was the most ancient of all that by report we know to have built a navy." With such new power he accomplished what none before him could have done: "He made himself master of the now Grecian Sea; and both commanded the isles called Cyclades, and also was the first that sent colonies into most of the same, expelling thence the Carians and constituting his own sons there for governors; and also freed the seas of pirates as much as he could, for the better coming in, as is likely, of his own revenue."[1] However one wishes to understand the probable increase the monarch thus achieved in "his own revenue," this much of the Thucydidean narrative can hardly be denied: it represents the king as erecting the dominion of his realm over the grave of common sea thieves. Such an image can be contrasted with another, which may also be found in works from the classical age. More than once, ancient authors present the rise of commonwealths as marking not the end of acts of depredation but their formal and lasting establishment. As evidence, one may refer to Plutarch's comments on the Dolopian regime on Skyros, built for the sake of organized robbery; one may also recall

the descriptions of the ways of pillaging peoples to be found in Diodorus Siculus, Polybius, and Livy. These Greek and Roman authors
all recount how individuals can come together, adopting customs
and agreeing on new principles, to prey on others over land and sea.

On the surface, the two accounts are quite evidently opposed.
The first casts the foundation of a public space as an event that will
assure the cessation of acts of plunder. The second, by contrast, presents the association of men as no more than a means for systematic
depredations all the more effective for being planned. But there is
also a third classical image of pillage and the city, and it may be that
it alone explains the others. This picture represents political authority as a power that decides on the rightful use of forceful capture,
thereby judging a single activity—pillaging—to be alternately licit
and illicit, imperative and forbidden, depending on the setting. One
finds such an account in book 2 of the pseudo-Aristotelian *Economics*, in a famous passage that describes how an ancient government
succeeded in relieving itself of a debt it could otherwise not have
settled. "The people of Chalcedon," we read, "had a large number
of mercenary troops in their city, to whom they could not pay the
wages they owed. Accordingly they made proclamation that anyone,
either citizen or alien, who had right of reprisal against any city or
individual, and wished to exercise it, should have his name entered
on a list. A large number of names was enrolled, and the people thus
obtained a specious pretext for exercising reprisal upon ships that
were passing on their way to the Pontus. They accordingly arrested
the ships and fixed a period within which they would consider any
claims that might be made in respect of them. Having now a large
fund in hand, they paid off the mercenaries, and set up a tribunal to
decide the claims; and those whose goods had been unjustly seized
were compensated out of the revenues of the state."[2]

As the author of the ancient treatise presents it, the solution to
the Chalcedonic state of impecuniousness lay in an ingenious use
of the "right of reprisals." Sealed within the history and sense of
that term is a large part of the problem of piracy and constituted
power—and not only in antiquity. A complex expression in English

translation, the designation of reprisals bore a simpler name in the original idiom of the *Economics*, where it was known by forms of the verb *sylan* (συλᾶν). Were one to leave the decisive terms untranslated, one might for this reason also render the Aristotelian passage in the following form, with reasonable exactitude, if also undeniable inelegance: the people of Chalcedon "made proclamation that anyone, either citizen or alien, who had a *sylon* against any city or individual, and wished to exercise it, should have his name entered on a list. A large number of names was enrolled, and the people thus obtained a specious pretext for enacting *sylai* upon ships that were passing on their way to the Pontus." In such an English version, at least one characteristic of the classical Greek diction can be clearly perceived. *Sylan* pertains both to an act and to the right to commit it, referring to a domain in which fact and law, events and claims, deeds and rules intertwine and grow difficult to tell apart.

Scholars of classical antiquity have dedicated considerable attention to this one lexeme and its cognates.[3] It has been noted that, as a rule, "the term *sylan* designates a violent action, which consists of seizing a person or the goods belonging to a person (including when the person is a divinity)."[4] Already in the Homeric corpus one encounters the expression with some frequency; in the *Iliad*, in particular, the term refers to the act of pillaging by which one despoils the enemy's corpse of his arms.[5] Numerous later literary works employ the expression to designate the sack of sacred sites and the theft of consecrated objects: texts by Isocrates, Herodotus, Aristotle, Plato, Polybius, and Diodorus all contain the term in this sense. In a concise analysis of the scholarship on the subject, Philippe Gauthier has identified four distinct senses among the classical mentions of the term.[6] A first acceptation is that of Homer, which may be found as late as in Polybius. Here *sylan* refers to the act of "despoiling, pillaging, and more precisely, pillaging sacred treasures" (arms being, in the archaic world, often of divine provenance).[7] Such deeds regularly imply the conjunction of two ideas: sacrilege and vengeance. In book 6 of Herodotus' *History*, the Persians, having conquered Eritreia, set out to "commit *sylan*," in this sense, against

43

the sacred things of the vanquished people.[8] A second meaning is more clearly legal. In this sense, the term signifies a "right of reprisals," which entitles individuals to redress a wrong committed against them by taking possession of persons or goods belonging to those responsible, be they compatriots or foreigners. In literary as well as epigraphic sources, the nominal form *sylon* (τὸ σῦλον) may then refer to the just claim to capture or, alternately, to the spoils seized as the vindication of that claim.[9] In a third meaning, the verb *sylan* evokes a procedure that has been called less legal (or "pseudo-legal") than "pre-" or "para-legal": the detention of a person or a good as a guarantee of or deposit on a claim to be fulfilled.[10] And in its fourth and final acceptation, the term may refer to "seizures that one may qualify as post-judicial," namely, the actions that constitute the proper execution of a judgment. In accordance with a decision of the law, goods and persons could be captured, from individuals and collectivities, both forcibly and rightfully.[11]

The textual and epigraphic evidence of these terms for violent acts of taking is abundant, and it has attracted the attention of the ablest scholars of classical antiquity. Among them was Louis Gernet, who famously discussed the multiple senses of *sylan* in his path-breaking *Recherches sur le développement de la pensée juridique et morale en Grèce* (*Studies on the Development of Legal and Moral Thought in Greece*). Gernet argued that the history of this word illustrates the passage from "magical thinking to positivist thinking," which, in time, led from the Homeric age to the birth of moral, legal, and economic individualism in the classical world.[12] Admitting that "the insufficiency of our documents" does not allow for the establishment of successive moments with exactitude, Gernet nevertheless held that the "progression" in the meaning of the term "must have been rapid." "We find ourselves," he wrote, "obliged to note the following three stages in the evolution of the word: *sylai* associated with *genē*, dominated by the notion of familial and religious vengeance; private *sylai*, functioning in the incipient economic life and dominated by the notion of individual and magical vengeance; properly 'secular' *sylai*, bearing on the goods of the debtor and bearing, in

44

international relations, on the goods of the compatriots with whom he shares solidarity."[13] Such an analysis admirably accounts for the alterations in the meaning of *sylan* over time, which are doubtless multiple. The forceful seizure signified by this single expression and its cognates may be alternately reviled, as sacrilegious, and required by custom. It may be enacted by individuals and by groups and inflicted on one as on the other. It may belong, finally, not only to the developed system of classical Greek right but also to the various domains that precede, accompany, and follow it. But in all these meanings, one observes the persistence of a single trait. This violent capture of persons and goods always remains in the closest proximity to the law, be it human or divine. There is a simple reason for this fact: *sylan* is sanctioned plunder, pillaging permitted and even commanded by law. Were it not endowed with this public distinction, it would be mere thievery.

The Greeks themselves harbored no illusions about the nature of the old practice of condoning captures. On this matter, the passage from book 2 of the *Economics* leaves little doubt. There the "right of reprisal" furnishes the clever Chalcedonians with what the ancient author does not hesitate to term "a specious pretext [μετὰ προφάσεως εὐλόγου] for exercising reprisal upon ships that were passing on their way to the Pontus," in a context in which the word "reprisal" (*sylan*), as Gauthier has observed, bestows no more than "an appearance of legality" on an act which would otherwise be "pure piracy."[14] Demosthenes also recalled that a title to depredation could be a troublesome institution. Discussing the liturgical service by which Athenians set sail upon the warship known to the classical world as the "trireme," the orator declared to his audience: "When a man who has taken the trireme for hire sets sail, he plunders and pillages everybody; the profits he reaps for himself, but whoever it may chance to be of you citizens pays the damages; and you alone of all people are unable to travel anywhere without a herald's staff of truce because of the acts of these men in seizing hostages and in provoking reprisals."[15] It was no doubt on the basis of considerations of this kind that the ancient people developed several juridical means to limit the field of lawful plunder. Against the rights of reprisals among individuals of differing peoples, the Greeks instituted the claims of "symbols" (σύμβολον and συμβολή): international agreements by which the security of the citizens of foreign cities and their goods was to be guaranteed.[16] And to restrict the violence of the pillaging that could be authorized by the law, they declared certain persons and places—sanctuaries, ports, on occasion even cities—to be inviolate: free of any *sylan* or, to employ the Greek term that has since remained in use, sites of "asylum" (ἀσυλία).[17]

These were doubtless noble inventions in the field of law. But one should make no mistake as to their aims: such measures never sought to abolish rights of seizure and their consequences altogether. That much was to remain, for a long time in the history of the West, unthinkable. As Rodolphe Dareste once observed, to the peoples of antiquity, as to most of those in the modern period, the institution of sanctioned seizure remained "justified by its absolute necessity."[18] Claims to violent capture could be restricted, but they could hardly be denied. That the regions declared places of asylum in antiquity may in practice often have been sacked is, from this perspective, of relatively minor importance. More crucial is that, in principle, the very delimitation of one region free of pillaging necessarily confirmed the practice to which it marked an exception: by definition, *sylai* remained licit in all those spaces not expressly protected by statutes of asylum. The law that forbade practices of depredation in certain conditions was no different from the one that permitted it in all others. Both originated in a single power, which remained at least as effective in peace as in war. The moderns would call this power "the state"; the ancients naturally gave it different names, depending on the circumstances. The essential point may be that, from the beginning, this power did not limit itself to seizing goods and persons, like the pillagers who roved beyond its borders. It also captured something else: the right to capture, with force no less than with legality.

CHAPTER FIVE

Greater Empire

Classical history abounds in tales of confrontations between rulers and robbers. It may be that they are as old as accounts of the institution of political authority itself. One may consider, as an example, the story of the first Cretan king. According to tradition, Minos was the earliest master of the seas. Thucydides reports that that archaic sovereign was also the first to punish pirates.[1] That assertion is ancient and venerable, yet there are good reasons to consider it with some caution. Herodotus, for one, wrote also in his *History* of the formidable Minoan navy, but curiously he said nothing of its suppression of sea thieves.[2] It is worth noting that in the famous opening of his *Archaeology*, Thucydides, in any case, specified that the Cretan sovereign "freed the seas of pirates as much as he could."[3] That qualification could be decisive. If one believes the report from Cleidimus contained in Plutarch's *Life of Theseus*, one has little choice but to conclude that even during the heyday of the Minoan realm, thieves continued to roam over the waters, for had they not, Jason could hardly have distinguished himself among the Greeks by his resolution to set sail aboard the Argo as he did, "scouring the sea for pirates."[4] The evidence suggests that the encounter between the monarch and the outlaw may not have issued in an unequivocal conclusion.

It is certain that even in archaic times, marauders could prove useful to sovereign powers. Herodotus relates that long before the classical age, there were Ionians and Carians who sailed from Greece to Egypt to plunder the shores of the Near East kingdom.

Doubtless they did so with distinction, for soon they found themselves recruited by the first Saite pharaoh, Psammeticos I; he convinced the Hellenic pillagers to take up residence in Egypt and to fight with their bronze weaponry in his army.[5] They may have been among the first maritime depredators to join the ranks of official armies. They were certainly not the last. In the classical period, the practice of hiring pirates was to grow increasingly widespread. The people who witnessed the thirty years of uninterrupted conflict in Peloponnesus and lived to see its consequences noted the phenomenon more than once. Xenophon described how, in public and declared conflicts, ships were often openly hired to plunder enemy vessels. Isocrates, discussing the rising recruitment of professional pillagers, commented on how many individuals in his time were "compelled through want of daily bread" to fight for pay.[6] Soon the institution, once remarkable, could be considered well established. By the Hellenistic age, "mercenaries had crept into the warfare of Greece and stayed there," as Guy Thompson Griffith has observed, and maritime bandits were well represented among them.[7] In the third century BC, the Macedonian monarch Antigonus Gonatas could thus avail himself in his battles of a warrior such as the Phocian Ameinias, a personage of dubious legality, whom the ancient authors dub "general" (στρατηγός) and "chief pirate" (ἀρχιπειρατής) in alternation.[8]

This was the age in which Rome appeared in the classical world as a redoubtable force in international affairs. The peninsular nation, to be sure, had never allowed itself fully to ignore the promise and the perils of the sea. Livy recounts that the port of Ostia was built by Ancus Marcius as early as the sixth century BC, and from Polybius we learn that even in its beginnings, the Republic of Rome traded actively with Sicily, Sardinia, Carthage, and its colonies in Africa. But these were the transactions of a city of relatively modest importance in the Mediterranean. Towards the end of the fourth century, the situation changed. As Rome expanded its suzerainty over the Greek colonies of Italy and allied itself with the states along its western coast, it developed a fleet. There are reports of Roman maritime

magistracies (*duoviri navales*) from 311 BC, and one year later sources
tell of a squadron formed by naval associates (*socii navales*), united
under an officer entrusted with the defense of the Italian coasts.[9] By
the third century, the republic could confront major naval powers
and extend its might across the waters. The First Punic War, which
lasted from 264 to 241 BC and from which Rome emerged stronger
at sea than ever, contained the proof.

That the waters to the west of Italy were lawless is a fact often
recalled by ancient authors. The bandits who famously abducted
Dionysus before he changed them into dolphins were, after all,
"Tyrrhenian pirates," as Homer and Ovid both relate. Strabo claims
that the Greeks were long afraid to establish settlements along
Italy's western coasts.[10] This was, however, the first region of Roman
expansion. To the east of the Latin capital, the dangers were equal,
if not greater. The Adriatic was a grave threat. Modern scholars,
versed in the Greek and Latin classics, have often recalled that
"piracy had free play in these waters," as Maurice Holleaux once
wrote.[11] Their "eastern shores," Ormerod explained, were "inhabited by wild, uncivilized tribes, who were active marauders by land
and sea, and were constantly reinforced from the interior."[12] The
historical veracity of such claims has been disputed in recent years.[13]
But there can be no doubt that by the end of the third century, if
not sooner, the peoples of the eastern Adriatic posed a challenge to
the economic ambitions of the Roman Republic. The histories of
Appian and Polybius both contain reports of repeated depredations
committed by one people of the region, the Illyrians, against Roman
merchant ships. In 229 BC, the Italian city protested formally on
behalf of its traders, but it was in vain. Later that year, it declared
war on the Adriatic kingdom. The sources differ in their accounts
of the occurrences, but it is certain that the Roman victory was
swift and undeniable. In its first entry onto the political stage of
the eastern Mediterranean, the Italian city had triumphed, claiming for itself a new title: that of the supreme antagonist of piracy.[14]
As a consequence, the Latin republic naturally expected the Greek
nations, like all others, to applaud its actions. In the eyes of Rome,

"the Illyrians," Polybius explained, "had become not the common enemy of one but the common enemies [κοινοὺς ἐχθροὺς] of all."[15]

This was but the first of a series of conflicts in which lesser maritime powers in the Mediterranean, dubbed piratical by Rome, were quickly crushed. After the Illyrians, the unruly Dalmatians, Ligurians, and Balearic islanders, all judged to be fostering insecurity at sea, were soon suppressed.[16] A new age of maritime dominion had begun. The final chapter in the rise of Roman supremacy at sea belongs, however, to the last century of the republic. It was played out in a region far from Italy, along the easternmost coasts of the Mediterranean, in the province of southern Asia Minor known to the ancients as Cilicia.[17] Numerous classical authors, including Appian, Dio Cassius, and Plutarch, portray this portion of southern Anatolia as a center of piracy.[18] Strabo, to whom we owe the fullest description of the area, proposes a compelling explanation for this fact. "It was above all the exportation of slaves [ἀνδράποδα] that incited them to commit criminal acts," he writes, "for this traffic was attended with very great profit, and the slaves were easily taken. Delos was at no great distance, a large and rich mart, capable of receiving and transporting, when sold, the same day, ten thousand slaves; so that hence arose a proverbial saying, 'Merchant, come into port, discharge your freight—everything is sold.'"[19] As the geographer presents it, the sordid business was directly tied to Rome. "The Romans," Strabo writes, discussing the market, "having acquired wealth after the destruction of Carthage and Corinth, employed great numbers of domestic slaves, and were the cause of this traffic. The pirates, observing the facility with which slaves could be procured, issued forth in numbers from all quarters, committing robbery and dealing in slaves."[20]

The Italians may have originally encouraged the marauders' market, but by the turn of the first century BC the situation in Cicilia clearly did not favor Rome. Garlan has argued that Marius Gaius's victories against the Celtic Cimbri and the Teutonic peoples of the north may have relieved the republic of its former need for slave labor from the east.[21] The Cilicians, however, were never submissive

50

subjects. As early as 140 BC, Diodotus Tryphon, the "Syrian usurper," staged a revolt against the Seleucid monarchy that then controlled the region. One consequence of his victory was the establishment of a base in Coracesium from which raiders could move freely from Anatolia to the coasts of Greece and Syria.[22] It seems that sometime close to 102 BC, Rome therefore resolved to act, putting an end to the banditry that flourished in the region. The governance of the eastern area was assigned to Marcus Antonius, who was entrusted with the task of overseeing a campaign against the marauders of Asia Minor. The praetor was, in Livy's words, "to pursue the maritime plunderers in Cilicia, that is, the pirates."[23] Today little evidence remains of Antonius's endeavors, but inscriptions from Delphi and Cnidos bear witness to a *lex de provinciis praetoriis* passed in these years that instituted new rules to facilitate the "prosecution of the pirates" (*persecutio piratarum*). Romans and their allies were henceforth strictly forbidden from assisting the freebooters and from tolerating their bases in any of their territories.[24] A "common war" (κοινὸς πόλεμος) had been declared.[25]

Plutarch suggests that Antonius was soon applauded by the authorities for his "triumphs" in the region, but there is little indication that his victory was lasting.[26] Cilicia, to be sure, was now technically a province of Rome, and a permanent command was assigned to its waters. But in the Mediterranean, Italian dominion was, if anything, less certain than before, not least because of the alliance soon established between the many groups of pirates based in Cilicia and Mithradates VI Eupator, King of Pontus, who waged a series of wars on Rome between 88 and 63 BC.[27] These were years in which, by all accounts, piracy flourished unchecked, and not only in the most distant East. It was the age of the famous abduction of Julius Caesar, captured and ransomed, according to tradition, near the island Pharmacusa.[28] Yet that was in truth but one of many episodes of violent acts of maritime depredation. All the waters the Romans called "our sea" (*mare nostrum*) were at stake, as were the regions of land that lay along their shores. Plutarch names thirteen sanctuaries pillaged in the first half of the first century BC. "For, you see," he relates, speaking of this time, "the ships of the pirates numbered more than a thousand, and the cities captured by them four hundred."[29] Dio recounts how the robbers who had once limited their acts of violence to ships now pillaged harbors and entire cities, almost organized as nations: "they no longer sailed in small forces, but in great fleets; and they had generals, so that they had acquired a great reputation."[30] Appian claims that in these years the pirates "dominated not only the eastern waters, but the whole Mediterranean to the Pillars of Hercules [....] No sea could be navigated in safety, and land remained untilled for want of commercial intercourse."[31] Cicero decries the plundering of sacred sites in Cnidos, Colophon, and Samos, the repeated raids on Sicily, the sack of Delos, and the pillaging of Caieta, Misenum, and even Ostia.[32] "We used to guarantee not just the safety of Italy, but were able, through the prestige of our imperial power, to preserve unharmed all our distant allies. Yet we are now cut off not only from our provinces and from the sea coast of Italy; we are even driven off the Appian Way!"[33]

In the winter of 67 BC, the situation attained a new degree of urgency. Livy and Appian recount that the pirates succeeded in cutting off the supply of grain to Rome. In the past, they had attempted such a feat; this time they were more effective, and the threat of famine in the capital became acute.[34] Appearing before the senate, the tribute Aulus Gabinius responded to the crisis with an extraordinary proposition. He suggested that a new office be created: among the ex-consuls, one general, he wagered, could be chosen and accorded vast powers and means to suppress the maritime menace to Rome. His motion was met with instant outcry among the members of the assembly. Dio reports that "the body preferred to suffer anything whatever at the hands of the freebooters" rather than put so great a command into any individual's hands.[35] Plutarch comments that "the chief and most influential men of the senate thought that such unlimited and absolute power, while it was beyond the reach of envy, was yet a thing to be feared."[36] Many understood the law to be a barely masked bid to return the republic to the monarchy of Romulus. In a first vote, the assembly therefore flatly refused it. But it seems not all those present in the senate shared that view. "When the people learned the feeling of the senators," Dio recounts, "they raised an uproar, even going so far as to rush upon them as they sat assembled; had the senators not got out of the way, the people would certainly have killed them."[37] With only a single member of the assembly, Julius Caesar, in support of the law, the frightened officials thus resigned themselves to accepting the motion, and a new title was bestowed on the man for whom the proposal, as all knew well, had been intended: Gabinius's own friend, Gnaeus Pompeius Magnus.

The ancient authors relay several accounts of the special capacities that the *lex Gabinia* accorded Pompey. Dio asserts that it granted the general "full power against the pirates," a title to "command [...] and have the use of a huge force, with many lieutenants."[38] Appian's report is more detailed: "When the Romans could no longer endure the damage and disgrace, they made Gnaeus Pompey, who was then their man of greatest reputation, commander by law [στρατηγὸς αὐτοκράτωρ] [...] with absolute power over the whole sea within the Pillars of Hercules, and of the land for a distance of 75 kilometres from the coast."[39] But it is to Plutarch's *Life of Pompey* that we owe the fullest description of the proceedings in the Roman senate. "Gabinius, one of Pompey's intimates," the biographer relates, "drew up a law which gave him, not an admiralty, but an out-and-out monarchy and irresponsible power over all men [νόμον οὐ ναυαρχίαν, ἄντικρυς δὲ μοναρχίαν αὐτῷ διδόντα καὶ δύναμιν ἐπὶ πάντας ἀνθρώπους ἀνυπεύθυνον]. For the law gave him dominion over the sea this side of the Pillars of Hercules, over all the mainland to the distance of four hundred furlongs from the sea. These limits included almost all places in the Roman world, and the greatest nations and most powerful kings were comprised within them. Besides this, he was empowered to choose fifteen legates from the senate for the several principalities, and to take from the public treasuries and the tax-collectors as much money as he wished, and to have two hundred ships, with full power over the number and levying of soldiers and oarsmen."[40]

The ancient chroniclers and commentators suggest more than a single interpretation of Pompey's extraordinary powers. Velleius asserts that the *lex Gabinia* accorded the general "a command equal [*imperium aequum*] to that of the proconsul in so much of every province as within fifty miles of the sea."[41] But the vast majority of the sources claim that the law instituted something else: a "greater command" (*imperium maius*), authorizing Pompey to make use of the exceptional military forces accorded him at sea, in the islands, and in a significant portion of the provinces assigned to Roman praetors.[42] It is possible that from a strictly constitutional perspective, Pompey's title had a precedent in the command bestowed seven years earlier on Marius Antonius Creticus, son of the former praetor of Cilicia, who may have been declared "guardian of the whole sea-shore" (*curator tuendae totius orae maritimae*) in 74.[43] But "in the manner of its grant and details of vital meaning," that earlier motion, as Hugh Last has written, "formed no precedent for the *Lex Gabinia*."[44] Pompey's means and right were without parallel in the history of the republic. "In 108 BC the People had given the African command to Marius without reference to the Senate: now they had created a power which nothing but the self-denial of the general could prevent from dominating the whole government of Rome."[45]

When the senators accorded Pompey his "greater empire," they were unequivocal in their stipulation that it last no more than three years. During that period, the seas, they hoped, would be at last purged of the pirates that infested them. But Pompey's action was far swifter than expected. The classical sources concur on this startling fact: less than two months after the institution of the extraordinary command, the pirates of the Mediterranean—from Mauritania to Cilicia, from North Africa to Macedon and Liguria—had ceased to pose any major threat to Rome.[46] Today it is not known how exactly this could have been. Ormerod cites Pompey's admirable organization and strategic deployment of the fleet, arguing that "the pirates were taken by surprise owing to the rapidity of the Roman movements, operations beginning at the earliest possible season."[47] Other scholars, however, are less certain of the extent of the Roman

54

victory. In his recent study, *Piracy in the Graeco-Roman World*, de Souza comments that "the remarkable speed with which Pompey cleared the seas before heading for Cilicia makes it unlikely that a thorough operation was carried out"; he concludes that "in spite of the numerous superlatives that have been used to describe Pompey's campaign of 67, a close scrutiny of the sources leaves the distinct impression of a 'rush job.'" [48]

More is known of the methods by which Pompey brought the enemies of Rome to justice. Dio explains that Pompey's military strength, albeit great, was no less than his clemency (φιλανθρωπία). [49] Velleius, Servilius, and Caesar had punished sea thievery by savage means; the marauders they fought could all expect with good reason that, if vanquished, they would be speedily executed, if not crucified or enslaved. According to many of his contemporaries and later biographers, Pompey had another habit. Plutarch reports that the general "did not once" think of putting his many antagonists to death. [50] Instead he offered them a settlement: were the pirates to surrender at sea, the general proposed, they would be granted titles to land in Cilicia and Achaia. [51] Facing the prospect of considerably less pacific ends from other Roman generals, such as Quintus Caecilius Metellus, many marauders appear to have accepted Pompey's proposition. "Even the Cretans," Cicero reports, calling to mind that most piratical of ancient nations, "when they sent emissaries to Pompey in Pamphylia to plead their case, learned that there was hope for their surrender, and were ordered to give hostages." [52] Some erstwhile enemies of the Roman people seem to have found fortune even in the navy of the republic itself. As Egon Maróti has indicated, there is evidence that two of Pompey's own admirals, Menocrates and Menodoros, had been themselves, in a former time, maritime depredators of Cilician origin. [53]

This much, in any case, can hardly be doubted: thanks to the combined novelties of the *lex Gabinia* and Pompey's policy towards the pirates he was to subjugate, the most spectacular episode in the ancient history of confrontations between the bearers of territorial authority and the bandits of the sea came to an end. The Roman

Republic followed only a few years later. "A milestone on the road to monarchy," as Last remarked, the new command given Pompey in the common war on piracy announced "the end of one epoch and the beginning of another."[54] It "paved the way," as scholars since Theodor Mommsen have observed, for the many measures of legal exception that were soon to follow in the constitutional history of Rome. In less than half a century, it would lead directly to the new dominion Augustus established: the Principate, a power "unrestricted in scope, which gave its leader the supreme command over the whole army of the empire, so that all troops took the military oath of allegiance to him and obeyed his orders."[55] That was to be the inception of another Roman *imperium*, greater even than Pompey's greater empire. That this dominion may have shared certain traits, in its aim and in its structure, with the marauders for whose persecution it had been instituted was a possibility no less conceivable at its end than at its beginning. In the last days of Rome, when no one believed the common war would end and that the roaming plunderers would ever be resettled, Augustine of Hippo did not hesitate to pose the question: "What are kingdoms but great robberies? And what are robberies themselves, but little kingdoms? The band itself is made up of men; it is ruled by the authority of a prince, it is knit together by the pact of the confederacy; the booty is divided by the law agreed on. If, by the admittance of abandoned men, this evil increases to such a degree that it holds places, fixes abodes, takes possession of cities, and subdues peoples, it assumes the more plainly the name of a kingdom, because the reality is now manifestly conferred on it, not by the removal of covetousness, but by the addition of impunity. Indeed, that was an apt and true reply which was given to Alexander the Great by a pirate who had been seized. For when that king had asked the man what he meant by keeping hostile possession of the sea, he answered with bold pride, 'What thou meanest by seizing the whole earth; but because I do it with a petty ship, I am called a robber, whilst thou who dost it with a great fleet art styled Emperor.'"[56]

CHAPTER SIX

Crossings

An institution, no less than an individual, may cross one line while retreating before another. It can expand the range of its force without passing beyond the limits of the law, increasing in its power while still not transgressing the boundaries set by right. An empire, too, must respect the titles that precede it, even if it is solely to show the excess of its own might with respect to the claims recorded in past traditions. The history of the domination of the sea illustrates this fact as few others do, and in this field, as in so many others, classical antiquity furnishes the perfect example. By the first century BC, if not sooner, Rome had proved herself the undisputed mistress of the seas. After Pompey's campaign against the pirates, it could hardly be doubted that the Latin control of the waters far exceeded that of any other ancient state, both in extent and in intensity. Now the Romans dominated trade and the fishing industry and, with the certainty of their unmatched maritime control, they lent to the Mediterranean in its entirety a new name, the telling expression of their imperial Latinity: *mare nostrum*, "our sea." Today that appellation may startle on account of its immodesty, but in its day it simply stated the obvious. Far more remarkable is that despite this common usage and the reality it reflected, in official settings the Roman statesmen never claimed—explicitly or programmatically, publicly or formally—that the sea could be, in accordance with any right, the established possession of their polity. Despite the force it exerted on all the waters around it, Rome continued, even in its age of empire, to defer to one archaic principle of law, which demanded that flowing water, both within the territory and beyond the shores, be by nature free from claims of ownership.

One might retort that matters of fact, in such a domain, carry greater weight than explicit pronouncements. It has been argued that the ancient Mediterranean was familiar with sovereign titles to possess the seas that long predated Rome. Some scholars have even asserted that such claims were once quite common.[1] But the evidence cannot be considered copious. It is said that the divine pharaoh defined his authority as stretching over water as well as land. Sources indicate that as late as the twelfth century BC, when the once indomitable Egyptian maritime might had vastly dwindled, Wes-Amon could still invoke his old prerogatives when challenged by King Byblus in Phoenicia. "The sea," the Egyptian monarch defensively declared, "belongs to the god Amon, and the Lebanon is his."[2] It has been speculated that the monarchs of Ugarit, also powerful in the Eastern waters, may have voiced similar pretensions; but today no documentary evidence of them remains.[3] Closer to Rome lay the famous Tyrian colony, Carthage, without doubt a maritime power of considerable proportions. Jonathan Ziskind argued that the Punic polity had no qualms about establishing its dominion over the sea: "Carthage used every diplomatic, military, and propagandistic resource at her disposal to assert and maintain a proprietary extension of her territories on the Mediterranean and Atlantic coast. The purpose of this policy was to protect and strengthen a far flung network of trading posts, mines, and supply stations."[4] But documents attesting to any Carthaginian pretensions to possess the waters, once again, are scarce at best. It may be that they are simply lost today. But it is also possible that the silence of the sources is more telling.[5] More often than not, the ancients may have accepted that the seas — no matter the occasional pronouncements of despots — could have no lawful master.

There are several reasons to draw such a conclusion. Some derive from documentary sources in the simple sense: claims made or omitted in ancient texts. Others, however, can be found in works in which the ancient authors discussed which things could be owned and which could not. Roman law, the most systematic and developed in the classical world, provides the decisive evidence. Earlier ancient legal codes defined the relations between objects (whether natural or artificial) and the subjects who would lay claim to them, in such a way that titles to possession, for instance, could be judged and secured according to clear and established principles. But when compared with the Latin legal system, the older codes seem minimal in their titles. In private law, the absence of any single Hellenic term for the rights of ownership that the Romans called *dominium* and *proprietas* is perhaps the most famous example of this fact.[6] But it is one detail among many, and it would be an error to seek to understand it on its own. The Latin legal order may be distinguished from all those institutions, including the Greek, that preceded it on account of one simple fact: the Romans sought to offer a fully articulated account of the legal "thing" (*res*) in the totality of its relations to the rights of which it may be made an object. For this reason, the Latin jurist availed himself of a technical arsenal of a kind known to none before him. He possessed a systematic typology of the various forms by which any thing could be submitted to the form of right.

Like every aspect of the Roman law, the theory of the legal thing developed over the course of centuries, and scholars have had little difficulty in identifying differences of origin and doctrine in the four parts that compose the *Corpus Iuris Civilis* commissioned by the Emperor Justinian in the mid-sixth century AD, the *Code, Institutes, Digest,* and *Novels.*[7] For the purposes of economy, however, one may present this domain of the Roman legal doctrine as a coherent whole, defining, at a single glance, the varieties of things with which the Latin jurists were familiar.[8] Naturally, the Romans admitted the existence of useful things (*bona*) within the realm of human law which private individuals could lay claim to owning. Such goods, they taught, form the set of objects that may rightly be said to be "in our patrimony" (*in patrimonio nostro*). But had the exponents of the Latin law restricted themselves to the analysis and classification of this one set, they would have admitted in their doctrine only entities susceptible of being privately owned by men. In reality, the ancient authors went much further. Concentrating on the legal thing less in its positive determination than in its mere determinability, they included in their system things bound to the right of possession by the barest and most minimal of all forms of relation — namely, exclusion. Thus the jurists of the *Institutes* and the *Digest* distinguished those things that they considered to be in our patrimony from all those that they deemed, with perfect symmetry, to lie "outside" it (*res extra nostrum patrimonium*).[9]

Such things were of more than a single kind. A first class can be defined by the fact of belonging to divine law (*res divini iuris*) and being, for this reason, withdrawn from the purview of all human claims. Among the members of this group, one may in turn distinguish several types. In the fullest surviving presentation of the Roman doctrine of things, which we owe to the *Institutes* of Gaius, the first subset is that of "sacred things" (*res sacrae*). Temples, shrines, holy groves and artifacts are all of this nature, incapable of being owned by men on account of consecration to the higher gods (*superi*).[10] Second among the objects of divine law are "religious things" (*res religiosae*), which belong to the souls of the underworld (*Manes*), the deceased ancestors venerated by Roman tradition.[11] The ground of the burial site, for the jurists, is of the type; from the moment it contains the body of the dead, it may no longer be assigned any rightful human master. Finally, various Roman sources admit the existence of a third class of things belonging to divine law: sanctified things (*res sanctae*). The walls of the city exemplify this type, which are as incapable of being appropriated by any single human subject. To violate sanctified things was, therefore, to incur a punishment of an exceptional nature, such as that said to have been meted out to Remus, put to death for having tried to scale the walls of Rome.[12]

Not all things that might not be owned were considered to belong to the gods. Many entities fell squarely within the province of human law, despite their essential resistance to appropriation. Among them, one must count first of all those which are by definition "public" (*res publicae*). These belong to the Roman people and so, by extension, to its institutional form in the state. Some among these things are destined to shared use, such as streets and squares, theaters and thermal baths; others, such as slaves, mines, and money, serve the administrative ends of the Roman republic.[13] Many Roman authors write also of "universal things" (*res universitatis*); formally these resemble those objects termed "public," yet still they can be identified on account of belonging not to the capital but to the other cities with which it stands in relation.[14] Finally, for the jurists a third set of things outside our patrimony can be found in nature itself. These are the beings that are, by definition, "common to all" (*res communis omnium*). Unmentioned by Gaius in his *Institutes*, this last class of things appears in many statements of the *Corpus Iuris*, where it is consistently characterized by the same striking features. "Common things," unlike all others, belong neither to the human law nor to the divine. For this reason, no single being—be it private or public, human or divine, living or dead—may rightfully claim them. They derive directly from a juridical realm more archaic than civil law (*ius civile*) and the law of peoples (*ius gentium*), a realm which the Roman jurists named "natural law" (*ius naturale*). For the lawyers, if not the philosophers, this was a legal order common to all living things, animals no less than human beings. The *Corpus Iuris* consistently describes it in negative terms. The ancient authors say little more of it than that it is lacking in all the positive conventions instituted by cities, such as ownership.[15]

The oldest recorded legal document on the status of the waters in the West tells us that the sea is a being of this kind, irreducibly common, by natural law, to all living things. The crucial statement can be can be found in book 1 of the *Digest* of Justinian, where it is attributed to the *Institutes* of Marcianus, an author of the second century AD whose pronouncements were widely held to represent the position of the law. Briefly recalling the doctrine of the possible determinations of objects with respect to the rights of ownership, the jurist explains in this fragment that most things belong to individuals separately (*pleraque singulorum*), being susceptible of being acquired by various means. But Marcianus then specifies that things may also be of other kinds. They may be "universal" (*universitatis*), belonging to an entire community; they may be "no one's" (*nullius*), still to be acquired by a private individual; finally, they may be "common to all" (*communis omnium*). Marcianus then declares: "The following things belong in common, by natural law, to all: air, flowing water, and the sea, and on its account the shores of the sea" (*quidem naturali iure omnium communia sunt illa: aer, aqua profluens, et mare, et per hoc litora maris*).[16]

Of the common things mentioned by the jurist, only air does not derive its specific legal quality from the character of water in movement. The principal thing of all, to the jurist's eyes, seems therefore to be the open sea; the others are those bodies inland, such as sources, streams and rivers, which most closely resemble it. In a single gesture, Marcianus thus establishes that all such entities outstrip the form of belonging to any single legal subject — including, we must infer, the august entity he so well knew, that is, the Roman state. But the excess of the sea with respect to ownership is hardly absolute. It can be measured by a single, albeit crooked and sometimes shifting line: that of the littoral. As Marcianus presents it, the last and finest edge of dry land before the flowing water traces a contour that is in every sense crucial for the determination of the domain of civil law. There, at the shore, the juridical order that admits of exclusive forms of belonging meets a legal region altogether unlike it. There, instituted right — be it of the city or of peoples — encounters its limit: that immense, unfounded yet still somehow legal order that the Roman scholars, acutely conscious of the artificiality of their civil law, called "nature."

That the ancient jurists found this limit provocative as well as troubling can be gleaned from their complex and conflicted theory of the shore, which was to have a lasting influence on almost all subsequent efforts in the West to define the law of the seas. Like its many modern counterparts, this domain of Roman law sought to respond to several thorny legal questions. Naturally, for the Latin jurists the first among such issues concerned the status of the shore itself as an entity in the legal sense. Not all agreed with Marcianus that the littoral was a "thing common to all by nature." The first jurist to have dissented appears to have been his illustrious near contemporary, Celsus, whose statement on the subject can also be found in the *Digest*. It is unequivocal in its form: "the shores," Celsus states, "in which the Roman people holds its power, belong to the Roman people" (*litora, in quae populus romanus imperium habet, populi romani esse arbitror*).[17] This judgment clearly identifies the shore as a thing submitted to human law, being the rightful possession of the Roman state.

The legal dissent was not only between Marcianus and Celsus. A survey of the *Corpus Iuris* as a whole reveals repeated formulations of the same two opposing views, which echo each other in contradiction. Thus Ulpian, after Marcianus, holds the shore to be "common to all," like the sea, and Neratius, in similar terms, declares the littoral incapable of being definitively appropriated.[18] But Pampinius and Paulus, by contrast, second Celsus; they both classify the shore among "public places" (*loca publica*).[19] The difference of opinion certainly seems stark. One may even say that the two judgments exclude each other as a matter of principle. If a thing may be ascribed to natural law on account of being common to all, then the city can hardly claim it as its own public thing; if, by contrast, it may be submitted to civil law, being the proper possession of the state, it can hardly be said to resist all appropriation, belonging by natural law to all.[20] But such a contrast, although clear, may be misleading, for from a different perspective, the two types of things may also be seen as the inverted images of each other. It is striking that both common things and public things are "outside our patrimony" (*extra patrimonium*), which no individual may own: the first, because they cannot be joined in any way to the city, the second, because, with perfect symmetry, they may not at all be disjoined from it.

At times, historians of the Roman law have sought to reconcile the legal positions. In an influential article published in 1890–1891, "Sulla condizione giuridica delle rive del mare in diritto romano e odierno: Contributo alla teoria delle 'res communes omnium'" ("On the Juridical Condition of the Sea Shores in Roman and

Contemporary Law: A Contribution to the Theory of the 'Res communis omnium'"), Muzio Pampaloni thus argued that both classical claims may hold, provided one grant the littoral a composite juridical status. It suffices, the scholar explained, to posit a legal partition within the shore. Then one may recover, within one natural region, two juridical things: one "internal," comprising, for example, ports and harbors, which are the rightful property of the State, the other "external," lying beyond them and so being, by natural law, common to all.[21] Such an account undoubtedly succeeds in reconciling the dicta of these authorities, but it does so only at a price. Within a single limit, a second now emerges, as if, to be grasped as such and qualified by law, one littoral must become two. It is difficult to avoid the impression that such an explanation resolves the question of the classical divergence of opinion only by restating it.

Whatever the legal status of the shore as a thing, however, a further and perhaps more pressing question can hardly be avoided: where, exactly, are the shores? At what point does the land border on the sea, such that the sphere of civil and international law ends along a clear line, where that of nature in turn begins? To this query, at least, the *Institutes* of Justinian furnish one unequivocal answer: "The shore of the sea extends to the point attained by the highest tide in winter" (*est autem litus maris, quatenus hibernus fluctus maximus excurrit*).[22] Aquillius Gallus and Cicero may have expressed a similar view.[23] It was certainly to be lasting in its force. In France, to cite but one example, it remained the accepted criterion for the delimitation of the public domain along the Mediterranean until 1973.[24] Despite its authority, however, the judgment of the Roman jurists is far from self-evident. It is striking that this definition of the littoral presents its object as a thing determined not by the proper extent of the territory but by the shifting movements of the water. The jurist, in other words, chooses to observe the land from the point of view of the sea, drawing the borders of the field of civil law from a region in which such a law, by nature, cannot hold. It is also worth noting that the classical definition of the shore of the sea as extending "to the point attained by the highest tide in winter" treats its object as essentially a portion of the waters beyond it, the relation between the littoral and the sea being, for the Romans, that of part to whole.[25] The shore, in such terms, may have no autonomy as a legal entity; deemed no more than the furthest extension of the water towards the land, its own status fades, as a consequence, into that of the sea. Between firm ground and moving water, between the terrain of the city and the domain of nature, there would seem to be no intermediary.

The semblance, however, is deceiving. It suffices to consider the coast at any time other than that of "the highest tide in winter" to observe an incontestable fact: a space opens between the land and sea, which is wide enough, in certain cases, to be occupied. Despite its legal definition as no more than sea extended to the land, the shore then allows itself to be considered, at least provisionally, as dry ground, and it can be treated much as land that may be owned. Well aware of this fact, the Roman jurists discussed the questions it raised at some length. Pomponius tells us that as a general rule, when the tide retreats, what belongs to all may indeed become the property of one. The reason is quite clear: while the sea itself cannot be owned, "anything built into the sea becomes private property."[26] "If I drive piles into the sea and build upon them," he explains elsewhere in the *Digest*, "the edifice will immediately be mine."[27] On the same grounds, the ancient lawyers held that anything erected on the shore may become the object of a claim to possession. As Neratius puts it, "whatever anyone builds upon the shore of the sea will belong to him,"[28] or, as Ulpian has it, "if anyone constructs a building in the sea or on the shore of the same, although he does not build upon his own land, he renders it his."[29] To this degree, the littoral may be viewed less as a "common thing" than as "no one's thing" (*res nullius*). By nature, it lacks an owner. But it nonetheless remains susceptible to being assigned to an individual, provided he claims it as his own.[30] The shore, in other words, can be "captured," exactly like a wild animal, which, once seized, may be rightfully appropriated.[31]

From belonging to all—and so to none—to belonging to one with exclusivity: the passage leads from the absence of rightful possession to its presence. Maritime or mythological, perhaps maritime and mythological, the transition merits some reflection. A statement by Paulus suggests that such a displacement contains the "trace" (*vestigium*) of the far older and more momentous movement that led, in immemorial times, from the law of nature, where everything was in common, to that of cities, where possession was officially instituted.[32] But one fundamental difference separates the seizing of the shore from the appropriation of goods that, for the Romans, accompanied the foundation of civil right. The securing of the city was to be permanent, allowing for the lasting establishment of justified claims to possession. The taking of the littoral, by contrast, must be provisional. In this regard, the parallel with the capture of the wild beast proves especially illuminating. A man, the jurists teach, may always lose his right to possess the feral beast he has caught: it suffices for the animal to run or fly away from its master without returning. Then, if another finds it, it will be his, for the law supposes that the beast has reverted, in the interim, to its natural state of being "no one's thing" (*res nullius*). In structure, the vicissitudes of the shore are no different, though, bound in part to the movement of the tides, they may be more regular. Should a building erected upon the shore cease to stand, Neratius explains, the ground immediately recovers its natural state: it "reverts to its former condition," "just as if it had never been built upon."[33] Having been temporarily detained for the exclusive use of an individual, the common thing, after passing from natural law to civil law, now crosses back again. Nature, by right, thus returns to itself. Marcianus tells us that the process is much like that of a prisoner of war, who recovers his freedom as he crosses the border of his homeland. Speaking of the shore on which a building has collapsed, the author explains: "the place reverts to its former condition by the law of *postliminium*, so to speak, and if another party builds a house in the same place, the soil becomes his."[34]

Postliminium was the name given by the Romans to the branch of their legal system that dealt with the rights of restitution and the principles by which goods and persons were to be reassigned their original status after capture, usually following a war.[35] Here Marcianus's invocation of this field of legal science may seem little more than an ornament of personification added for the purposes of illustration: the building in ruins, the shore, in his words, "so to speak" (*quasi*) claims the right to return, like a soldier after battle. But the likeness is of profound import. It clearly reveals what might otherwise have remained merely implicit in the doctrine of the juridical status of flowing water: namely, that the boundary between the land and the sea is of the nature of a threshold. That proposition could not otherwise be directly derived from the discussion of the seas in the *Digest*. The fact that a line separates those legal things that may be in our patrimony from those that lie outside it needs no recalling. That this line may sometimes move, at least in matters of maritime law, follows from the implication of the flow of the tide in the classical definition of the shore. Now, however, the jurist says much more: he tells us that the shifting limit that divides the land from the sea is in truth a line of passage, which a single thing, like the freed captive, may sometimes cross. Wherever the official barrier is to be situated—at the mark of high tide, as the *Institutes* declare, or at the mark of low tide, as some authors in the *Digest* also suggest—the decisive point may be that the line may be crossed, that the water mark, in other words, can be unmarked, if only for the time it takes to pass it.

Since it was impossible in ancient times for human beings to survive at sea except by returning, time and time again, to the land, those who moved across this line in the classical age did so not once but repeatedly. They lived by crossing the moving limit which the Roman jurists systematically *demarcated*, in every sense of the word. When such seafarers took goods aboard their vessels, they carried them from the juridical realm in which they could be rightfully attributed to their masters into one in which claims to ownership, by right, must cease. They transported things, in this way, from the region in which they could be said to lie "in our patrimony" to that outside it (*extra patrimonium*): a maritime dimension without ownership, itself incapable of being rightfully possessed. By definition, such individuals, therefore, could not claim to be and to remain masters. They could certainly be transmitters, rightfully relaying property, according to established legal rules, from persons to persons through the medium of the moving waters. They might also be thieves, taking goods from the land into a region in which they could no longer clearly be assigned their owners, in order to insert them later, at a price, into new chains of legal commerce. Such individuals — one might call them "pirates" — were in any case always agents of the threshold, who crossed the moving border at which things pass from belonging to someone to belonging, alternately, to no one and to everyone. Hence their indispensability to so many: to those who wished to subtract goods from the legal orders in which they had an established place; to those, too, who wished to exert their own force beyond the claims of the law, without, for that matter, annulling it. A means to cross from the field of civil right into the domain outside it may well be of interest to an individual. Fictional or real, artificial or natural, such a means is certainly an asset to an institution, especially one that claims sovereignty, like Rome and the many states that followed it, over land bounded by the sea.

CHAPTER SEVEN

Afloat

Things at sea pose a number of delicate questions for the law, at least from the point of view of the land. The classical jurists were well aware of this fact, and they noted it more than once: once a good falls into the hands of pirates, who take it beyond the shores with them, its legal status as the object of a claim often proves difficult to define. It is true that sea thieves in the strict sense appear relatively infrequently in the *Digest*. But Justinian's was a late compendium. By the age of the Christian emperor, maritime thieves had long ceded their distinguished place as the preeminent outlaws of the sea to the likes of port robbers and petty wreckers, piracy having "practically disappeared from the Mediterranean," as Walter Ashburner put it, "in the palmy days of the empire."[1] Books by Roman lawyers of earlier times paint a different picture. There, the plunderers are numerous, perhaps as many as the problems they raise for the experts trained in the domain of private right. Seneca the Elder's *Declamations* are exemplary in this regard. Composed toward the end of the first century BC and the inception of the first century AD, they contain accounts of various instances in which pirates could give the lawyers cause for debate. The exact cases recorded by Seneca were most likely invented for the purposes of training young lawyers in the rhetorical arts of argument. But this casuistry of piracy was no less serious, in jurisprudential terms, for being fictional.

A brief summary of the contents of several of these controversies is instructive. One may begin with the striking case of "The Pirate Chief's Daughter" (*Archipiratae Filia*). It follows on the heels of various unseemly acts at sea. Pirates captured a man, for whom they expected to obtain a considerable ransom. But the unflinching father refused to pay to regain his lost son. Over the waters, meanwhile, another transaction came to pass. The daughter of the pirate chief furnished the captive with a means of escape: were he to marry her when back on land, she promised to lead him to safety. The son accepted. Once back in his city, accompanied by his new wife, the young man found himself, however, promptly disinherited by his progenitor. Hence the question debated by the lawyers: does the son now have a right to sue his father?[2] The opinions of the specialists were divided. There is also the case of the "Man Who Adopted His Disinherited Brother and Was Himself to Be Disinherited." A Roman citizen, Seneca reports, "had two sons, a good one and a debauched one. He disinherited the debauchee. The good one set off abroad. He was captured by pirates, and wrote to his father to get a ransom. The father was dilatory; the debauchee acted first and redeemed him. The good son returned home and adopted his brother."[3] May the father rightfully now disinherit him? The scenario recalls that of another case, "The Man Who Was Released by His Son, the Pirate Chief."[4] This time, a man has remarried after the death of his wife and convicted one of his two sons by his former spouse for parricide, on the grounds that the youth sought to kill him. Implacably, the father punished the delinquent son by sending him out to sea on a boat without rigging. The son "drifted into the hands of pirates" and, in time, became a "pirate chief" himself. The quandary arose later: "The father set out abroad and was captured by his son and sent back to his country." Now the father—with clearly questionable right—disinherits his other son.

The most remarkable case, however, may be that of "The Prostitute Priestess" (*Sacerdos Prostituta*).[5] This is the tale of a virgin captured by pirates, bought by a pimp and forced, as a consequence, into prostitution. "When men came to her," Seneca writes, "she asked for alms. When she failed to get alms from a soldier who came to her, he struggled with her and tried to use force; she killed him. She was accused, acquitted and sent back to her family."[6] The legal question proves unavoidable once the daughter finds herself again in her own city, having crossed from servitude to freedom in passing from sea to land. Now she resolves to pursue a calling to which she could certainly have laid claim before setting out to sea, but to which her access may be barred. She demands to be accepted as a priestess, in full knowledge of the Roman principle according to which that function demands she be "chaste and from the chaste, pure and from the pure" (casta e castis, pura e puris).[7] The lawyers deliberate over her case at length before reaching their verdict. It is unequivocal. Despite the purity and chastity that may have belonged to the young woman before her abduction, the representatives of the law deem her now, after captivity and killing, ineligible for the priesthood, recalling—not without some outrage—that there can be no place in the temple for one who has been both "practicing whore" and "murderess." That conclusion can hardly be considered startling. More remarkable is the very fact of the inclusion of this case in the anthology of legal quandaries. Had the events leading to the petition to join the priesthood come to pass on land, they would certainly have occasioned no debate. But that which occurs over the moving waters cannot easily be determined by the lawyers, and its juridical import remains, at least for the time of this debate, open to dispute. Momentarily, the legal procedure slows and stalls before a case in which grounds for judgment must be sought at sea.

The Romans were not alone, in their age, in hesitating to apply their law to events which take place on the open waters. For evidence, one may look to the texts of Seneca the Elder's Greek contemporaries, who made of the juridical questions raised by things at sea an essential element of a new literary form: that variety of narrative work known to the literary tradition as the "ancient novel." Pirates and their companions, to be sure, are far from absent in Hellenic letters before this period. There are scattered sea bandits throughout classical Greek literature, from the Homeric "plunderers" (ληϊστῆρες) to the slave-trading "sailors" (ναῦται), for instance, who intrude on the action of the Hypsipyle to bring the tragedy's eponymous hero speedily from Lemnos to Nemea.[8] At times they

71

may well be striking to the modern reader. But their appearances remain, by and large, those of minor characters and strategic middlemen. It is only in the novels of the Hellenistic period—from Heliodorus, Longus, and Xenephon to Apuleius and *Apollonius of Tyre*—that sea bandits begin to proliferate in classical letters, taking characters, mainly against their will, to the easternmost regions of the Hellenic world. Now, for the first time in Western literature, "we find that pirates and lawbreakers," as P. A. Mackay observed, "have virtually taken over the running of the story."[9]

Chariton's *Chaereas and Callirhoe* may be the oldest ancient prose romance to have survived to the modern age intact, and it revolves entirely around a perilous passage to the seas, which bears more than a passing resemblance to the piratical abduction imagined by Seneca in his *Declamations*.[10] The action of the novel begins in Greek Syracuse, where Callirhoe, "the pride of Sicily," a girl of "more than human beauty," "not that of a Nereid or a mountain nymph but of the maiden Aphrodite herself," marries Chaereas, a youth "surpassingly handsome, like Achilles and Nireus and Hippolytus and Alcibiades as sculptors and painters portray them."[11] Envious neighbors conspire against the exceedingly lovely couple soon after they are wed, convincing Chaereas, by a malevolent ruse, that his bride has betrayed him with another. Suitably enraged, the athletic youth fiercely kicks his wife, who falls to the ground, as if never again to rise. Callirhoe receives a lavish public funeral, at which her mourning relatives place her in a monumental tomb of many treasures. They do not see that among the grieving masses at her interment, a sea thief lies concealed on land: "a man called Theron, a scoundrel whose criminal trade it was to sail the seas and have thugs handily stationed with boats in harbors under cover of being ferrymen; from this he made up pirate crews."[12] Conscious of the riches it contains, Theron and his pack enter the tomb that very night to steal its treasures. But they soon discover more. As his henchmen investigate the sepulcher, seizing its many goods, the dead woman stirs. "As for Callirhoe," the narrator writes, "she came back to life! Her respiration had stopped, but lack of food started it again; with difficulty, and gradually, she began to breathe. Then she began to move her body, limb by limb."[13]

Taking the frightened beauty together with the costly objects that adorn her tomb, the pirates set sail in search of gain across the seas. They encounter little difficulty in disposing of their new loot in Asia Minor, where they reap considerable profit by inserting things that were to belong to the dead into the commercial exchange of men. They also sell Callirhoe to an Ionian, Leonas, who remits her, in turn, to his master in Miletus, Dionysus, "the wealthiest, noblest and most cultured man" in the region.[14] Naturally, the cultivated aristocrat finds himself consumed with passion for the forsaken Greek. Callirhoe wards him off at first, faithful to her dear Chaereas. But upon learning that she is pregnant with her husband's son, she fears for the future of her child, concluding, after some reflection, that she must marry her rich suitor.

Meanwhile, in Syracuse, the once murderous, now mournful Sicilian husband discovers the desecrated tomb, carelessly left open by the savage plunderers. He sets off in search of his lost spouse and happens, by a stroke of luck, upon Theron and his men drifting at sea, without water yet still in possession of some of the funeral offerings they pillaged in Callirhoe's tomb. Chaereas has them rounded up and brought back to Syracuse. Chained in the city theater, Theron now confesses his iniquitous deeds—though not before being tortured by "the rack, fire, and wheels," "the proper prize," Chariton notes, "for his efforts."[15] The lawful citizens proceed to crucify the pirate before the site of his crime, "in front of Callirhoe's tomb, and from his cross he looked out on that sea over which he had carried as a captive the daughter of Hermocrates."[16] In possession of the precious news he had sought, Chaereas sets sail for Miletus, where he demands the restitution of his erstwhile wife at the court of Dionysus. Predictably, however, the second husband refuses to recognize the rights of the first. As rumors of the quarrel between the litigious husbands begin to fly, Dionysus's superior, the King of Persia, intervenes. He orders that all the participants in the suit come hastily to an audience with him in Babylon, where he will decide the crucial question: who, beyond the tomb and seas, may rightfully lay claim to Callirhoe.

Readers of *Chaereas and Callirhoe* have often remarked upon the attention lavished by the novel on the legal proceedings that ensue. In a classic study of the romance, P. E. Perry noted that the final trial "overshadows in interest and importance everything that has preceded, and what follows consists in the unraveling of the situation thereby developed [....] It is the culminating point of a suspense which has been gathering momentum for the space of an entire book."[17] Chariton himself seems to have held no illusions about the extraordinary nature of the legal discussions before King Artaxerxes of Persia: "Who could fitly describe that scene in court?" the author asks. "What dramatist ever staged such an astonishing story? It was like being at a play packed with passionate scenes, with emotions tumbling over each other—weeping and rejoicing, astonishment and pity, disbelief and prayers."[18] Chaereas charges Dionysus with adultery on the grounds that he has taken possession of a thing belonging to another: "You're laying hands on another man's wife." The legal status of the woman who was his own, he maintains, could not have changed in being seized from him and taken across the waters. It was a compelling point, later to be accepted as a matter of principle by the jurists of the modern age. Following Bartolus, the founding fathers of modern international law famously would declare, in terms close to those of Chaereas, that "the pirate does not alter ownership" (*pirata non mutat dominium*).[19]

Dionysus cannot defend himself except by countering the allegation of theft with a more serious accusation still. He calls to mind the near fatal kick, by which Chaereas, he contends, attempted to murder his own wife, before burying her, in full accordance with religious law.[20] May a woman who has been assassinated and given a proper funeral, Dionysus wonders, still belong to the husband who once rightfully laid claim to her? That argument would merit some discussion. But before the question can be treated at any length, the plot of the novel takes another turn: a third pretender steps onto the stage. Artaxerxes confesses that which the reader may have

74

anticipated: he, too, declares himself smitten by the Sicilian beauty. He cannot bring himself, for this reason, to assign the contested woman to either of the men who would claim her as his own. Thus the legal deliberations continue, day after day—until an uprising in Egypt obligates the monarch to set forth to quell the insurgents. In the absence of any judgment, Dionysus absconds with Callirhoe. But he is soon overtaken at sea by Chaereas, who captures the captured wife and returns her by force, if not by right, to their home in Sicily.

Chariton's novel may have been the first extended fiction to follow, step by step, the vagaries of a subject of civil law loosened from all claims to mastery in being sent off across the seas. It was hardly the last. Over a millennium later, Boccaccio followed a similar course in a novella of the *Decameron*, though it led him to a different destination. The medieval writer's tale was not that of a woman who, like the "prostitute priestess," must be reconciled while on land to a new legal status acquired at sea. Nor was it that of a woman whose many voyages at sea rendered her, like Callirhoe, susceptible to being claimed by more than a single master. It was, instead, the narrative of a woman who passed—as always, by the pirate's hand—from the individual who claimed her as his own to a region in which she remained felicitously without any lawful master, afloat, so to speak, with respect to the law, if only for a while.

Bartolomea was married to a distinguished judge of Pisa, Riccardo di Chinzica. The latter proved noticeably more devoted to his legal studies than to his exceedingly beautiful bride, "not without," we learn, "grave melancholy on the part of his wife."[21] One hot day, near Leghorn, the judge granted his spouse the small pleasure of going out to sea in a fishing boat. Paganino the pirate lurked nearby and, catching sight of the boat and its passenger, quickly captured both, bringing the married woman with him to his home in Monaco. Bartolomea, we learn, was at first understandably distressed, "crying heavily" as she was taken off her expected course. But the pirate "softly comforted her," and with considerable speed and success, for "even before they arrived in Monaco," the narrator tells us, "the judge and his laws had entirely left her mind, and she began living in the most joyous way imaginable with Paganino, who, having brought her to Monaco, in addition to all the consolations that he gave her day and night, held her honorably as his wife."[22] When the Pisan official at last discovered the location of his wife and made the journey across the waves to retrieve her, Paganino amiably allowed the representative of the law to converse freely with his spouse. But Bartolomea would not return: proclaiming her husband less a judge than a "banisher of rites and holidays" (*banditor di sagre e di feste*), she assured him that, even were Paganino cruelly to abandon her, still she would never return to her husband.[23] Thus the Pisan judge left the illicit couple empty-handed, returning to Tuscany to die soon afterwards. As the pirate well knew, that event, in turn, opened one new possibility: "Aware of the love that the woman had for him, Paganino took Bartolomea to be his legitimate wife."[24]

After piratical capture and abduction, the protagonist of Boccaccio's tale thus returns to the order of possession that is lawful marriage. The path is indirect, even winding, but still the medieval novella follows it to its certain terminus. In death and marriage, Boccaccio's comic controversy may then find its resolution. In this, it departs from the itinerary of the Greek novel, interrupted before any rightful decision comes to settle that which the tomb and a second marriage set in motion. Bartolomea's course lies closer to that of Seneca's *Declamations*. Like the Roman lawyers, she steers a route, knowing or unknowingly, from land to sea and back, albeit with a pause, again to land. There, in the home of the lawfully married pair in Monaco, rightful conjugal relations may be reestablished after their suspension, as legal things return to the shores and to the ties that will then bind them fast to land. There, however, the tale can only end; no more of it may be said. The novelistic invention sustains itself elsewhere, in a region in which claims do not clearly hold, and into which even the distinguished judge, despite his studies, might not venture. Only there, between one shore and another, can a fiction — legal or literary — stay afloat. The rest, for it, is shipwreck.

CHAPTER EIGHT

Dialectic of the Sea Dogs

It would be an error to consider all roving seafarers, without distinction, lawless. To be sure, innumerable sources indicate that maritime plunderers are often to be feared. It may also be that, given a choice, few would claim the title of sea bandit for himself. Both times that Odysseus and his companions are asked whether they are not "pirates" (λῃϊστῆρες), who roam the seas, "risking their lives and bringing harm to others," the Homeric hero, for one, declines to answer in the affirmative.[1] There can be no doubt that the question put to him was comprehensible. The actions of the great Achaeans during war bore more than a passing resemblance to those of robbers, and in the Homeric world it was no easy thing to distinguish between the varieties of armed men traveling by ship. Once at least, Odysseus joyfully recalled how he forsook the land for the sea: "I reveled in long ships with oars; I loved polished lances, arrows in the skirmish, the shapes of doom that others shake to see. Carnage suited me; heaven put those things somehow in me. Each to his own pleasure!"[2]

Then, admittedly, the crafty Ithacan was in disguise, claiming, as he did more than once, to be a Cretan.[3] That mask fit the Homeric hero almost too well. For Odysseus competed with the other Greeks for a fame that would depend, at least in part, on the booty to be seized from the sacked city of Troy, and his distinction in battle was to be measured by the magnitude of that which he would take back with him from his raids. As a scholar has recently remarked, "it would seem, therefore, difficult for the modern student of Homeric society to determine exactly, or even approximately, where any boundaries between warfare and piracy might be drawn."[4] This much seems to have changed little in later antiquity. It appears that the people of all the early ages of the West, like Goethe's Mephistopheles, held "war, commerce and piracy" (*Krieg, Handel und Piraterie*) to be essentially "three in one" (*dreieinig*), "not to be disjoined" (*nicht zu trennen*).[5] From the archaic age of Greece through to the end of the Roman period, the promise of plunder remained, as Servius observed, the most common reason why anyone — citizen or criminal — would set sail.[6] The ancient lexicon of seafaring is to this degree significant. In Greek as in Latin, a reference to "pirate ships" (λῃστρικὰ πλοῖα, *piratica navigia*) remains resolutely ambiguous. It may point to vessels of two very different sorts: those belonging to bandits and also to those belonging to the appointed representatives of a lawful state.[7]

The ancient authors show every sign of having been well aware of the formal difference that may separate the two varieties of violent seafarers. Numerous sources indicate that the writers of the classical age could distinguish, when necessary, between the roving standard-bearers of cities who sacked and pillaged their enemies, on the one hand, and, on the other, the raiders who preyed on the sedentary inhabitants of the Mediterranean without claiming any rights. Some scholars have argued that the awareness of this distinction is as old as the records of Greek culture and that already in the Homeric world, the warrior and the bandit were considered not to be of the same kind. It suffices, some have argued, to recall the relatively marginal place of the term "pirate" (or "plunderer," λῃστής) in the epic vocabulary. In the *Odyssey* and the *Iliad*, this expression refers exclusively to characters of minor status and negligible dramatic importance, and although many of the major Achaean and Trojan figures commit rapacious acts at sea in search of booty, none suffers the dishonor of finding himself designated by the iniquitous epithet. The philological evidence suggests a conclusion, therefore, that cannot but perplex: although perfectly aware of the distinction between the legitimate and the illegitimate pillagers of the sea, the ancients did not assign to it any single name. The classical authors disposed of no term, be it Latin or Greek, by which they might divide the wide expanse of roving sailors, separating, in a single gesture, the lawful maritime raiders from the lawless.

That was to be an achievement—for better or for worse—of modernity. But the sources of the post-classical innovation lay, as so often, in the long interval that followed the end of Antiquity. The Middle Ages witnessed the emergence of a term unknown to the ancients, which, once coined, would accompany that old noun, "pirate" (*pirata*), in Latin, Greek, and all the emerging vernaculars of modern Europe. The novel medieval expression was *cursarius*, "corsair." This Latin noun derived from verbal expressions indicating the maritime "course" (*cursum*) run by ships as they raided goods along the coast of the Mediterranean (*cursum facere, ire ad cursum*, and simply *currere*). Numerous medieval administrative and legal documents refer to such "corsairs" and their "course," employing a variety of related forms in Latin and Greek (*cusarii, cursales, corsalia*, κουρσάριοι).[8] By the last centuries of the Middle Ages, if not sooner, the usage could also be found in literary works. This includes the pirate Paganino, introduced in the *Decameron* as "a very famous corsair" (*molto famoso corsale*), and that other rover of the second day of Boccaccio's tales, Landolfo Ruffolo.[9] The medieval author describes this seaman's exploits in some detail, relating that after he lost his boat at sea, Landolfo "bought a light wooden ship to run the course [*da corseggiare*], arming and decorating it with every thing suited to that purpose," such that "within a year, he had stolen and taken so many ships from the Turks that he had not only regained the goods he had lost but had more than doubled them."[10] Similar expressions for the "course" soon acquired common currency in the other Romance languages. Such terms lasted well into the modern period, furnishing works of literature of the seventeenth, eighteenth, and nineteenth centuries with many of their most memorable figures. Of countless cases, one might recall, as a single example, the infamous *corsaire de Salé* who boards and raids the ship of a hapless Candide in Voltaire's exemplary tale.

By the early twentieth century, the medieval distinction had long become a staple element in the technical vocabulary of European international law. In jurisprudential terms, the term "corsair" was not to be confused with that older word, "pirate," though, if one believes the specialists, many of the age continued to do precisely that. "Every day, in common speech," Henri Brongniart deplored in a monograph published in 1904, *Les corsaires et la guerre maritime* (*Corsairs and Maritime War*), "we see the most enlightened people indifferently using the words *corsair* and *pirate*. This," he continued, not without some severity, "is to confuse the voluntary soldier with the thief, the hero with the bandit. The *course* is one means among others to wage maritime war. Its legitimacy in natural right, at least, may not be contested. Piracy—all authors agree on this point—is a crime against the right of nations. The pirate can be captured by any warship and even, under certain conditions, by merchant ships."[11] In such a sense, the "corsairs" of the Romance jurists corresponded with precision to the legal and political figure the Anglo-Saxon experts regularly termed "privateers." These, as one could read in William E. Hall's 1924 *Treatise on International Law*, are "vessels belonging to private owners, and sailing under a commission of war empowering the person to whom it is granted to carry on all forms of hostility which are permissible at sea by the usages of war."[12] As such, they could be clearly contrasted with pirate ships, whose aggressive actions bear no such legitimacy, being "done under conditions which render it impossible or unfair to hold any state responsible for their commission."[13]

One might well wonder when the pirate and the privateer, the common sea thief and the legal rover, definitively parted ways. Historians and lexicographers provide no single answer to the question. Discussing the development of the English terminology of sea plunder, J. G. Lydon has noted that "before 1700, in referring to vessels, the terms *freebooter*, *buccaneer*, *sea rover*, and *privateer* were used almost synonymously with the word *pirate*. With the passage of time, the name *privateer* lost its stigma of illegality."[14] In the opening pages of *Elizabethan Privateering*, Kenneth R. Andrews similarly cautioned, despite his title, that the term *privateering* "did not come into use until the seventeenth century and was therefore unknown to the Elizabethans."[15] It is certain, in any case, that when the term "corsair" first appeared in the Middle Ages, its signification could not be clearly opposed to that of "pirate." Numerous medieval documents refer to measures taken "against corsairs and pirates" (*contra cursales atque pirates*), treating under a single rubric activity deemed to be "corsair-like or piratical" (*corsaria ouero piratica*).[16] In his pioneering edition of the maritime code of Rhodes, Ashburner long ago commented on this fact: "the indiscriminate use of the two words," he observed, "points to a close similarity in the characteristics of the two classes [....] When the Pisans in AD 1165 asked Trepedicinus, a distinguished Genoese corsair, where he was going, 'I am going,' was the answer, 'to capture you and your goods and persons and to cut off your noses.' It must have been at least as difficult for Pisa or Genoa to keep their corsairs within the bounds of legality as it was for the British Government in the eighteenth century to keep their privateers within the terms of the strict instructions which were given them when war broke out."[17] Nevertheless, it seems that towards the end of the medieval period, a single criterion emerged, which would henceforth allow for the rigorous separation of institutions, if not of terms. "By the late thirteenth century," Frederic L. Cheyette has argued, "lawyers, ambassadors, and scholarly theorists had made the required distinction."[18] To the question of the point at which illegitimate plundering at sea could be told apart from legitimate depredation—that of "the line," in other words, "where wrong became right"—these various authorities furnished one answer: "it is not the act that renders itself legitimate, nor the actor, but the authorization."[19]

In time, the consequences of this simple principle proved to be immense, for it allowed the medieval and modern authorities to confer formal legitimacy on banditry at sea, producing a legal thing unknown to the ancient world: a veritable license to plunder. Classical Greek and Roman law, to be sure, were familiar with rights that could permit one party forcibly to seize, in peace and in war, things belonging to another. As evidence, it suffices to recall the practices of reprisals illustrated by the law of "capture" (συλᾶν) and its suspension in sites declared places of "asylum."[20] Such institutions had hardly vanished in the Middle Ages; and, with the development of trade between the Christian and the Muslim coasts of the Mediterranean, rights of reprisal had become, if anything, more various and more effective. But once it could be argued that a violent action at sea could be considered licit or illicit according to no rule other than that of its sanction by a sovereign power, the law of maritime raiding acquired a distinct and recognizable new form. It did so in the later medieval period, through the institution of a branch of jurisprudence that was to play a notable role in the history of Europe: that field, namely, involving what the jurists of the epoch termed the "letter," "patent," or "license of marking" (licentia marcandi).

Records of this convention in France can be found as early as the first decade of the thirteenth century. By the fourteenth, they abound throughout the European continent.[21] The first document of such "patents" in the administrative history of England dates from 1295. This was the year Edward I officially allowed and even commanded a captain in his service to plunder from the Portuguese as much as had been already spoiled by "the men and subjects of the realm of Portugal."[22] In times of peace, the English sovereign thus granted the lawful seafarer a "letter," which would enable him to transgress the borders that separated one state from another, passing beyond the limit—the "mark," from the Old High German marcha—that restricted the field in which he could otherwise act with legitimacy.[23] An early type of "passport" to the sea, as Jean Merrien has suggested,[24] the license thereby allowed the rover to board vessels belonging to the sailors of another state, for a single purpose: to carry out an act of licit raiding, to whose institution the jurists of medieval Europe, developing the vocabulary of their art, soon gave a host of Latin names (marca, pignoratio, represaliae, pignorationes, pignora, clarigatio, queminae, cambium, laus, and laudes represaliarum).[25]

Such "letters" were declared in times of peace. Licenses of a similar nature could be issued during war. In an epoch in which state navies, in any modern sense, did not exist, this much was, to a certain degree, inevitable. Private vessels manned by seafarers who worked for gain were the classic instruments of war at sea, and no sovereign power could forgo them. Hired seamen had naturally been common in maritime warfare for some time. Griffith has noted that already in the Hellenistic period, "pirates could be, and were, used as mercenaries through the connivance of their leaders."[26] With time, the force of that convention had not waned. Examples in the field of maritime and political history are hardly lacking, but medieval literature also contains its records. One might recall, as a single example, how in the *Saga of the Faroese*, King Olaf employs Karl, the Moere-man, who "had been a great Viking and the worst of robbers" (*hinn verið víkingur og hinn mesti ránsmaður*) to set sail to subjugate the unruly inhabitants of the Faroese archipelago to the Norwegian crown.[27] By the end of the Middle Ages, however, the juridical condition of the hired sea bandit underwent a decisive change. Pirates who acted in the name and interests of the state now acquired, for the first time, an accepted place in the field of public law, even if it was not to be formulated, in its specificity, for some time still. One must await the eighteenth century for the most precise, if subtle, definition of these lawful raiders. Then, jurists such as Christian Wolff knew to name that which most properly characterized the lawfully hired pillagers: namely, the fact of "waging, by private means, not a private but a public war" (*non privatum sed publicum privatim bellum gerunt*).[28]

One of the earliest and most striking records of the altered legal status of the sea bandit can be found in an Old French romance of the thirteenth century, *Wistasse le Moine* (*Eustace the Monk*).[29] Thought to have been composed sometime between 1223 and 1284, this anonymous work recounts the life and deeds of a churchman of unusual distinction.[30] A French nobleman by birth, Eustace, the romance relates, travels in his youth as far as Toledo. There he studies necromancy and, once a master in its arts, spends a winter and a summer "under ground, in a pit" (*sous terre en/abisme*), in constant communication with no less an authority in the field than "the

Devil, himself, who taught him the tricks and the ruses [*l'enghien et l'art*] that deceive everyone."[31] Returning to northern France, Eustace resolves to cultivate a different social circle: he enters a Benedictine monastery, which, however, he must soon forsake to avenge the unexpected murder of his father. That obligation exemplarily discharged, Eustace devotes the remaining years of his life to a career as soldier-seafarer in the service of French and English monarchs. This is the period on which the medieval romance focuses with the greatest attention. In the central portions of the work, Eustace finds himself commissioned by King John of England, Philip Augustus and, still later, Prince Louis of France. The seaman battles and plunders in the Channel for both states, in often startling alternation, yet always on the official command of at least one sovereign legal authority. The romance closes with the decease of its eponymous protagonist, put to death on his own ship. The Devil, we learn, had long before prophesied that event, announcing from his Spanish crypt that Eustace would be "killed at sea" (*en la mer occis seroit*) having "waged war against kings and counts" (*rois et contes guerriëroit*).[32] But the most notable fact in the narrative went unmentioned by the evil one, despite his foresight. It seems the thirteenth-century Devil was still bound, in his imaginings, to rules of combat soon to be outdated. The truth is that the erstwhile monk waged war not only "against kings and counts"; with far greater novelty, he did so lawfully, and on their command. Eustace was to be, for this reason, not only pirate but privateer, the first seafarer in French letters to plunder and to pillage by the right of kings.

Historians have observed that the rights to plunder granted seafarers in the Middle Ages were not all of a single kind. Two varieties of letters, in particular, may be distinguished. Some letters, or "marques," were issued to individual merchants, enabling them to secure transactions that could not otherwise be guaranteed. Once licensed to pillage for the sake of commerce, seamen, for example, could lawfully exact reparations for economic wrongs that they had suffered or that, alternately, they might still suffer; one such instance was the right-termed *pignoratio*, "the taking of security by an injured party to guarantee payment of damages."[33] A second type of patent, by contrast, was explicitly political. Licenses to commit *depredationes*, *rapinae*, *extorsiones*, and *represalia* were of this order. These were all weapons of war, which permitted the pillaging of enemy ships during times of battle; after the end of hostilities and the reconfiguration of alliances, the "problems" they raised had, therefore, immediately to be "settled."[34] To the modern eye, the distinction between such rights to pillage seems in principle quite clear. One belonged to times of peace, the other pertained to warfare; one facilitated transactions in the private sphere, the other involved the actions of the public domain; one implied, in all rigor, no more than a reprisal, the other, by contrast, authorized privateers.

There are several reasons, however, to doubt that the medieval licenses could so neatly be opposed. In his valuable study of the legal institutions of depredation in the fourteenth century, Frederic L. Cheyette argued that in the Middle Ages "the right of reprisal or marque existed in a no man's land between judicial action and war."[35] One could point to numerous such cases drawn from the maritime histories of England and France in particular.[36] But it is perhaps more important to recall several fundamental facts, which in the Middle Ages rendered any rigorous distinction between the two types of authorized pillagers at sea difficult, if not impossible, to achieve. It is worth noting that those who held a letter of reprisal for commercial reasons and those who, by contrast, were formally hired for battle were, in any case, drawn from a single class of rovers, which included pirates. Among such seamen, a variety of legal offices could easily be exchanged. Moreover, the deeds committed by sailors with private patents and by sailors with public licenses were, as a rule, of one nature. Despite their juridical variety, these seafarers — again, in this, much like their lawless counterparts — were all specialists in violent depredation.

But there is more. Even when carried out by seafarers who could be distinguished among themselves in form, the two varieties of legal plundering, private and public, could also fade into each other. What began as a punctual "reprisal," delimited by private law, could slide into public conflict, rendering the legally armed trader, *de facto* if not *de jure*, a privateer. Such developments long outlasted the Middle Ages; they remained commonplace in the early modern period. Historians of the fifteenth, sixteenth, and seventeenth centuries have devoted considerable scholarly attention to the "indiscriminate" legal use — or abuse — of licenses to plunder at sea in the early modern period.[37] It is certain that the people of these centuries held few illusions about the delicacy of the distinctions among legal pillagers. For evidence, it suffices to look to the books of the founding figures of modern international law, which distinguish the rights of private and public plunderers while simultaneously pointing to the multiple possibilities of their confusion. In his *Law of War* of 1539, Francisco de Vitoria thus alluded, albeit discretely, to the fact that belligerent privateers could be employed to carry out private reprisals. Any prince who orders a war "for his own profit," "appropriating public revenues for his own aggrandizement," he wrote, deserves to be denounced as not a legitimate king but a "tyrant."[38] The inverse, too, could all too easily come to pass; a martial operation authorized by a sovereign, in other words, could acquire the unmistakable characteristics of a common reprisal. Hugo Grotius recalled this possibility in his *Law of War and Peace* of 1625. "It sometimes happens," he observed, "that on the occasion of a public war, a private war is born; for example, when someone, confronted by his enemies, runs the risk of losing his life and possessions."[39] Between the two classes of legal plunderers — those private individuals commissioned for the public good, and those publicly licensed to redress a private wrong — the lines of demarcation, for various reasons, could be difficult to draw.

One major phenomenon of the early modern age testifies, perhaps more vividly than any other, to the intractability of all distinctions between types of lawful pillagers at sea. It is the long and complex span of skirmishes between the sailors of Europe and North Africa traditionally designated as the "Barbary wars."[40] Chroniclers have often described these maritime battles as the instances of a single conflict, which divided the two shores of the Mediterranean

for centuries. Christian and Muslim corsairs, it has been said, confronted each other from the end of the Middle Ages up to the eighteenth century to wage a war at sea, if not a series of successive wars.
From an historical as well as a legal perspective, however, references
to belligerent activity in any accepted sense run the risk of propagat-
ing some confusion in this setting. The conflict of the Mediterranean corsairs, while open, was quite dissimilar to any other. "Unlike
normal wars," Peter Earle has written, "the war of the corsairs had
neither beginning nor end. It was an *eternal war*."[41] "The maritime
prolongation of the holy war between the Cross and the Crescent,"
this long series of encounters at sea "displayed two features that
brought it very close to piracy," as Michel Fontenay and Alberto
Tenenti have argued. "Perpetual and permanent, it did not admit of
any truce; total and universal, it could hardly bear the notion of neutrality. Yet the people of the time were formal and generally refused
to employ the word 'pirate' to designate its protagonists."[42]

For centuries, Christian and Muslim seamen plundered freely in
the Mediterranean, capturing goods as well as persons according to
legal principles that, while widely accepted to be valid, could not
easily be defined. The historical and ideological complexities of this
"course" were multiple, as numerous historians have shown. First
there was the question of the dubious identities of the seafarers.
Earle has commented that the Christians, while licensed by public
authorities, were "often little more than pirates who sought their
fortunes under the star-spangled green banner of Algiers rather than
the Jolly Roger."[43] The "war" in which they fought, moreover, could
hardly be defined in the terms of any established and respected *ius
belli*, for while the conflict was stable, the "enemies" whom the
Christians were to fight consistently eluded any precise determination. "Even after specific treaties had been signed in the 1620s,"
for instance, "the question of whether Turkish and Algerine should
be treated as pirates or public ships of a sovereign power was still
undecided."[44] Finally, the theological dimension of the holy battle,
though in principle apparent, assumed historical forms far more
obscure than has often been recalled. The activity of the Maltese,

the greatest of the Christian corsairs, is especially telling in this regard. The appointed defenders of the Cross at sea, the Christian islanders dutifully pillaged whatever Muslim ships they could. But the pious corsairs did not limit their efforts there, for the Maltese of the sixteenth and seventeenth centuries, much to the consternation of their Eastern coreligionists, also raided the vessels of whatever Greek merchants they could intercept at sea.[45]

The Mediterranean corsairs may present the most searing example of pillagers whose legality, while in some sense established, could not be defined with any satisfactory legal exactitude. They were far from being the only such authorized depredators in the modern age. In the conflicts between England and Spain, the British "sea dogs," for instance, played a somewhat similar role to the Christian corsairs; licensed by the English crown, these Elizabethan seafarers famously wrecked havoc on the Dutch, the Spanish, and the Portuguese.[46] "Privateers" to the English, they were naturally no more than "pirates" to their opponents. After them came many waves of violent sailors in the Atlantic and the Indian Oceans, from the Jacobean pillagers to the Buccaneers, the Madagascar seafarers, the "corsairs of the French Republic," and beyond, each of whom claimed rights of some kind to plunder at sea in the service of a European sovereign state.[47] That the savage seamen could turn against the interests of the power that had sponsored them was a fact demonstrated more than once. One might recall, as an example, the fate of Captain Kidd, once "privateer," then "pirate," finally judged for his exploits at sea and hanged in 1701.[48] There was a logic to these early modern phenomena, which Janice Thomson has defined, in its basic pattern, with admirable lucidity: "The state would authorize privateering, which was legalized piracy, during wartime. When the war concluded, thousands of seamen were left with no more appealing alternative than piracy. The state would make desultory efforts to suppress the pirates, who would simply move somewhere else. With the outbreak of the next war, the state would offer blanket pardons to pirates who would agree to serve as privateers, and the process would start all over again."[49]

In the Middle Ages and the early modern period, this movement seemed inevitable. But the situation was soon to change. Privateers would not last forever. The states of modern Europe were soon to consolidate the "monopoly on the legitimate use of physical violence" that Max Weber would one day grant them as their defining trait.[50] By the end of the eighteenth century, not one but several European sovereign powers would conclude that licensed plunderers caused a host of ills that far outweighed any benefits they could provide. It is worth recalling how, in the later eighteenth century, the formidable British insurance companies formally protested to their government the losses they suffered on account of raiding privateers.[51] Their complaints were taken seriously. For reasons of their own, the Russians, to be followed by various other nations, subsequently issued declarations against the practice of allowing their ships conveying goods to be boarded by foreign privateers.[52] The first great blow to the old institution of licensing sea raiders came in 1856. This was the year that the representatives of the governments of Britain, France, Prussia, Russia, Austria, Sardinia, and Turkey all signed the Treaty of Paris, at the same time signing the Paris Declaration Respecting Maritime Law, the aim of which was "to establish a uniform doctrine" on the divisive question of "Maritime Law in times of War." The first statement of the declaration sounded the decisive judgment: "Privateering," it read, "is, and remains, abolished."[53]

That bold assertion did not pass unchallenged. The United States, notably, objected immediately to the terms and intent of the Paris Declaration, replying formally that "the right to resort to privateers is as clear as the right to use public armed ships, and as uncontestable as any other right appertaining to belligerents."[54] That claim was not surprising, for long before, the legal charter of the American nation had established in no uncertain terms its prerogative to hire pirates. Article 1, section 8, of the United States Constitution invested the Congress with the power "to declare War, grant letters of Marque and Reprisal and make Rules concerning Capture on Land and Water."[55] The Americans were not alone in clinging to the medieval institution. In France, too, dissenting voices could be heard. As late as 1904, Brogniart thus insisted "not only on the legitimacy, the necessity and the possibility, but also the *fatality* of employing corsairs at the present hour."[56] "Wrongly viewed as an inheritance of barbaric times," the legal scholar argued, "the privateer, nonetheless so fitting to the modern democratic idea of the armed nation, is essentially suited to humanizing maritime war. While a battleship can be sunk in an instant, pierced by an invisible submarine, the privateer is only after merchandise. He has no need for bloodshed [....] To develop the 'course,' to make it into the principal basis of maritime war—could one not find there a solution to the problem of imagining maritime war without the sacrifice of human life?"[57]

That striking question had been formulated vivaciously and with real enthusiasm. But by 1904, any call to defend the privateer must already have sounded somewhat quaint. Only a few years after objecting to the judgment of the Paris Declaration, the United States, plunged into civil war, had retreated before its initial stance. Invoking the decision to which it had once taken issue, the American government called on Britain and France to treat the Confederate privateers as no more than pirates, outlawed by the law of nations.[58] The seizing of goods at sea by private vessels employed by states was fast becoming a practice no modern power would officially condone. In 1897, Francis R. Stark, an American jurist writing on the history of the right to privateers, could comment, without any trace of hesitation: "The right of capture of private property on the high seas in time of war was once universally recognized. At some time in the future, it will not be recognized at all."[59] One year later, in 1898, at the time of its war with Spain, the United States formally issued a presidential proclamation indicating that it would henceforth abide by all the stipulations of the Paris Declaration of 1856, including the outlawing of privateers.[60] By the end of the nineteenth century, the situation, therefore, appeared to many, if not all, indubitable: centuries after being named, identified, diversified, and variously contested, the legal pillager had run his course. The dialectic of the sea dogs was at an end.

This fact may once have seemed remarkable, but in retrospect it is not astonishing. With sufficient time and effort, it is possible, after all, successfully to remove from the books of jurisprudence a positive right, especially one instituted (as was the privateer's) at a date in relatively recent memory. The same can hardly be said of the ambiguous person of the law who so long predated the licensed plunderer in the law of nations. Since the Middle Ages, that immemorial pillager—the privateer's old double—had hardly vanished. For several centuries, the unlicensed rover had, perhaps, receded from clear view, concealed behind the more modern seaman and his sovereign letter. But the pirate and his exceptional criminality had nonetheless persisted, both in the open seas, where illegitimate depredations did not disappear, and in the law of nations, which never ceased to reserve a special place in its titles for the outlawed raider of exceptional illegality, who in ancient times had been declared "the common enemy of all" (*communis hostis omnium*) and who was now more often dubbed, in the increasingly precise terms of modern international law, "the enemy of the human species" (*hostis generis humani*). The inverted image of the licensed plunderer, the pirate remained in the law at least as long as the official privateer. Indeed, this shadow figure—if it ever was one—was to last far longer.

CHAPTER NINE

Elder Foes

The modern authorities in the law of war teach that the enemy is by nature of more than a single kind. There are, we learn from their books, two types of antagonists. An exemplary expression of the doctrine of the founding modern jurists can be found in Wolff's *The Law of Nations Treated According to a Scientific Method* of 1749. The sixth chapter of this treatise contains a concise treatment of the question of "who enemies are," which furnishes the reader with an unequivocal answer: "Those are called enemies [*hostes*]," the philosopher writes, "who are at war with each other."[1] That statement seems to resolve the issue with a clarity admitting of no commentary; but in truth it is not so. A note placed immediately after the pellucid affirmation explains that enemies of war must be distinguished from adversaries of another sort. "Enemies [*hostes*]," the enlightened work continues, in smaller print, "are different from private enemies [*inimici*]. A private enemy pursues another with hatred; consequently his mind is inclined to take pleasure from the unhappiness of another. But a just war is not waged in hatred towards the opposing party but from a sense of right, and one whose war is unjust at least thinks that he has the right, or wishes to seem to others to think so."[2] Emerich de Vattel reaffirms the same principle in his own influential compendium of international right of 1758, *The Law of Nations, or the Principles of Natural Law Applied to the Conduct and to the Affairs of Nations and of Sovereigns.* "The enemy [*l'ennemi*]," Vattel specifies, in terms that owe much to Wolff, "is he with whom one is at open war."[3] The Swiss jurist does not end his treatment with that first declaration. Like his Prussian predecessor, he added that a further qualification must be made: "The Romans had a special term, *hostis*, to designate a public enemy, and they distinguished him from a private enemy, *inimicus* [....] A private enemy is a person who seeks to hurt us and takes pleasure in doing so; a public enemy makes claims against us, or refuses ours, and maintains its rights, real or pretended, by force of arms."[4]

Several distinctions between the two classic types of enemies may be discerned. A first involves the presence and absence of affect, on which Wolff strenuously insists. The German philosopher states that a private adversary "pursues another with hatred," while a public antagonist takes action solely on account of a pure "sense of right." Vattel concords with that judgment, albeit in less forceful terms. He admits that "it is possible" for the public enemy to act in battle without passion. It may be that a *hostis* wishes no ill upon his adversary, even as he seeks, according to legitimate principles, "to defend his rights."[5] Not so the private enemy: his combat aims to bring harm to his antagonist. Impelled "by malice and by hatred," the *inimicus*, by definition, cannot be "innocent."[6] But a more decisive difference still separates the two orders of antagonists. It is not psychological but juridical, and it concerns the category of legal persons at issue in the two varieties of combat. On this matter, too, the eighteenth-century theorists of the law of nations are essentially in agreement. Both Wolff and Vattel maintain that a public adversary must be political; more exactly, this enemy must be identifiable with a state in so far as a sovereign ruler represents it. A private antagonist is a legal being of another order. No more than an individual, he fights for a cause that could hardly be termed political, and he remains bound, as a single subject, to the rule of the larger nation to which he belongs.

For this reason, the difference between the two types of antagonists necessarily involves more than affect and the status of the person. It also entails a logical distinction, which touches on a question of number. The conflict of public enemies, the jurists claim, is that of totalities; the battle of private adversaries, one of mere individuals. In war, an entire nation pits itself, in the person of its sovereign representative, against another; as a consequence, all the subjects of a state may be said to be opposed to all those of its antagonist. The combat of *inimici*, by contrast, finds single elements of society set against each other; it may involve one or more private persons, but it cannot ever rise beyond the unit of the individual. Wolff draws this conclusion in the paragraph of his work that immediately follows the definition of the legal status of enemies. "Since those are enemies who are at war with each other," he writes, "and since when war is declared by the ruler of one state against the ruler of another, war is understood to have been declared against the entire nation by an entire nation. When war is announced, all the subjects of the one against which it is announced are declared to be enemies of the subjects of the one announcing war; when there is a resort to arms on either side, the subjects of each are enemies of the subjects of the other."[7] Vattel advances the same claim in his own terms. "When the leader of the State, the Sovereign, declares war on another Sovereign," he asserts, "it is to be understood that the whole nation declares war on another nation. For the Sovereign represents the nation and acts in the name of the entire society."[8]

Both Wolff and Vattel note that the distinction between the two types of enemies, though in principle categorical, has been in fact often confused, starting with the facts of speech. "By an inaccuracy of language which scientific method does not tolerate," Wolff observes, not without some severity, "it happens that those who are public enemies [*hostes*] are likewise said to be private enemies [*inimici*]."[9] Such an imprecision surely could be avoided in Latin; but as Wolff and Vattel both well knew, in the idioms of the eighteenth century, the difficulty was a good deal more complex, since there the terminological distinction was hardly known at all. The German *Feind*, by which Wolff translates the Latin *hostis* "into the idiom of our fatherland," can refer to a private enemy no less than to a public antagonist.[10] To this degree it is no different from the French term *ennemi*. In his *Law of Nations*, Vattel leaves no doubt that if one is truly to respect the legal distinction between antagonists, the Latin idiom alone will do, for where it contains to that end two different terms, the French language knows only one. "The Romans," Vattel observes, "had a special term, *hostis*, to designate a public enemy [*un ennemi public*], and they distinguished him from a private enemy [*un ennemi particulier*], *inimicus*."[11] For the proper definition of the legal status of the adversary, classicism, it seems, proves indispensable.

The vocabulary of the ancient language, however, was in truth more ambiguous than the enlightened authors suggest. It is true that the Latin word employed by the modern jurists as the name of the "private enemy," *inimicus*, remains bound in its structure to the lexical field of the word of which it constitutes a simple negation, namely "friend," *amicus*.[12] There is ample evidence that Roman authors could employ the word *inimicus* in this sense to refer to an "intimate" or "inner adversary," or, in other words, an antagonist within the walls of the ancient city.[13] The classical term invoked by the modern scholars as the title of the "public enemy," for its part, could in antiquity clearly also designate an antagonist of an official sort: sources evoke *hostes* of the fatherland, the Republic, and the Roman people, and the expression *hostis publicus* itself can be found.[14] But if one considers that last title, one must concede that it belies the very distinction proposed by the moderns, and for a simple reason: if some *hostes* may be specified as "public," it can only be because others of a different kind may well also be conceived. Roman sources confirm the doubt. Surveys of the Latin lexicon have amply demonstrated that the two terms invoked by the modern jurists appear in ancient times in multiple senses. Despite Vattel's claims, *inimici* in Rome could also be political; classical authors wrote frequently of wars (*belli*) waged against them.[15] Conversely, various sources suggest that *hostes* were for the Romans antagonists of an undifferentiated legal status, "private" or "public," in the terms of the modern thinkers, depending on the occasion.[16] On close scrutiny, the strict distinction between types of adversaries reveals itself, in short, less classical than classicizing. No less an authority than Livy employs *hostis* and *inimicus* in alternation and almost interchangeably.[17]

The truth is that the Romans had not two but many terms to

designate the enemy. In addition to referring to the *hostis* and the *inimicus*, the classical Latin authors regularly wrote of the *adversarius*, *perduellis*, *rebellis*, *usurpator*, and *tyrannus*.[18] The Romans were not unaware that the signification of these multiple terms had changed over the course of time and that some lexical elements could be derived from others. Festus, for instance, affirms that "among the ancients, 'enemy' [*hostis*] meant 'stranger' [*peregrinus*], and what we now call 'enemy' [*hostis*], they called 'opponent' [*perduellio*]."[19] But despite such lexical diversity, the exponents of the Roman law propose a simple taxonomy. Like that employed by Wolff and Vattel, this classification admits of no more than two elements. The first of them was the same term that would later be invoked by the moderns: *hostis*. The second, however, appears never to have been *inimicus*. When the Latin lawyers define the "public enemy" (*hostis*), they do so by opposing him to a combatant of changing name yet constant traits: a figure one may call, for the sake of brevity, the "bandit."[20] A dictum in book 50 of the *Digest* is in this regard decisive. In the section of this concluding fascicle dedicated to clarifying Roman legal terms, Pomponius offers the following definition of the legal adversary: "'Enemies' [*hostes*] are those who have publicly declared war on us or on whom we have publicly declared war; the others are 'brigands' [*latrones*] or 'plunderers [*praedones*]."[21] Elsewhere in the *Digest*, Ulpian's *Institutes* establish the same doctrine: "The 'enemy,'" we read in the section of the legal compendium on military matters, "are those on whom the Roman people has publicly declared war, or who themselves [declare war] on the Roman people; the others are termed 'thieves' [*latrunculi*] or 'plunderers' [*praedones*]. Therefore, a person who is captured by plunderers is not the plunderers' slave, nor does he need *postliminium*; after capture by the enemy, however, as say, by the Germans and Parthians, he is the slave of the enemy and recovers his former status with *postliminium*."[22]

To grasp the full meaning of the distinction proposed by the Roman jurists, it is necessary first to understand the technical value of the term "enemy" as they employed it. As Festus indicates, the Latin *hostis* seems originally to have meant simply "foreigner"; the word appears in this sense in a passage of the oldest of surviving Roman legal documents, the Twelve Tables.[23] More precisely, Latin sources suggest that the term *hostis* signified a foreigner of a specific legal status, capable of claiming a set of rights. In his influential study, *Le vocabulaire des institutions indo-européennes* (*Indo-European Language and Society*), Émile Benveniste thus argued that in Rome, "a *hostis* is not a foreigner in general. Unlike the *peregrinus*, who resides beyond the limits of the territory, a *hostis* is 'the foreigner in so far as one recognizes in him rights equal to those of Roman citizens.' This recognition of rights implies a certain relation of reciprocity and presupposes a convention; not everyone who is not Roman may be said to be a *hostis*."[24] To this extent, the status of the Roman *hostis* initially resembled that of the Greek "foreigner" (ξένος), rather than that of the non-Greek "barbarian" (βάρβαρος), as Gauthier has also indicated.[25] When, at a later point in the course of the Latin language, "through a change whose precise conditions we do not know, the word *hostis* acquired a 'hostile' meaning and referred only to the enemy," this legal and linguistic principle continued to hold.[26] Despite antagonism, the *hostis* could still lay claim to being, at least in certain respects, the "equal" (*aequus*) of his Roman adversary before the law.[27]

The brigands, thieves, and plunderers of the *Digest* are juridical beings of a different sort. They are opponents to whom the privileges of enemies do not apply. They may well assault the polity from beyond its borders, but still they cannot be considered to wage a "war" against it in the legal sense; that form of public combat obtains only between enemies, a "strict correlation," as Peter Haggenmacher has written, "existing between *bellum* and *hostis*."[28] In Rome "a clear difference was established," Gabriele Steinmayr has observed, "between legitimate war, which is legally sanctioned, and illegitimate and abusive war; between *bellum iustum* and *bellum iniustum*, in which, as is often the case in Livy, brigands (*latrones*) are opposed to 'legal enemies' (*iusti hostes*)."[29] The contrast is stark. On one side, one encounters "war," waged by legally symmetrical "enemies," each possessing privileges in principle equal to those of its adversary;

on the other, one finds mere "brigandage" (*latrocinium*), carried out by plunderers whose combat, by definition, cannot be lawful. In one case, battle must be announced before it can come to pass, for the rules of lawful combat stipulate that war must be declared. In the other case, military action may be taken without such precautions, since it does not pit one public antagonist against another. Hence the legal difference between actions committed by the two types of adversaries. An "enemy" may legitimately capture goods and human beings, to be returned to the opponent, after seizure and slavery, according to the rules of *postliminium*. In the eyes of the Roman jurists, a brigand, however, can hardly alter the legal status of things and persons. Just as Bartolus establishes that, no matter what act of theft he might commit, "a pirate does not alter ownership" (*pirata non mutat dominium*), so Paulus solemnly declares, in willful ignorance of extra-legal fact, "persons captured by pirates and brigands continue to be freemen" (*A piratis aut latronibus capti liberi permanent*).[30]

The position of such plunderers within the legal order merits some reflection. While they did not possess the privileges of foreign antagonists such as "the Germans and the Parthians," the bandits were also denied the rights of common criminals. Roman citizens, when accused, had access to defense at court. The brigand, by contrast, did not. A juridical "non-person," he was close, in legal status, to the slave and the insane.[31] As Brent D. Shaw has argued in an extended study of bandits in the Roman Empire, in the Roman legal code "there existed quite separate definitions of them that placed bandits in a penumbral category between persons within the scope of the law (criminal and civil, largely overlapping) and enemies of the state. They were, quite literally, 'out-law.'"[32] The action taken by the authorities against such combatants, therefore, could be assimilated as little to criminal prosecution as to war. When an officer prevailed in battle against a band of plunderers, his success could not but have a special status. It was barely victory. After defeating his opponent, the general would enter the city unaccompanied by trumpets, without a scepter, not in a chariot but on horseback or on

foot. He could not be accorded the crown of gold or laurel marking
the military achievement that was the Roman "triumph" (*triumphus*).
In its place, the general would be given a crown made of myrtle, the
proper token of the "lesser triumph," (*minor triumphus* or ελάττων
θρίαμβος) that the Romans named "ovation" (*ovalis*). "The occasion for awarding an ovation, and not the triumph," Aulus Gellius
reports, "is that wars have not been declared in due form and thus
have not been waged with a legitimate enemy, or that the adversaries' character is low or unworthy, as in the case of slaves or pirates
[*ut servorum piratarumque*]."[33]

The Latin authors who allude to the ways of inferior and improper
adversaries are best understood in light of this classic doctrine of
opponents. Cicero is the perfect example. In his tirades before the
Senate, the orator did not hesitate to cast Mark Antony as an adversary of the lowest kind, a "barbarian" (*barbarus*) and "robber" (*latro*)
unworthy of the respect shown public enemies in the past: "Your
ancestors, Romans," he declared, "had to deal with an enemy who
possessed a state, a senate, a treasury, unanimity and concord among
its citizens, some principles on which, if the occasion admitted, to
found peace and a treaty. But this enemy [*hostis*] of yours attacks your
state, while he himself possesses none; he is eager to obliterate the
Senate, the council of the world, but he himself has no public council. As to concord among citizens, how can he who has no citizenship
possess it? But as to peace, what reckoning can there be with a man
whose cruelty is incredible and whose good faith is non-existent?
The whole conflict lies between the Roman people, the conqueror
of all nations, and an assassin, a bandit, a Spartacus."[34]

In the intensity of its polemic against one distinguished "enemy"
unworthy of that legal title, Cicero's invective may be without equal
in his voluminous work. But it is not without an echo in the thinker's
philosophical reflections. Reading the impassioned condemnation of
Mark Antony's "criminal brigandage" (*nefarium latrocinium*)[35] and its
difference from acts of lawful warfare, it is difficult not to think also
of the terms with which Cicero defines the exceptional adversary
in his treatise on obligations. There the "pirate" (*pirata*) illustrates,

in shorthand, the special status of the improper antagonist. The "common enemy of all" (*communis hostis omnium*), the plunderer is, of course, an opponent of the city and its people; but nonetheless, a bandit by both nature and right, "he is not included in the number of lawful enemies" (*non est ex perduellium numero definitus*).[36] It is true that in its final theses, Cicero's discussion in the *De officiis* may not represent "any considered legal opinion," pertaining instead to the terrain of moral and political philosophy.[37] At least since the age of Grotius, if not earlier, scholars have at times questioned the good reasons for Cicero's startling conclusion that "with a pirate, there ought not to be any pledged word nor any oath mutually binding."[38] But in its mere reference to an antagonist too base to deserve the rights owed a "public enemy," the Ciceronian assertion remains, if memorable in its details, absolutely traditional in its meaning. It reflects one juridical axiom essential to the rules of war in Rome: that, namely, some combatants be exempted from the count of law-ful "enemies" (*hostes*); that some be taken into account, if one may say so, without ever being counted.

That arithmetical operation was complex, but it would be an error to conclude that its function in the ancient account of war was ever inessential. One may go so far as to assert exactly the contrary: the procedure may have furnished the classical statesmen with the very condition for their doctrine of public enemies. One antagonist could be accorded a set of rights and treated as an equal precisely because he could be clearly distinguished from others in the large class of opponents: those who, while doubtless adversarial, lacked the positive characteristic of equality. One opponent could be securely established within the law of war as the enemy of the Roman state and people because others could always also be envis-aged, others who were no less antagonistic for being without "a state, a senate, and a treasury," and without, therefore, the right to claim that which must be accorded properly public enemies. The definition of the legitimate adversary, in this sense, could hardly have come to pass without the simultaneous constitution of the juridical figure of the bandit. "Brigand," "thief," "plunderer," or "pirate," the name, from this perspective, matters little. What is decisive is that a single structure remained in place. It dictated that, where the law cleared a space for the rightful adversary, the shadow of the unlawful combatant continued to be close at hand. This was to remain the case for far longer than the Roman jurists may ever have anticipated. Long after the end of the ancient world, the classic account of counted and uncounted enemies proved to be of great consequence for the modern European authorities in the law of war — including for those enlightened thinkers, such as Wolff and Vattel, who preferred not to write of it directly.

CHAPTER TEN

Younger Antagonists

Like so many other branches of classical legal doctrine, the ancient taxonomy of enmity long survived the fall and fragmentation of the Roman Empire. Even when the people who dwelt in the regions of Europe that had once partaken of a single state no longer lived under a common rule, and even when foreign antagonists, therefore, could not be said to oppose any one "Roman people," the jurists of the Middle Ages continued to teach and to transmit the classical theory of the two types of opponents recorded in the *Digest*. One may take as evidence how in the late twelfth century Azzo of Bologna recalled in the *Summa Codicis* that not every antagonist in battle may properly be termed a "public enemy" (*hostis*), just as not every conflict deserves the name of "war."[1] One may equally recall how Azzo's pupils, Odofredus and Franciscus of Accursius, each took pains, in various settings, to distinguish legal adversaries representing polities from mere bands of "brigands" (*latrones*) and lesser "robbers" (*latrunculi*).[2] Bartolus of Saxoferrato, the great Italian glossator of the fourteenth century, even introduced into his *Apostilla* on the *Digest* the following remark on the formal difference separating the bandit of the seas from the lawful enemy: "enemies [*hostes*] are not to be compared to pirates [*pyrate*], for the latter have renounced [*diffidati*], by the law itself, the very principle of faith." Employing a turn of phrase not found before him but that was fated to have a long life in the law, Bartolus then explained, rewriting Cicero, that such unworthy opponents are most properly said to be "the enemies of the human species" (*hostes humani generis*).[3]

There is also in the medieval period no lack of historical records deploring the illegality of maritime depredations attributed to groups of bandits sailing in the Mediterranean and the northern seas of Europe. From Aragon to Genoa and Venice, from England to the Hanseatic League and Scandinavia, legal authorities repeatedly condemned violent acts of roving sailors as deeds in violation of the law of nations.[4] The medieval denunciations of maritime thieves and plunderers, to be sure, did not always explicitly invoke the terminology of brigandage familiar to the Romans. No doubt this was at least in part because the law of the age still lacked a means to distinguish common bands of roving warriors from armed seafarers who might represent a public entity, laying claim, as a consequence, to the title of proper "enemy." Violent and rapacious sailors could not be securely identified as brigands as long as they might always also claim to act in the service of a sovereign power, be it that of a city, kingdom, or empire. Gradually, however, and with the emergence of the legal distinction between the sanctioned and the unsanctioned combatant, a juridical space emerged for a new bandit, one who was at once pirate and unlawful opponent.

The jurists of the early modern age perceived this space, and they constructed within it a theory of the inferior antagonist more complex than any imagined in antiquity. The first treatises of the modern law of nations contain the evidence, and it is copious. These works offer extended accounts of the rights of warfare that obtain between the sovereign states of Europe, but not without remarking, with differing length and detail, on what need not be accorded opponents of a lesser variety. In his pioneering *Treatise on Military Matters and Warfare*, published in Venice in 1563, Pierino Belli, for instance, dwells forcefully on the classic principle that "hostilities should not be begun except after a proclamation or declaration of war, as it is called," before adding, in terms reminiscent of Bartolus: "But it is customary to make an exception in the case of pirates [*solent tamen excipi Piratae*], since they have both technically and in fact already broken faith [or, as the published English translation has it, "they are technically and in fact already at war" (*enim sunt ipso facto iure et facto diffidati*)]; for people whose hand is against every man should expect a like return from all men, and it should be permissible for any one to attack them. So Baldus."[5]

Less than two decades after Belli, the exceptional combatants appear again in Balthazar de Ayala's *Three Books on the Law of War and on the Duties Connected with War and on Military Discipline*, published in Antwerp in 1582. In his opening definition of the conditions that must be satisfied for a war to be deemed just, the Flemish scholar recalls in passing that not all bands of armed fighters ought to be classed as enemies. "Rebels," for instance, fall outside that set; the action taken against them, therefore, constitutes not war but the mere "execution of legal process, or prosecution."[6] From the juridical point of view, pirates, we learn, belong to such a class. While undeserving of the title of enemies of war, they may nonetheless rightfully be crushed by all the lawful means of battle—and this, if necessary, with greater intensity than that to be shown to public antagonists. "For this reason," Ayala continues,

the laws of war and of captivity and of postliminy, which apply to enemies, do not apply to rebels, any more than they apply to pirates and to brigands [*nec pirates et latronibus*] (these not being included in the term "enemy" [*qui hostium numero non continentur*]). Our meaning is that these persons themselves cannot proceed under the laws of war; that is, they do not acquire the ownership of what they capture, this only being admitted in the case of enemies [*hostes*]; but all the modes of stress known to the laws of war may be employed against them, even more than in the case of enemies, for the rebel and the robber merit severer reprobation than any enemy who is carrying on a regular and just war, and their condition ought not to be better than his.[7]

Though more developed than those of the ancients, Belli's and Ayala's discussions of the legal status of the bandit seem of modest proportions when compared to those that were soon to come, starting with the publication, in 1589, of the first edition of Alberico Gentili's *Three Books on the Law of War*.[8] This influential treatise made of the Italian jurist, in Alfred P. Rubin's words, "the first writer of lasting eminence to convert the confusions of the time to legal principle, to argue that the label 'pirate' carries with it the meaning of outlawry and that what 'pirates' do is forbidden by international law."[9] Gentili's treatise opens with the famous formal definition of the state of war as "a lawful and public contest of arms" [*bellum est publicorum armorum iusta contentio*]."[10] It proceeds to stipulate, on the basis of the classic Latin legal sources, that in such a "contest" only sovereign potentates may properly take part, since only they stand above the laws and processes that regulate the deeds and misdeeds of lesser persons and associations. "Reason shows," the jurist explains, "that war has its origin in necessity," and more exactly in a situation of extreme duress from which no other issue can be conceived.[11] "Private individuals, subject peoples, and petty sovereigns are never confronted with the necessity of resorting to the arbitrage of Mars," Gentili recalls, "because they can obtain their legal rights before their superiors' tribunal."[12] Not so free peoples and supreme sovereigns. When those authorities do not concur, no power may resolve their discord, since by definition "the sovereign has no earthly judge, for one over whom another holds a superior position is not a sovereign."[13] Public and official figures must resort, in such cases, to decisions made by arms.

The definition of war as a public, official, and armed confrontation of supreme sovereigns evidently leaves little room for bandits, at least as acceptable belligerents. But lest the matter be misunderstood, Gentili devotes an entire chapter to the elaboration of the principle that "brigands do not wage war" (*latrones bellum non gerunt*). "With pirates and robbers," this section begins, "a state of war cannot exist [*cum piratis et latrunculis bellum non est*]." Here the jurist founds his claim on two established arguments, each of which effectively excludes the bandit from the domain of war. On the one hand, Gentili argues, brigands may not legitimately lay claim to the title of "enemies" (*hostes*), which belongs solely to those who have "emancipated themselves" from the jurisdiction proper to private individuals. "One who is a subject does not by rebellion free himself from subjection to the law, as says Baldus, and no one improves his legal status by transgression, as says Paulus."[14] On the other hand, Gentili reasons, one must recall that the law of war derives from the law of nations, a code that pirates and robbers, by their acts, intransigently oppose. "Malefactors," we read, "do not enjoy the privileges of a law to which they are foes. How, as Florus says, can the law, which is nothing but an agreement and a compact, extend to those who have withdrawn from agreement and broken the treaty of the human species?"[15] At last, the jurist invokes the classic judgment of the *De officiis*: "Pirates are the common enemies of all human beings and therefore Cicero says that the laws of war do not apply to them."[16] A war, therefore, could no more be declared against them than a pact or truce could be signed with them. "A war with plunderers [*bellum cum praedonibus*]," Gentili writes, with manifest imprecision, "has never been terminated by agreement or brought to end by a treaty of peace, but the pirates have either saved their lives by victory, or have been conquered and compelled to die."[17]

The argument of *Three Books on the Law of War* may to this point be considered traditional, though in extent it is doubtless novel. But soon Gentili's treatise takes a new turn. The Italian scholar writes that "we must beware of confounding a brigand with a military commander, and brigandage with war," as many authors before him, it seems, have done: thus "Justin speaking of Aristonicus, Frontinus of Viriathus, Appian of that same Spartacus and the pirates, of a certain Apuleius who was proscribed, and of Sextus Pompeius."[18] Those classical writers all erred in writing of "enemies" where, strictly speaking, there existed simple combative collectivities. More, in truth, is needed for war: there must also be, the jurist maintains, "the assumption of a public cause" (*adeptio publicae caussae*).[19] Now Gentili alludes directly to the Fourth Philippic, citing the good grounds that led Cicero to condemn Mark Antony. "He is an enemy," we read "who has a state, a senate, a treasury, united and harmonious citizens, and some basis for a treaty of peace, should matters so shape themselves."[20] Not all groups may claim as much. "Charles Martel said of the Saracens, that although they roved about in great numbers and had leaders, camps, and standards, they were none the

less plunderers [*praedones*], since they had no cause for war."²¹ In this
regard, the bandits of the sea, Gentili specifies, are no different from
those of the land. They are united before the law in illicit plunder,
whatever the deeds that they may, in fact, commit. "Pirates may
follow the customs of war, and not those of brigands, as Paterculus
writes of those against whom Pompey made his campaign; yet they
do not wage war."²² Gentili concedes that in some cases, the ancients
did extend the name of "enemy" (*hostis*) "to those who are not equal,
namely, to pirates, proscribed persons and rebels." But he immediately excuses that usage. "Nevertheless," he writes, "it cannot confer
the rights due to enemies, properly so called, and the privileges of
warfare," for such brigands, while many and mobilized as armies,
still lack any "public cause."²³

One can wonder only for a moment what element furnishes that
"public cause." "It seems clear," Rubin has written of Gentili, "that
the license of an established sovereign was the key to his thinking."²⁴ Spartacus and his men obviously lacked precisely that, as
did the "Saracens" for Charles Martel. On that matter, the Italian
jurist shows no signs of doubting the sound judgment of the Roman
authorities, or that of the pious Frankish ruler of medieval times.
But Gentili suggests that the European peoples of the sixteenth
century furnish cases of greater legal complexity. "What are we to
think," he asks in conclusion, "about those Frenchmen who were
captured by the Spaniards in the last war with Portugal and were
not treated as lawful enemies? They were treated as pirates [*piratae*],
since they served Antonio, who had been driven from the whole
kingdom and never recognized by the king of the Spaniards."²⁵ That
legal decision would seem, by Gentili's standards, sound. "But history itself proves that they were not pirates," the jurist continues,
"and I say this because no argument derived from the number and
quality of the men and ships, but from the letters of their king which
they exhibited; and it was the king whom they served, not Antonio,
although this was especially for the interest of Antonio: a consideration, however, which did not affect their status."²⁶ Thus we learn
that the thorny question cannot be resolved by appeal to the acts and

characters of the violent agents: neither the "the number and quality" of the men nor that of the ships will suffice for deciding whether
the combatants in question are to be judged as pirates. One must
appeal instead to the legal statement that is the sovereign "letter."
According to the Italian jurist, it alone traces the line that separates
the lawful from the unlawful belligerent; it alone, more precisely,
institutes it.

The consequences of Gentili's doctrine were to prove far-reach-
ing. As Rubin observes in *The Law of Piracy*,

> if it were generally accepted, whatever the weaknesses of the appeal
> to classical writings in support of it, that all takings were in some
> sense "criminal" unless authorized by a person whose legal power to
> issue such an authorization were acknowledged, no degree of politi-
> cal organization or goal could make a "rebel" into a lawful combatant
> or require the application of the laws of war to the struggle against
> a rebel army. A tool of enormous power was placed in the hands of
> "sovereigns."[27]

A single ruler could, by fiat, decide which enemies were legitimate
representatives of a state and which, by contrast, were mere "bandits," even when the combatants seemed, by all appearances, to wage
a war on behalf of an established polity. The issue was of particular
importance for the definition of the legal status of the rulers and
armed sailors of the southern shores of the Mediterranean. "The
Barbary states could be rendered 'piratical' by simply withholding
recognition of his governmental position from a new Dey or 'rec-
ognizing' a rival, thus depriving the one not liked of the power to
issue the Turkish equivalent of letters of marque and reprisal."[28] That
implication, for Gentili, was far from troublesome. A Protestant in
England, he not only taught civil law at the University of Oxford,
but also worked, from time to time, as the official advocate of the
Spanish crown in the Royal Council Chamber in London. There the
question of the states of North Africa arose more than once, and the
legal doctrine of the "public cause" could prove most instrumental.[29]

In 1625, Hugo Grotius, "the miracle of Holland," published the first edition of what is surely the single most important work in the modern law of nations, *On the Law of War and Peace*.[30] It naturally contained a discussion of the varieties of enemies, to be found in the third chapter of its third book, "On War That is Lawful or Public according to the Law of Nations, and Therein, on the Declaration of War." "Authors of repute," the jurist recalls, "have called war lawful [or "just," *justis*] not from the cause from which it arises, nor, as is done in other cases, from the importance of its exploits, but because of certain peculiar legal consequences."[31] One such "peculiar legal consequence" is the status of the antagonist involved in the armed struggle. Faithful to the classics, Grotius admits two types in the field. There is the public and lawful opponent, who may be termed "enemy" (*hostis*) in the strict sense. Then there are the others. Like Gentili, Grotius calls them "brigands," "robbers," and "pirates," in blithe disregard of the difference between plunderers of the land and of the sea.[32]

Grotius declines to mention his illustrious Italian predecessor by name, but it can hardly be doubted that *On the Law of War and Peace* constitutes, among other things, a sustained response and partial refutation of Gentili's own *On the Law of War*. One point in particular sets the two jurists apart, and it concerns the legal grounds for the qualification of an armed opponent of the state as either enemy or bandit. *Contra* Gentili, Grotius will not grant that the juridical distinction between lawful and unlawful combatant may be established solely by a sovereign license. One may take, as illustration of the difference, the vexed legal case of the so-called Barbary states. In Gentili's view, were a supreme European public person to invalidate the title to raid of certain North African corsairs, those seafarers could be judged, by consequence, piratical. Grotius dissents. He suggests that one must determine the character of the antagonists with reference to the nature of the association to which they belong. One must consider whether the community of the opponents has been formed, like the pack of robbers, "for the sake of wrongdoing" or, like the commonwealth, "for the enjoyment of rights."[33] Such argumentation was to lead Grotius's successor and compatriot, Cornelius van Bynkershoek, to differ publicly from Gentili in his *Questions of Public Law* of 1737, writing that "I do not think that we can reasonably agree with Alberico Gentili and others who class as pirates the so-called Barbary peoples of Africa, and that captures made by them entail no change of property. The peoples of Algiers, Tripoli, Tunis, and Salee are not pirates, but rather organized states, which have a fixed territory in which there is an established government, and with which, as with other nations, we are now at peace, now at war."[34]

That particular case of legal qualification was to be debated for some time, since the consequences of the question—political, economic, and military—were great. But Grotius's treatise complicated any simple opposition of actual commonwealths and bands of robbers for a simple, startling reason: unlike many who wrote before him, the Dutch jurist admitted in principle that a single group of individuals may pass from one legal category to the other. Despite the categorical difference between types of antagonists, a legal "mutation," we learn, may nonetheless occur. After presenting the classic distinction between opponents, Grotius added a comment: "A transformation [*mutatio*] may take place, not merely in the case of individuals, as when Jephthah, Arsaces and Viriathus, instead of being leaders of brigands became lawful chiefs, but also in the case of groups, so that those who have only been robbers upon embracing another mode of life become a state."[35] The consequences of such a principle of alteration are great: he who was a pirate may, in time, become a lawful chief of state, and those who were no more than bands of plunderers may still one day form a commonwealth "for the enjoyment of rights." But that new rule of historical alteration still remains subordinate to a higher legal principle, which continues to discriminate, according to the classic Roman terms, between two types of antagonists. The fact that those individuals who occupy the position of "brigands" and "enemies" may exchange their roles in no way contests the difference that separates the two legal categories. Indeed, one may go so far as to assert that the "mutation," to be perceptible, requires that the two classes of antagonists remain in principle distinct.

The legal scholars who wrote after *On the Law of War and Peace* certainly show few signs of doubting the distance separating the two varieties of opponents. Their catalogues of antagonists are at times more complex than those of Gentili and Grotius; but they are rarely as precise in their specifications of the legal grounds on which one may attribute legitimacy and illegitimacy to the armed adversaries of war. An example can be found in Richard Zouche's *An Exposition of Fecial Law and Procedure, or of Law between Nations, and Questions concerning the Same* of 1650. The section of his treatise dedicated to "The Status among Belligerents" appears to depart from tradition, distinguishing between not two but three types of opponents: those who are "lawful enemies" (*justi hostes*); "unfriendly" (*inimici*); and "plunderers" (*praedones*).[36] But beneath the tripartite taxonomy one still finds the old bipartition. One must admit, Zouche argues, a class of conflict involving persons lacking "friendship or legal intercourse," joined in mutual "unfriendliness" (*inimicitia*). Those who belonged to this category in ancient times were called "aliens" (*exteri*), such as "barbarians and pilgrims," as well as "adversaries" (*adversari*). Of those two, modern jurisprudence since Jean Bodin recognizes only "adversaries," defined as those "with whom friendship or legal intercourse has existed, but has been dissolved, for example, by civil dissension": examples include Caesar and the Pompeians and, one presumes, persons united in modern civil strife. Then there are the foreign opponents of war, "some of whom are of a worse and others of a better condition." Only two kinds of antagonists can thus be conceived. "Lawful enemies are those to whom are due all the rights of war," such as the old official opponents of the Roman state and people. Brigands, by contrast, are "those to whom the laws of war do not apply." Zouche presents such others as a motley class, composed of "traitors" (*perduelles*), "rebels" (*rebelles*), "deserters" (*defectores*), "thieves" (*latrones*) and "pirates" (*piratae*), such as "the Cilicians, who, breaking the treaty of the human species [*rupto foederis generis humani*] and destroying commerce, swept the seas with war like a tempest, as Florus says, and were first checked by Servilius, and afterwards utterly crushed by Pompey."[37]

The writers of the seventeenth century who codified the maritime law of the age could naturally permit themselves to discuss
the pirate with greater economy. Passing over in silence the full
cast of brigands known to the modern jurists, they concentrated
their attention on the status of the exceptional plunderer of the
seas. There the opposition between the enemy and the pirate, stark
and solitary, remained. The terms of Charles Molloy's *A Treatise of
Affaires Maritime and of Commerce in Three Books* of 1682, which recall
Sir Edward Coke and anticipate William Blackstone at once, are to
this degree representative:

> A Pirat is a Sea Thief, or *Hostis humani Generis* ["enemy of the human
> species"], who for to enrich himself, either by surprise or open force,
> sets upon Merchants and others trading by Sea, ever spoiling their lad-
> ing, if by any possibility they can get the mastery, sometimes bereaving
> them of their lives, and sinking of their Ships; the actors wherein *Tully*
> calls Enemies to All, with whom neither Faith nor Oath is to be kept.
> By the Laws of Nature Princes and States are responsible for their
> neglect, if they do not provide Ships of War, and other remedies for
> the restraining of these sort of *Robbers* [....] Though Pirats are called
> enemies, yet are they not properly so termed: For he is an Enemy, says
> *Cicero*, who hath a *Common-wealth, a Court, a Treasury, Consent and
> Concord of Citizens, and some way, if occasion be, of Peace and League*; and
> therefore a Company of *Pirats* or *Free-booters* are not a Commonwealth
> [....] Pirats and Robbers that make not a Society, *i.e.* such a Society as
> the Law of Nations accounts lawful, are not to have any succour by the
> Law of Nations.[38]

It is not surprising that the lawyers most directly concerned with the
regulation of the seas should have shared that abbreviated doctrine
of the illegitimate opponent. Disserting upon "some sorts of *Felonies
and Offenses* within the Jurisdiction of the Admiralty," Sir Leoline
Jenkins warned in the same years against "the chiefest in this Kind,
[...] Piracy," declaring "all *Pirates* and *Sea-rovers* [...] in the Eye of the
Law *Hostes humani generis*, Enemies not of one Nation or one Sort of
People only, but of all Mankind. They are outlaw'd, as I may say, by

the Laws of all Nations; that is, out of the Protection of all Princes and of all Laws whatsoever. Every Body is commissioned, and is to be armed against them, as against Rebels and Traytors, to subdue and to root them out."[39]

More than once, historians of the law of nations have recalled how the age of these early modern jurists and thinkers brought about a host of fundamental changes in the rules and conventions of warfare. It has often been asserted that, starting with the sixteenth century, scholars of martial law began to focus their attention not on privileged individuals and their licensed combatants, as in antiquity and the Middle Ages, but on recognized sovereign states and their increasingly professional military forces, which were now to be subject to an ever more recognized set of regulations. Combatants had always been, in a sense, enjoined to conform to certain principles. But now those principles gradually ceased to concern what the medieval thinkers and jurists had understood to be the "lawful cause" (*justa causa*) of war. The rules of warfare began to bear instead on an entity that could be much more easily perceived: that legal being that was the "lawful enemy" (*justis hostis*), the public combatant who, to be worthy of the name, must visibly conform to the same set of outer conventions respected by his symmetrical opponent.

This was the age of "war in due form." Vattel, in the second half of the eighteenth century, famously proclaimed its first principle: "War in due form must be viewed, in its effects, as just by both sides" (*La guerre en forme, quant à ses effets, doit être regardée comme juste de part & d'autre*).[40] That new doctrine of war could also be related to the developing material conditions of battle in this period. Military and civilian populations came to be separated in space, as warfare acquired its own domain. Increasingly housed in barracks rather than in towns, soldiers donned uniforms to indicate that they belonged to the sphere of public combat between states. It was to be understood that wars were legal confrontations between peoples, publicly declared by their sovereign representatives and openly carried out by official combatants. "The result," Stephen C. Neff has written in a recent history of the law of war, "was to reduce, if only modestly, the degree of suffering of civilian populations, which had been such a ghastly feature of the Thirty Years War" and to "promote moderation in warfare as between the contending fighters themselves."[41] Carl Schmitt went so far as to argue that, between the Peace of Westphalia in 1648 and the inception of the Napoleonic wars, modern public law even achieved its central aim: "the containment of war" (*die Hegung des Krieges*).[42]

It has less often been observed that the very thinkers who conceived the doctrine of war as a formal duel between equal parties also elaborated a detailed theory of an antagonist too iniquitous to deserve the title of proper opponent. There is a reason for this peculiar fact, and it is to be found in the old ambiguity and even instability of the juridical and political concept of the "enemy." On the one hand, a *hostis* in the technical sense must by definition be lawful; the modern distinctions between "enemy" and "brigand," like the ancient, stress nothing else, denying to some antagonists the formal rights of "enemy of state." On the other hand, however, the jurists who record those rights, from Gentili to Grotius, Wolff, and Vattel, never fail to specify that such prerogatives belong to the opponent who may also be defined, with greater precision, as the "lawful enemy" (*justis hostis*). That phrase could certainly be considered simply pleonastic, attributing a quality to a being that must, by definition, already imply it. But the phrase could also be more significant. Taken seriously, it suggests a possibility that cannot easily be dismissed: the possibility that the category of the "enemy" is neutral with respect to legal qualification, that, in other words, it is no less obvious or permissible to conceive an enemy as "unlawful" than as "lawful." Repeatedly, the modern sources of the modern law of nations imply that the distinction between the enemy and the bandit traverses the idea of the "enemy" itself. Hence the constant reemergence within the category of the official opponent of two types of antagonists: *justus* and *injustus*, the "unjust" no less than the "just," the "unlawful" no less than the "lawful."

Only if one grants this possibility can one understand how the modern authorities on the law of war can — and must — find a place in their books for an antagonist whose definition so resists the legal and political categories they advance. They extend their many rights to an "enemy" whom they have qualified and conditioned. This is an "enemy" (*hostis*) who will be considered worthy of that classical name only as long as he fulfills the various criteria that render him "lawful" or "just" (*justus*). But that legitimate adversary, as the scholars know well, is but one of several opponents that can always assail the sovereign state. Then there are also others: groups of combatants who, lacking an established title to represent a sovereign potentate, may also not be defined as common criminals; bands of antagonists, conversely, who, while outside territorial jurisdiction, nonetheless cannot be prosecuted according to the rules that are to obtain between separate nation-states. Faithful to a long tradition, the jurists thus clear a space for a foe beyond the line. Neither *inimicus* nor *hostis*, neither private nor public, and neither criminal nor political, this antagonist can hardly be represented in the dominant terms of the modern law of nations, starting with the seemingly straightforward terms of quantity recorded by Wolff in his *Jus gentium*. Such an opponent, who is no more an individual than a constituted collectivity, cannot, strictly speaking, be considered either "one" or "all." All that may be certain is that there are some, "not included in the number of lawful enemies."

These unlawful and uncounted antagonists haunt the bright house of modern European public law well into the eighteenth century. It should therefore come as no surprise that the same authors who stipulated in famous terms that there are no more than two types of adversaries, the "private" (*inimici*) and the "public" (*hostes*), were well acquainted with the exceptional "enemy of all." The classicizing thinkers did not deign to mention that foe when they proposed their systematic doctrine of enemies; but at other times they bethought themselves and named him in no uncertain terms. Writing of wars that do not conform to the rules of proper combat, Wolff thus recalls that "he who wages an unjust war is a robber, an invader, and a bandit [*praedo, invasor, ac latro est*]," adding in a note:

116

"in every period, the more civilized nations have recognized that unlawful belligerents [*injustos bellatores*] are to be classed with robbers, invaders, and bandits [*praedonibus, invasoribus et latronibus*], and that those things which are done by them in a war waged without any right are to be considered robbery and brigandage."[43] Evoking in another passage the dire case of "those who from no justifying reasons are carried into war," the philosopher goes further. Such adversaries, he writes, "cannot be said to wage war, but to practice brigandage, [...] destroying the security of all nations." "Therefore," the enlightened author concludes, "the right to punish them belongs to all nations, and by this right they can remove from their midst those wild monsters of the human species [*ista fera generis humani monstra*]."[44]

Vattel said no less. The doctrine of the two types of enemies was perhaps never formulated as clearly as in *The Law of Nations or Principles of Natural Law*, but that work also contained an allusion to a third antagonist of indeterminate number. "Nations which are always ready to take up arms when they hope to gain something thereby," Vattel writes, "are unjust plunderers; but those who appear to relish the horrors of war, who wage it on all sides without reason or pretext, and even without other motive than their savage inclinations, are monsters, unworthy of the name of men [*monstres, indignes du nom d'hommes*]. They should be regarded as the enemies of the human species [*les ennemis du genre-humain*], just as in civil society persons who follow murder and arson as a profession commit a crime not only against the individuals who are victims of their lawlessness, but against the state of which they are the declared enemies. Other nations are justified in uniting together as a body with the object of punishing, and even of exterminating, such savage peoples."[45] The jurist did not hesitate to give multiple examples of such "savage peoples," some drawn from his own time. "Who would doubt," he asks later in his treatise, "that the king of Spain and the states of Italy would be justified in destroying to their very foundations those maritime towns of Africa, those lairs of pirates, who are constantly molesting their commerce and afflicting their subjects?"[46] Before those who wage "an unformed and illegitimate war, which is more properly called brigandage," public authorities, we learn, are entitled to respond in kind: "a Nation attacked by enemies of this kind," Vattel writes, betraying once again the ambiguity of that term, "is not at all obligated to observe against them the rules belonging to formal war; it may treat them as brigands."[47]

Neither Wolff nor Vattel attributed a single title to the unlawful antagonist. Their terminological scruples lay elsewhere. It was the distinction of the eighteenth-century jurists to be concerned above all with the definition of the doctrine of the formal war and the sovereign peoples that might rightfully wage it, and the scholars had little desire to restate what their many predecessors had long before established. As Wolff noted, abruptly and with some discomfiture at the end of his note on the "monster of the human species" to be eradicated, "we do not wish to repeat what can be read in Grotius and the commentaries on his work."[48] When it came to the odious figure of improper enmity, Wolff and Vattel, in any case, hardly needed to say more. By the eighteenth century, the paradigm was securely in place. No matter how many official antagonists the scholars of the law might count, there would still be another, to be opposed not to a particular state, people, or commonwealth but to "the human species" in general: an age-old foe and "monster," "common enemy of all." With such an exceptional opponent, the many rules of combat were to be suspended: no battle was to be declared, no rules respected, no due form observed. Those protocols aimed to regulate the beginning, middle, and end of the legal, armed, and public process that was deemed war, just as they were to issue in the formal pact of peace. The public law of Europe could clearly prescribe no such interactions for the modern states when confronting their uncounted antagonists. Then the unlawful combatants, as Sir Leoline Jenkins put it, were simply to be "subdued" and "rooted out."

CHAPTER ELEVEN

Law of the Sea Camels

The sovereign states of Europe did not rise to their modern might without conceding one great limit to the jurisdiction that was to obtain within their territory. They accepted that, beyond the boundaries that marked the contours of their land, lay vast and uninhabitable regions of the earth that no single polity could claim for itself. These regions, of course, were those of flowing water and, as became ever more apparent with time, they covered the greater part of the surface of the common globe. By the second half of the seventeenth century, if not earlier, enlightened monarchs and publicists came to an agreement on the question of the legal status of the seas: such extraterritorial regions, it was accepted, were to be considered "free," that is, open to all those who wished to employ them for travel and the transport of goods. That decision doubtless recalled the judgment of the Roman jurists, who defined the sea as a legal "thing," like air, by nature "common to all" (*res communis omnium*). But it would be an error to surmise, therefore, that an unbroken tradition linked the modern maritime law to the ancient. Naturally, the medieval jurists and statesmen had been well aware of the place of the open seas in the juridical system of the Digest. Deferential to the tradition, they rarely contested the Roman doctrine directly. But the habits of sovereign powers in the Middle Ages possessed an eloquence all their own. By the thirteenth century, the Genoese, for instance, were known to enforce a policy of taxation that left little room for commentary, exacting payments from all seafarers who passed through the Ligurian sea, be they Italian or

Provençal.[1] The Danes, Swedes, and Norwegians had each adopted similar customs along their coasts. And long before them all, Venice, singularly powerful at sea in war and trade, had set an audacious precedent in the field. Despite the fact that it never possessed more than one of the two long shores of the Adriatic, the insular republic had officially asserted its dominion over the entire "Gulf of Venice." To record its exclusive prerogative, it had even developed wedding liturgy of a special kind, which allowed a thing the ancients placed beyond possession to enter the realm of medieval civil law. On Ascension Day, the Doge would be rowed from his palace in San Marco towards the channel of the Lido in an official gilded barge, the *Bucentaur*, where, to strains of music, he would cast a ring into the lagoon and proffer a solemn oath on behalf of his city-state: "We espouse Thee, O Sea, in sign of a real and perpetual dominion!" (*Desponsamus te mare in signum veri perpetuique dominii!*).[2]

The modern European law of the seas broke above all with such institutions, starting with the famous treatise published in 1609 under the unmistakably polemical title *Mare Liberum Sive de Jure quod Batavis Competiti ad Indicana Commercia Dissertatio* (*The Freedom of the Seas, or A Dissertation on the Right that Belongs to the Batavians to take Part in East Indian Trade*).[3] This "little book of Grotius," as Thomas W. Fulton long ago remarked, "was at once a reasoned appeal to the freedom of the seas in the general interest of mankind, and the source from which the principles of the Law of Nations have come."[4] The work was occasioned by the juridical and political controversy that arose once the Dutch reached the eastern Indian Ocean in 1597. The "Batavians" found that large body of water to be claimed by the Spanish and Portuguese, who did not hesitate, therefore, to denounce the merchants from Holland as pirates illegally sailing in Iberian waters. To such charges, Grotius responded strenuously, defending the rights of his countrymen on the grounds that "navigation, by the law of nations, is free [*liberum*] to all persons whatsoever."[5] That thesis, to be sure, was not altogether novel. As early as the sixteenth century, two Spanish authors, Fernando Vázquez de Menchaca and Alfonso de Castro, had advanced like arguments, particularly against the maritime pretensions of the Genoese and the Venetians.[6] But Grotius's was a more forceful and systematic essay, and it provoked reactions throughout Europe. Drawing at once on Roman law, the law of nature, and the law of nations, the *Mare Liberum* offered a comprehensive treatment of the legal status of flowing waters as such, be they in Europe or beyond it. The Dutch jurist conceded that small inland seas no broader than rivers might well be owned, as could straits and bays. Waters in close proximity to the territory of a state, he maintained, can also be legitimately appropriated, since it is possible for a fleet or naval army effectively to occupy them.[7] But the uninhabitable and inexhaustible oceans of the earth, Grotius argued, are of another legal status altogether, closer, as the Romans knew, to that of air. No sovereignty may be acquired over such elements. Claims to possess the open seas, whether from titles of "discovery," papal bulls, the law of war and conquest, or occupancy and prescription, are all, he therefore concluded, equally invalid.

Grotius's bold claims did not go unchallenged. Although a treaty signed in Antwerp less than a month after the publication of the *Mare Liberum* decided the case in the East Indies in favor of the "Batavians," rebuttals of the jurist's tract were soon in print, and they were many.[8] The years 1617–1620 witnessed the appearance of works by Venetian scholars asserting the rights of the Adriatic republic to its gulf.[9] In 1625, Seraphin de Freitas published a defense of the Iberian cause, *On the Just Asiatic Dominion of the Portuguese, against Grotius's Freedom of the Seas*.[10] Perhaps the most famous replies to Grotius came from a maritime power the Dutch jurist had hardly mentioned in his treatise, namely, England. A first response came in 1613, when the Scottish mathematician and jurist, William Welwood, recalled the rights of the British crown to its waters in an *Abridgment of all the Sea-Lawes* dedicated, with good reason, to King James I. In a long chapter, "The Community and the Propriety of the Seas," Welwood answered, point by point, the argument of "the Author of *Mare Liberum*."[11] Two years later, Welwood amplified his claims in a Latin treatise dedicated to Queen Anne, *De Dominio Maris*.[12] But the most extensive reply to Grotius was to appear in 1635, with the publication of a monumental work of juridical scholarship commissioned and printed by King Charles I: John Selden's *Mare Clausum, seu de Dominio Maris Libri Duo (Of the Dominion, Or, Ownership of the Sea)*.[13] Here the learned English author sought to establish firmly that, according to natural law and the law of nations, English sovereignty covers the entire "British ocean" (*Oceanus britannicus*), a body of water Selden described as bounded to the south and west by the coasts of neighboring continental states and to the north and east by limits that still remained to be determined.[14] Grotius appears to have known Welwood's work and held it in high esteem, but he did not reply to Selden.[15] Dirck Graswinckel, Grotius's own relation and erstwhile secretary, composed an answer to the author of the *Mare Clausum*, but the Dutch authorities resolved, for reasons of political prudence, not to print it.[16]

The next years were to witness the appearance of more tracts on the question of the dominion of the seas, but in comprehensiveness and argumentative force none exceeded the levels set by the authors of the *Mare Liberum* and the *Mare Clausum*. The juridical controversy, while protracted, would in any case also not last forever. Ernest Nys wrote, in this regard, of a "battle of the books" that lasted one hundred years.[17] The confrontation had begun in the middle of the sixteenth century, when Fernando Vázquez de Menchaca and Alfonso de Castro contested the claims of sovereign states to appropriate the seas. With Selden, the debate had entered its last stages. In matters of maritime politics, the English were soon to confront the Dutch directly and to prevail. In 1650 and 1651, acts passed in Parliament and signed by Cromwell forbade foreign ships from transporting goods from North America that were not produced by their nations or manufacturers, measures that targeted the Dutch traders above all.[18] Ultimately, however, the official publicists of Europe were to second not Selden but Grotius, judging the seas to be by nature "open." In his *Law of Nations* of 1672, the German jurist Samuel Pufendorf thus considered the question of the ownership of flowing water at length before reaching an unambiguous judgment: "There can then be no probable Ground or Colour be alledged why any one People should pretend to the Dominion of the whole Ocean, so as by virtue of this Right to aim at excluding all others from sailing there."[19] In his treatise *On the Sovereignty of the Seas* from 1702, Bynkershoek concurred. Developing a suggestion that could be found in Grotius, the later jurist stipulated, in influential terms, that territorial sovereignty may be extended from the land into the sea no further than the point where "the force of arms ends" (*ubi finitur armorum vis*).[20]

By the eighteenth century, it could be considered an established legal principle that the world's oceans lay beyond the rightful reach of any single sovereign power. Wolff's *Law of Nations* is in this regard exemplary. It treats the question of the dominion of the seas in terms whose clarity almost conceals the earlier controversy. Wolff recalls that ownership, properly defined, consists in the right to occupy a thing and to define the extent to which others may, or may not, legitimately make use of it. Were a nation to somehow occupy the open sea, we read, it might claim such rights of possession, deciding, as on land, whether others might also employ its own property. But the open waters are vast and inhospitable, and they resist all effective occupation. "It is impossible to compel all nations, or any one from another nation, not to do whatever he wishes to, without the consent of the other, anywhere at sea; a thing," the jurist added pointedly, "which no one can call in question, provided only he consider everything with sufficient care. Therefore it is inconsistent that any nation should have ownership in the sea."[21] Vattel reaffirmed that verdict in his *Law of Nations*. "The open sea is not of such a nature as to be occupied," he wrote, "since no one can establish himself in the open seas in such a manner as to exclude others from passing through them [....] No Nation, therefore, has the right to appropriate the sea, or to attribute to itself its use, to the exclusion of others."[22] But Vattel then went one step further. Having demonstrated the justice of the Grotian law of the seas, he briefly considered the status of a sovereign force that would dare to break it. Such a nation, he argued, would by that act prove itself a "common Enemy" of all. "Moreover," he specified,

> we say that a Nation that wishes to arrogate to itself an exclusive right to the Sea, and to defend it by force, insults all Nations, whose common right it violates. All have good grounds to unite against it to suppress it. Nations have the greatest interest in ensuring that the Law of Peoples be universally respected, since it is the basis of their tranquility. If someone openly troubles that law, all may and must arise against him. Uniting their forces to punish that common Enemy, they will acquit themselves of their duties to themselves and to the human Society of which they are members.[23]

The principles established by these early modern jurists have remained in force. It suffices to open such a classic of twentieth-century legal studies as C. John Colombos's *The International Law of the Sea* to measure the extent to which the terms and arguments of Grotius, Wolff, and Vattel continue to hold in our age. "Today," we read in that primer, which dates from 1947 but has since been reprinted many times, "it is universally recognized that the open sea is not susceptible of appropriation and that no State can obtain such possession of it as would legally be necessary to entitle it to a claim of property over it."[24] It is perhaps needless to recall that from the seventeenth century to the twentieth , however, not all the basic rules of maritime law stood still. One thorny question, in particular, continued to be debated until it was at last resolved. The enlightened jurists, like the Romans, distinguished the "open" seas from the "closed," and while they granted that the first lay beyond the jurisdiction of the state, they insisted that the second, composed of waters inland and around the coast, must be considered as falling under the jurisdiction of the territory. But the early modern legal scholars, like the ancient, possessed no single criterion for deciding on the line of demarcation between the two types of seas. Vattel could thus remark that "it is no easy thing" to determine at which point the waters near the land pass into the free expanses beyond them.[25] Doubtless he was well aware that earlier authorities had emitted more than one judgment on the issue. In the Middle Ages, Bartolus taught that territorial jurisdiction extends one hundred miles from the land, or less than a two-day journey from it.[26] His pupil, Baldus, by contrast, argued that "territory extends into water" (*territoriam in acquis se extendit*) as far as sixty miles into the sea.[27] When Bynkershoek suggested in the first years of the eighteenth century that maritime occupation might be asserted as far as arms released from land could reach into the sea, he proposed a compelling, albeit formal, solution to the old conundrum. In measuring territorial jurisdiction, jurists subsequently could appeal to the range of fire, or, as it has been called, the "canon shot rule" (*portée de cannon*, or *Kanonschußweite*).[28] In time, however, that principle could not define any stable line running parallel with the shore, and for a simple reason: with each advance in the technologies of warfare, the "force of arms" would change, and the line would need, therefore, to be redrawn. Only in 1782 did a jurist propose a modern rule that could be generally accepted without consideration for the strength of arms. Fernando Galiani, Sicilian Secretary of Legation at Paris, argued for a point of demarcation of three miles, the equivalent of a marine league.[29] His decision has remained to this day the most respected in the field. Up to the three-mile line, waters may still generally be considered "territorial," forming a "marginal sea" or "maritime belt" (*mare proximum, mare vicinum*, or *nächstangrenzendes Meer*). Beyond that point, the high seas begin, and claims to territorial jurisdiction must cease.[30]

That consensus resolved one legal question, yet it immediately raised another. Incapable of being inhabited and even occupied in any legal sense, the open seas might well be "free," beyond the reach of the various jurisdictions that obtain on land. The seas and oceans of the earth, however, could still be crossed. But what legal thing could traverse them, and wherever could such a thing, sailing in the open seas, be? With his customary acumen, Kant pointed to the crux in terms of memorable precision. "The community of human beings," he remarked in his essay "Toward Perpetual Peace," "is divided by uninhabitable parts [*unbewohnbare Theile*] of the earth's surface, such as oceans and deserts."[31] These "parts" may not be appropriated, being, as Kant noted, "no one's thing," or, to employ the German form of the Latin *res nullius*, "without master" (*herrenlos*).[32] But still, he explained, "it is possible for human beings to approach their fellows over these ownerless tracts [*herrenlose Gegenden*], and to utilize, as a means of social intercourse, that right to the earth's surface that the human species shares in common."[33] The philosopher observed that travel through the "uninhabitable parts of the earth's surface" is due, in case of the desert, to the exceedingly useful beast that is the dromedary. In the oceans, the possibility of the exceptional passage through "ownerless tracts" may be attributed, with perfect symmetry, to the camel of the sea that is the "ship."[34]

Once the modern jurists had granted the freedom of the open seas, they could hardly avoid the question of the legal status of that unlikely "camel." While in transit, at least, the ship must forsake the land. But what then became of its jurisdiction? To be submitted to the rule of any single code of law, the vessel would have to be exempted from the juridical principle that obtained beyond the line of demarcation; stated positively, the ship would have to be considered in some way as if it were still on land, despite the fact that it sailed across the open seas. In his *Law of Nations*, Vattel had encountered the difficulty while discussing the potentially troublesome legal question of the nationality of children born while their mothers traveled over the free and open seas. There he had also suggested a classic solution: "If children are born in a vessel of the nation," the Swiss scholar wrote, "they may be reputed born in the territory; for it is natural to consider the vessels of the nation as portions of its territory, especially when they sail in the free seas, since the State preserves its jurisdiction over those vessels."[35] From the "natural" legal point of view, the ship, he thus maintained, might be considered a simple "portion of the territory" of its sailors. The only consequential complication, of course, was that this "portion" by definition moved. Committed to precision in their diction, later jurists, for this reason, openly alluded to the fact in the standard epithets they attributed to the vessel. Nineteenth- and twentieth-century legal scholars defined the ship, with increased juridical exactitude, as "floating territory" (*territoire flottant*) or "swimming land" (*schwimmendes Gebietsteil*).[36]

Those terms, to be sure, involve a curious, if decisive, juridical operation. They imply the legal procedure the Romans long ago named "fiction of the law" (*fictio legis*): that device by which, for the purposes of reaching a judgment in court, "the false," as Baldus explained, may be "accepted as the truth" (*falistas pro veritas accepta*), such that, as Cinus of Pistoia more starkly wrote, the law comes to "take as true what is most certainly contrary to the truth" (*in re certa contrariae veritatis pro veritate assumptio*).[37] In the juridical theory of vessels, the mechanism of confabulation is flagrant: that which is, in fact, in motion and at sea is considered as if it were, by law, immobile and inseparable from the land. One may well assert that such a form of reasoning distorts physical reality, proposing, as Azzo wrote of the "figments of the law" (*figmenta legis*), "interpretations contrary to the truth."[38] But the legal doctrines of the ship as "floating territory" and "swimming land" do not merely negate reality, since, in disguising the extra-legal facts, they reveal a principle. It is one rule fundamental to the law, even if, in the absence of the fiction, it might never come to light as such. The truth is that the jurists may conceive of such a thing as "mobile land" only because they have already presupposed a purely abstract and formal legal being: a principle of "territoriality" that may, when necessary, be detached from any geographical segment of the surface of the earth. Once such a principle has been established, one may well loosen the domain of legal jurisdiction from the space of geographical extension. "Territory," as Baldus wrote, can "extend into water," albeit only from the perspective of the law. And, in the open ocean, beyond the line that demarcates the inner from the outer waters, a ship and those aboard it may therefore be considered to fall under the jurisdiction of a single state.

Since the eighteenth century, the fiction of the territoriality of the ship has proven of particular use to jurists when defining the legal status of vessels belonging to states, such as ships of war. International law has long accepted, as Hall records, that sovereigns and the armies of a state, when in foreign territory, and that diplomatic agents, when within the country to which they are accredited, possess immunities from local jurisdiction in respect of their person, and in the case of sovereigns and diplomatic agents with respect to their retinue, that these immunities generally carry with them local effects within the dwelling or place occupied by the individuals enjoying them.[39]

A principle of "exterritoriality" assures that, no matter where such officials may be, the law of nations will regard them "as detached portions of the state to which they belong, moving about on the surface of foreign territory and remaining separate from it."[40] Maritime vessels of war, the jurists teach, partake of this same legal régime. Even when they cross the "ownerless tracts of the earth," they and those they carry remain, for the law, as if firmly rooted in the territory of their state. Article 8 of the 1958 Geneva Convention on the High Seas states, without ambiguity, that "warships on the high seas have complete immunity from the jurisdiction of any State other than the flag State."[41] As Colombos explains, "the position of a warship on the high seas is that of complete exterritoriality in the sense in which the fiction of exterritoriality must be understood, namely, that the ship is not subject to the jurisdiction of any State other than her own."[42]

That qualification is not superfluous, for in the past the fiction of the territoriality of the ship has led to consequences that, while logical, are often startling. In the first half of the seventeenth century, Sir John Pennington, for example, ventured to suggest that since the king's ships counted for the law as an extension of the territory, they might be judged, like any other portions of firm land, to possess maritime belts about them, such that "any foreign ship attacked by another in the narrow seas might put herself under the protection of any of the king's ships coming under its lee, 'in the same manner as under a castle on shore.'"[43] As late as 1856, Baron de Cussy advanced a very similar argument, which followed, he maintained, from the "incontestable, ambulatory sovereignty" granted by the law to ships of state. "A warship in the open seas," he wrote in an influential study of the maritime law of nations, "carries with it over the Ocean an incontestable, ambulatory sovereignty. In such a situation it even has a kind of territory about it, its own atmosphere, which has as its measure the distance of the cannon shot. If a ship takes refuge in this belt, it will be safe from the prosecution of the aggressor, just as if it were in a cove or neutral port."[44]

Today, legal authorities attribute to the warship a more limited "exterritoriality," which confers territorial jurisdiction solely to the vessel and its members (with varying concessions, while ashore, to the laws obtaining in the port).[45] The territoriality accorded to private ships on the high seas is generally considered to be more restricted still. Some may hold it less "exterritorial" than "quasi-territorial."[46] Most jurists in our time, however, would deny the merchant ship even that unprepossessing title. Colombos thus flatly maintains that "the jurisdiction which a State may lawfully exercise over vessels flying its flag on the high seas is a jurisdiction over the persons and property of its citizens; it is not a territorial jurisdiction."[47] The reasoning supporting that judgment is simple. As Lord Finlay declared in the famous criminal case of the *Lotus*, a private French vessel stationed in Turkish territory, a merchant ship "is a moveable chattel; it is not a place; when on voyage it shifts its place from day to day, and from hour to hour, and when in dock, it is a chattel which happens at the time to be in a particular place."[48] If it absolutely must be conceded that the private vessel constitutes a "place," it is, as Henri Walther argued, one of the order of "a room or armchair, rather than a geographical location."[49] Provided that it conform to the regulations of a single state and fly its flag, a merchant ship on the high seas needs no greater territoriality. Territorial jurisdiction will extend not to the vessel but to the persons and things on board it. Should there be allegations that a crime has been committed while at sea, the case will be investigated and judged in accordance with the code of law of the ship's flag state. All those aboard the vessel will be considered to have been answerable to that single jurisdiction.[50]

THE ENEMY OF ALL

These principles of legal accountability at sea, hold, however, only to a point. "So long as acts of violence are done under the authority of the state [...], the state is responsible, and it alone exercises jurisdiction," Hall writes. "If a commissioned vessel of war indulges in illegal acts, recourse can be had to its government for redress; if a sailor commits a murder on board a vessel the authority of the state to which it belongs is not displaced, and its laws are able to assert themselves."[51] But the law of nations is also familiar with occurrences on the high seas of quite another type. Acts of piracy may also come to pass. "If a body of men of uncertain origin seize upon a vessel and scour the ocean for plunder," Hall continues, "no one nation has more right of control over them, or more responsibility for their doings, than another, and if the crew of a ship takes possession of it after confining or murdering the captain, legitimate authority has disappeared for the moment, and it is uncertain for how long it may be kept out."[52] Then persons and things aboard no longer fall under the jurisdiction of any single state, for offenses have been committed against all nations, and the crime is considered international. Any state authority, as a consequence, may legitimately take possession of the vessel, prosecuting those on board. The juridical grounds for that judgment are well established: as Colombos tersely explains, "the crew by becoming pirates render themselves 'the enemies of mankind' and the Courts of the captor State are competent to try them."[53]

It is worth reflecting on the legal status of the ship that bears such "enemies." Although it may once have belonged to a state or to an individual, from the moment a crime against the law of nations comes to be committed aboard it, a vessel must immediately "forfeit" the protection of its flag.[54] This much can hardly be doubted. As Alexander Müller observed in 1929, "the practice and science of the law of nations all agree in maintaining that the pirate ship is *ipso facto* denationalized. The ship that commits piracy loses, through that deed, its nationality. It is no longer justified in hoisting up its flag. If it does so nonetheless, no state is obligated to respect that flag."[55] But the pirate vessel's ultimate fate is considerably more obscure than this summary allows. Like other ships, it cannot be considered firm land, over which a single state jurisdiction might unquestionably hold. But neither is it "floating" or "swimming" land, which, detached from the borders of the state, could still be considered, by a fiction of the law, a rightful portion of the state's territory. Moreover, it is also no rightful possession — "room or arm-chair" — that might fall, as an object of ownership, under the juris-diction of a private code of law. The pirate ship is not a place, nor may it be considered from the point of view of the law as if it were within another place. Its legal status can hardly be told apart from that of the exceptional medium in which it moves. Like the high seas over which it sails, the vessel of the universal enemies is nowhere, no one's, and exposed, therefore, to being legitimately captured by all. A camel of the sea that has swum out of legal sight, it is as ownerless and as uninhabitable as the oceans that divide the dry parts of the surface of the earth.

CHAPTER TWELVE

Of Iron Cages and *U-Boots*

Melville once suggested that something in the nature of ships unsettles. Describing the apprehensiveness with which Captain Delano approached the foreign vessels he was to board, the narrator of "Benito Cereno" remarks that "both house and ship, the one by its walls and blinds, the other by its high bulwarks like ramparts, hoard from view their interiors till the last moment; but in the case of the ship there is this addition: that the living spectacle it contains, upon its sudden and complete disclosure, has, in contrast with the blank ocean which zones it, something of the effect of enchantment. The ship seems unreal; these strange costumes, gestures, and faces, but a shadowy tableau just emerged from the deep, which directly must receive back what it gave."[1] Some two decades earlier, in 1838, Melville's compatriot, Edgar Allan Poe, had also placed at the center of his novel, *The Narrative of Arthur Gordon Pym of Nantucket*, the portrait of a vessel of striking "unreality." This was a merchant ship of unknown origin that few readers are likely ever to forget. The exceptional brig, Poe's narrator surmised, had most likely once been a Dutch trader. But by the time he caught sight of it sailing in the Southern Seas, it moved all on its own, having become a phantom ship, belonging now to no one and no place. "There came wafted over the ocean from the strange vessel (which was now close upon us)," the narrator recalls in his ill-fated notes, "a stench, such as the whole world has no name for—no conception of—hellish—utterly suffocating—insufferable, inconceivable."[2]

Earlier literature, of course, had not been lacking in accounts of unusual ships. It suffices to think of the mythic feats Jason accomplished while aboard the Argo, or of the significantly less familiar report given by the narrator of Lucian's *True Story*, who recalls how he and his men were assaulted at sea by unlikely seamen soon after leaving Calypso's charming cove. "We were storm-tossed for two days, and on the third," he writes, "we fell in with the pumpkin-pirates [οἱ κολοκυνθοπειραταί]. They are savages from the neighboring islands who plunder passing sailors. They have large boats of pumpkin, sixty cubits long; for after drying a pumpkin they hollow it out, take out the insides and go sailing in it, using reeds for masts and a pumpkin-leaf for a sail. They attacked us with two crews and gave us battle, wounding many of us by hitting us with pumpkin-seeds instead of stones." No less propitious an event than the sudden appearance of those corsairs's worst enemies, the "Nut-sailors" (οἱ καρυοναύται), could save Lucian and his Grecian crews. Fortunately, he recalls, "it was evident that the Nut-sailors would win, as they were in greater numbers—they had five crews—and fought from stouter ships. Their boats were the halves of empty nutshells, each of which measured fifteen fathoms in length."[3]

In antiquity, even sovereigns allowed themselves to enter wondrous vessels. The Greek *Alexander Romance* records how, having once come across a crab of monstrous proportions inside whose shell there lay seven pearls the likes of which no man had ever seen before, the Macedonian monarch concluded that "they must originate in the inaccessible depths of the sea." That thought immediately led him to another. "Then," Alexander proudly recalled in an informative, if lengthy, letter to his mother, "I made a large iron cage, and inside the cage I placed a large glass jar, two feet wide, and I ordered a hole to be made in the bottom of the jar, big enough for a man's hand to go through. My idea was to descend and find out what was on the floor of this sea."[4] The classical and medieval traditions offer multiple accounts of Alexander's voyages beneath the waters.[5] In Greek literary sources, he observes "all kinds of fish," including one enormous swimming beast that dares to pull the sovereign's own cage through the sea, before wrecking it against the shore, spilling the king on the sand.[6] Medieval Latin and Romance versions of the tale find the sovereign in a glass jar, absorbed in contemplation of the strange spectacles before him: "he saw fish looking very much like men and women, walking on their feet on the sea-bed and feeding on other fish, just as men in this world feed on animals."[7] The Old French adaptation attributed to Alexander of Paris has the king commenting on the ways of belligerent fish in battle.[8] That rendition also suggests that Alexander's wish to fashion the marvelous jar may not have been altogether unrelated to his infamous imperial ambitions. "My lords," the weary monarch declares in the verse romance, before proposing his novel plan, "I have conquered widely. The inhabitants of Jerusalem do exactly as I will. I have destroyed the people of Tyre on account of their great cruelty. Because of me, Darius, King of Persia, has been put to death by his own people. Now I will tell you what I have thought: I have come and gone about the earth enough. I wish to know the truth concerning the people of the seas."[9]

"Cage" or "jar," the vessel Alexander invented to obtain that truth bears more than a passing resemblance to the sturdy and armed devices of underwater travel now commonly called submarines. It was not till the first half of the twentieth century, however, that common monarchs disposed of tools like Alexander's, and that the unlikely ships began to contribute significantly to the naval forces of sovereign states. The new vessels emerged most notably, so to speak, during the First World War, when the German empire employed them with considerable success against her enemies. Those who witnessed the appearance of the new technology of war naturally noted its remarkable stealth and destructive power, but they also saw immediately that this was a ship unlike those of traditional combats between belligerent public persons. The submarine marked a new departure for the international principles of war. Although the underwater vessel could be, and indeed was, employed against ships of state, it itself resisted, by its form, adherence to the rules established by the law. The modern doctrine of war stipulated that to be lawful, state vessels were to comply with certain principles.

They must, for instance, visibly affiliate themselves with their state, usually by means of the flag, if not permanently, at least always in the moments prior to attacking. When they waged war, they were to discriminate, at least in principle, between a neutral and an enemy vessel. They must also be willing to receive on board for safety the crew of the opposing vessel, and if they took captives, they were to do so in accordance with the jurisdiction of the prize court, whose crew they were always to transport.

By its design, the submarine, however, could respect no such imperatives.[10] Its action was secretive by definition; it disposed of no technology, at least at its inception, by which to distinguish under water between enemy and neutral ships; finally, its construction did not furnish it with any certain means for taking aboard captives, be they things or persons, and its own crew, in any case, was too exiguous to afford personnel for staffing prize vessels and visiting and searching passing ships. The new underwater vessel was no more, and no less, than a sealed and swimming sinking weapon. In the late nineteenth century, some jurists, such as the members of the *jeune école* in France, defended the new war vessels for this very reason, claiming that they were less of the form of the ship than that of the boat, particularly close in kind to the novel torpedo-boat; therefore "the existing rules relating to visit and search should not apply to them."[11] But their judgments were "promptly countered," as Colombos recalls, "by those of other sailors, especially by Admiral Bourgeois in 1886: 'the advent of the torpedo, whatever its influence on naval material, has in no way changed international treaties, the law of nations or the moral laws which govern the world. It has not given the belligerent the right of life and death over the peaceful citizens of the enemy State or of neutral States."[12] That judgment left little room for doubt. But the legal status of the seafarers of the new vessels in those years was still far from certain, as interested observers were well aware. With uncanny prescience, Jules Verne famously remarked upon the fact in his 1869 novel, *Twenty Thousand Leagues Beneath the Seas* (*Vingt milles lieues sous les mers*). When Captain Nemo and the underwater crew of the *Nautilus* abduct Dr. Pierre

Aronnax and his companions, the astute and learned, if understandably bewildered, protagonist exclaims: "With whom were we dealing? Perhaps with some pirates of a new variety, who exploit the sea
in their own fashion?"[13]

The question became most acute with the outbreak of the First
World War. One episode in particular attracted the attention of
publicists and lawyers everywhere. It was the sinking, on May 7,
1915, of a large and famous British transatlantic liner, the *Lusitania*,
as it made its way from the shores of the United States to England.
While expressing its "deepest sympathy" for the death of some two
thousand people on board, who were almost all non-combatants,
the German authorities publicly justified the act with reference to
the maritime blockade the British had imposed on Germany. The
English act of war, they claimed, was starving the German civilian
population and had, therefore, effectively obliged the well-meaning
representatives of their state "to resort to retaliatory measures."[14]
The legal authorities of Germany appear largely to have seconded
that judgment. They argued that, in any case, it was senseless to
demand that underwater vessels conform to the old laws of naval
warfare. "New situations," Max Fleischmann of the University of
Königsberg explained, with reference to "the case of the *Lusitania*,"
"necessitate new rules."[15] Ernst Zitelmann, from the University of
Bonn, was more explicit:

> Legal rules that are inapplicable to new conditions, must give way to
> new regulations. "As the reason for the law ceases, so, too, must the law
> itself cease" (*Cessante ratione legis cessat lex ipsa*). Technical science and
> polity may create new conditions which of necessity destroy the frame-
> work of the old rules of international law. Who would have thought
> at the time the old rules governing maritime warfare were formed,
> of the possibilities of submarine warfare? Had the use of submarines
> been anticipated, special rules governing their employment would have
> been devised.[16]

Anglo-Saxon jurists of the period tended to find such claims
unconvincing. Past practices in war, they recalled, set clear standards

that need not be lowered. "Even Semmes," James W. Garner commented in *International Law and the World War*, "who was variously described as a 'freebooter,' 'corsair,' and 'pirate,' never destroyed an enemy vessel without taking off the crew and passengers."[17] When he described his treatment of Northern captives in *Memories of Service Afloat During the War Between the States*, this Confederate Admiral had proudly declared: "We were making war upon the enemy's commerce, not upon his unarmed seamen. It gave me as much pleasure to treat these with humanity as it did to destroy his ships."[18] During the Great War, the President of the United States also pronounced himself on the question, stating that armies that availed themselves of submarines could make no such clear distinction. Responding to the torpedoing of the *Lusitania* in 1915, Woodrow Wilson stressed the "practical impossibility of employing submarines in the destruction of commerce without disregarding those rules of fairness, reason, justice and humanity which all modern opinion regards as imperative."[19] A year later, he went further, declaring the submarine, by virtue of its methods of activity, essentially "incompatible with the principles of humanity, the long-established and incontrovertible rights of neutrals and the sacred immunities of non-combatants."[20] A conference on naval tensions in East Asia organized by the United States in 1922 aimed to establish that judgment in the law of nations forever. "It is practically impossible," the opening article of the Washington Naval Conference read, "to utilize submarines without violating the generally recognized principles of international law."[21] Eight years later, the London Naval Treaty (formally titled the Treaty for the Limitation and Reduction of Naval Armament), signed by Great Britain, France, Italy, the United States, and Japan, aimed to submit the underwater vessels to the same legal principles that held for ships of war. "Submarines," the treaty declared, "must conform to the rules of international law to which surface vessels are subject."[22]

Restrictions on underwater vessels were incorporated into the so-called London Protocol, a treaty for the limitation of naval armament, of November 6, 1936, which was signed by many sovereign states, including Germany. Within months, however, the troubled question of the legal status of the submarine once more emerged. The Spanish Civil War had brought new insecurities to the Mediterranean seas. Although the military conflict was one of notable importance, the major powers chose not to intervene and, claiming complete neutrality in the conflict, they formally refused the rights of belligerency. Almost as soon as the civil war erupted, however, the waters surrounding Spain were affected. Submarines as well as airplanes began targeting maritime vessels bearing goods to and from the Iberian peninsula, with little regard for their legal status in the conflict. The perpetrators did not publicly identify themselves, but it could hardly be doubted that those acts of maritime destruction would entail consequences for the civil war. As one contemporary observer recalled, "the attacks were obviously of strategic importance in cutting the flow of supplies from Soviet Russia to the Spanish Government, as both those governments violently denounced the attacks and openly accused Italy of being responsible for them."[23] Soon the range of targets grew wider: not only merchant ships but also war vessels belonging to neutral powers were struck. To offer a united response to such maritime assaults on non-belligerent vessels, the British and French authorities summoned an international conference at Nyon in September 1937. Nine Mediterranean states, including Bulgaria, Romania, and the Soviet Union, but excluding both Italy and Germany, met to discuss the urgent issue: "attacks [...] repeatedly committed in the Mediterranean by submarines against merchant ships not belonging to either of the conflicting Spanish parties."[24] Referring to the London Naval Treaty of 1930, the authors of the Nyon Arrangement judged the recent acts to be "violations of the rules of international law." But then they went one step further. The assaults committed by submarines, they subsequently proclaimed, "constitute acts contrary to the most elementary dictates of humanity, which should be justly treated as piracy."[25]

That declaration introduced a new term into the discussion of submarines. Admittedly, the choice of diction was by 1937 not

entirely without precedent. Commenting on the Nyon Arrangement's wording, an unidentified contributor to the 1938 *British Yearbook for International Law* recalled that two decades earlier, "great
indignation was caused by the sinking by German submarines during the Great War, contrary to the rules of maritime warfare with
regard to the exercise of belligerent rights at sea, of the merchant
vessels of belligerent and neutral powers, and by the loss of non-
combatant and neutral lives and property involved. This action was
often described popularly as piracy."[26] But the author took pains to
specify that this was a resolutely nontechnical usage, which had been
without significance for the practice of the law: "no captured submarine officers, who had acted in accordance with the orders of the
government, were tried as pirates."[27] There were good legal reasons
for that fact, as commentators of several nationalities immediately
observed.[28]

The author of the unsigned article in the *British Yearbook*, for one,
noted that the law of nations admits no more than two varieties of
"piracy." The first, "piracy *jure gentium*," applies to certain forms of
violence at sea done by persons "in defiance of the laws of all states
for which no state can be held responsible"; these are acts committed
by persons who, on account of being "outside the pale of international law," may be arrested by any vessel and tried by the courts of
any state.[29] The second type is "piracy by treaty and/or municipal
law"; this variety may be established by one state over its subjects
and extended to the members of other countries, provided their own
legal representatives have, by signed treaty, accepted it.[30] That the
acts committed by the submarines surrounding Spain were not deeds
"for which no state can be held responsible" was all too evident; the
author of the *British Yearbook* article could therefore reject the possibility that the Nyon Arrangement bore on "piracy *jure gentium*." But
no articles in international accords provided for the trial and punishment of individuals guilty of such deeds as in cases of piracy, and the
unidentified attackers were therefore equally unfit to be accused of
"piracy by treaty."[31] "It would seem," the author concluded, "that
the references to piracy in the preamble [...] must be interpreted as

meaning that such attacks are morally as disgraceful as piracy, and that it *would* be justifiable to treat them as such, but the participating powers, while placing this on record, have thought it better to do something else, namely, to meet them by forcible direct naval action taken collectively and for the collective benefit of all vessels 'not belonging to either of the parties of the Spanish conflict.'"[32]

The same year, *The American Journal of International Law* published an article, "The Charge of Piracy in the Spanish Civil War," which advanced a similar thesis in greater detail. Its author, Raoul Genet, hailed from one of the other main signatory powers of the Nyon Arrangement, France, where he held a prominent post as the director of an important law journal. Genet opened his considerations by noting that one circumstance alone could have induced legal authorities to dub the recent maritime attacks in the Mediterranean "piratical": namely, that they had been committed by warring parties, such as those involved in the Spanish Civil War, who did not possess internationally admitted titles to belligerency.[33] But that fact, he argued, still did not suffice for them to be judged as "piratical." Violent acts by the nationalists might well be described from the point of view of international law as deeds committed by "insurgents" or "rebels"; but to call them "piratical" would be an error. "We may add," Genet wrote, "that to misqualify the act of rebel as that of pirate is to assume a singular responsibility, since one thereby passes from the municipal sphere and consequently from the sanctions provided and enforced solely by the internal law of the state, to the incomparably more severe sanctions provided by international law. A rebel, in fact, is subject only to punishment by the authority against whom he rebels, and to the extent to which that authority is in a position to exercise his right; the pirate, on the other hand, is beyond the pale of the *ius gentium*, is an outcast from mankind, an international criminal who may be pursued, destroyed or captured by any vessel, public or private."[34]

Lest the "abuse of language" be further propagated, Genet then briefly recalled three conditions that must be fulfilled for a deed to be defined as "piratical" with precision. It must involve (1) an "act of criminal violence"; (2) "an illegal attempt against goods or persons (with its implicit corollary, the *animus furandi*);" (3) "a menace directed against the security of general commerce."[35] Finally, the jurist noted two further and more obvious presuppositions: (4) "the scene of the piratical action is necessarily the sea"; and (5) "the ship engaged in acts of piracy is *ipso facto* denationalized, that is to say, withdrawn from the authority of any state whatever."[36] All such circumstances could not be said to apply to the situation near Spain, where the acts, though violent, maritime, and destructive of trade, lacked the "implicit corollary" of the second specified condition: the "*animus furandi*" or intent to steal for private gain that, in the eyes of the law, defines the felonious act of larceny. That absence proved decisive: "there is no piracy without the *animus furandi*," Genet argued, "and it is indeed impossible, even for the most disordered imagination, to conceive of a ship which would suddenly attack merchant vessels for the pure pleasure of shooting at a target, without committing acts of violence and rapine, and would send them to the bottom with no motive whatsoever."[37] To understand the acts of the deadly submarines, one could in any case resort to a far simpler explanation. Deeds of public vessels, the attacks were committed under the orders and responsibility of a sovereign state, which, legitimately or illegitimately, had resolved to participate in the political confrontation—rebellion, insurrection, or civil war—that divided Spain.

It is hardly surprising that the terminology of the Nyon Arrangement, which elicited such a critical commentary by British and French jurists, provoked at least as vehement a response from distinguished legal scholars in Italy and Germany. The most eminent among them was Carl Schmitt, who published a characteristically pithy and polemical essay on the international accord the very month it was signed.[38] His article, pointedly titled "The Concept of Piracy," appeared only a few months later in Italian translation.[39] Discussing the essay in a letter to his friend Ernst Jünger, Schmitt recalled several weeks later, on November 14, 1937, how this particular contribution to the law of nations had arisen from a moment of rare

142

passion. "The essay on 'The Concept of Piracy,'" Schmitt confessed, "emerged from the affect provoked in me when I see how cold-bloodedly the Anglo-Saxons are pursuing the World War, and how they seem to have succeeded at Nyon in achieving the very thing that, throughout the war, we sought to avoid—namely, the renunciation of the honor of the *U-Boot* weapon [*das Verzicht auf die Ehre der U-Boot-Waffe*]."[40]

Despite the unusual emotion that elicited it, however, Schmitt's essay was in its legal argument largely conventional. It aimed above all to establish the inapplicability of the title of "piracy" to political agents, demonstrating the irreducibility, so to speak, of the concept of the piratical to the concept of the political. Taking as his point of departure Paul Stiel's traditional statement that "an undertaking that pursues political aims is not piracy," Schmitt enumerated three qualities that define the classic crime of maritime depredation.[41] Each, he maintained, was essentially foreign to the submarine attacks carried out near Spain. First, he affirmed, acts of piracy must be committed in "a stateless space, which is not subject to territorial sovereignty."[42] But the European sea, he suggested, contained no such thing: "whoever calls to mind the specific state and political condition of the contemporary Mediterranean must immediately confront the question of where, then, the non-political sea-thieves could find an empty space of complete statelessness in which to run their business."[43] Second, he argued, whoever commits an act of piracy is "denationalized," "either as a presupposition or as a consequence of his deed; thus, if he is not stateless, he is in any case not supported or authorized by any state."[44] Such a status could not apply to the officers aboard Mediterranean submarines, who obviously acted with the weapons and also in the interests of sovereign states. Finally, Schmitt recalled that international law traditionally defined piracy, with respect to its intent, as an act committed for "private enrichment."[45] When discussing piracy in the old books of the law, he noted, "one spoke of *animus furandi*, etc.; and according to the correlation of the political and the state, one spoke of piracy as a typically non-political activity."[46]

Those three arguments were not all equally compelling. The first, which maintained that the Mediterranean was not a "stateless space," might well be contested. Tellingly, Schmitt did not propose it directly, asserting solely that this particular point involved a question to be confronted. He advanced the second and third arguments with greater assuredness. These both asserted the separation of the pirate from the sphere of politics; in implication, they were, therefore, substantially indistinct. They hardly did more than to underline the difference between the "pirate" and the "privateer." This was an authoritative distinction, to be sure, but it was also one of which Schmitt himself, it should be noted, was elsewhere far from certain: in *Land and Sea*, remarkably, he noted that "the various designations of pirate, corsair, privateer, merchant-adventurer can in practice be unclearly exchanged."[47] Schmitt's original contribution to the debate concerning the Nyon Arrangement in truth lay elsewhere. It consisted less in his refutation of the legal applicability of the term "piracy" to submarine depredations than in his analysis of the political significance of that usage, which, he argued, had as little to do with "old-fashioned and now romantic sea-thievery" as with "the resuscitation of the controversial questions of the 1914–1918 World War."[48] The terms of the 1937 international agreement, Schmitt maintained, "instead belong to the great domain of attempts at a new and genuine inter-state European order." This was one new "inter-state European order" that Schmitt enjoined his readers to oppose without qualification, on the grounds that it implied the hopeless confusion of a distinction fundamental to the modern law of nations: that between principles of international relations and principles of domestic jurisdiction; between categories of war and categories of crime; between "politics," in short, and "police."[49] Because pirates, he recalled, are not in any classical sense legitimate belligerents, the military operation undertaken against them cannot be defined in traditional terms as war: "The action taken against pirates is therefore equally non-political. It is not war; instead it is either criminal justice, according to the English conception, or, according to the continental system, a measure of international maritime police."[50]

That Schmitt believed he could uphold "the honor of the *U-Boot* weapon" by invoking the hallowed principles of the European law of nations is one startling fact. The same jurist who had famously explained in an article of 1934 how exactly "the *Führer* protects the *Reich*"[51] now strenuously warned his readers that the English conception of maritime piracy disturbed the classic order of European public law: "Should the English conception of submarine piracy be established as a general concept of the law of nations," Schmitt wrote, "the concept of piracy will have changed its place in the system of international law. It will have been displaced from the empty space of non-political action into the space of intermediary concepts between war and peace, which is typical of the after-war period."[52] One might certainly respond that a scholar of the law who had publicly justified Adolf Hitler's "right, as well as force, to found a new state and a new order" could not now credibly implore others to rise in defense of the traditional legal principles of war and peace.[53] One might doubtless allege that Schmitt's position was incoherent, even hypocritical. But such considerations do not alter one insight the jurist expressed in his brief tract. By the Nyon Arrangement of 1937, the legal status of warfare had undergone an irrevocable change: state vessels were no longer impervious to charges of criminality. In addition to the classic conception of war as the lawful conflict of sovereign nations, a new model of confrontation had emerged. It pitted not one public figure against its symmetrical antagonist but one collective term against its lesser, infamous opponents, setting the representatives of a universal code of law against the stateless criminals who sought to transgress it.

Schmitt understood that the sole term that would lend legitimacy to this new confrontation was one the jurists of the tradition had rarely employed: humanity. Only if war could be defined with respect to such an abstract and general notion as the common species would it become possible to treat the conflict of sovereign states as "either criminal justice, according to the English conception, or, according to the continental system, a measure of international [...] police." Only then could enemies be cast as criminals. In his vain and lucid attempt to recall the traditional doctrine of public law he had done so much to supplant with his legal theories of the National Socialist régime, Schmitt also intuited that one figure alone would be sufficient to summon such a generic collectivity: the figure of its archaic foe, "the enemy of the human species." "Against the pirate as 'the enemy of the human species' [*der Feind des Menschengeschlechts*]," Schmitt remarked, "all humanity—which is otherwise so disheveled—suddenly appears as if united on a single front."[54] Hence the intensity with which the erstwhile *Kronjurist* militated against references to piracy in war. Committed by "affect" no less than interest in defending the legitimacy of the German and Italian belligerents, he implored his contemporaries not to conjure, through the magic name of "the common enemy of all," the humanity he hoped might still continue to remain "otherwise so disheveled." But by 1937 it was already too late. The modern submarine was neither the iron cage of the ancient and medieval fables nor the state ship of war of modern times, whose movements across the surface of the seas, while threatening, could still be safely restricted by the old principles of law. The *U-Boot*, a creature of unsettled and unsettling times, penetrated a new dimension. Its destructive operations beneath the surface of the world's waters announced the age in which piracy would inevitably "change its place," and in which it would soon be quite impossible to keep that obscure presupposition of the law of the nations, humanity, from comng into view.

CHAPTER THIRTEEN

Justifying Humanity

"Humanity" is an obscure word, especially in the fields of law and politics. Today, however, it can hardly be avoided, for it plays a decisive role in many of the dominant phrases of our age. From discussions of human rights and crimes committed against humanity to controversies surrounding humanitarian associations, policies, wars, and "interventions," the name of our natural kind remains crucial. That there may be little about this designation that is self-evident can be gleaned from the rapid recollection of one fact in the history of words: in the West, "humanity" is a late addition to the set of basic legal terms. Not that the ancient authors, for example, lacked all understanding of the idea whose implications we now so easily assume. It is instructive, from this perspective, to consider the practice of the Roman lawyers, whose influence on legal terminology far exceeds that of any other single set of authorities. In their expositions of the code of civil law, the scholars of the Digest often employed the term "human being" (*homo*), and from their various usages one might well deduce a theory of such a general thing as "humanity." But that account would be fundamentally at odds with most contemporary conceptions. The expression "human being" (*homo*), for the Roman scholars, pointed neither to positive rights nor to their ground. On the contrary, it signified the near absence of juridical titles. "Human being" (*homo*) was for them the name of a dimension in individual existence that the law, in principle, excluded from its complex considerations.

This is why the ancient jurists consistently opposed the terms "human being" (*homo*) and "person" (*persona*). They wrote of "human beings" when designating living individuals, considered in the near absence of legal qualification, while they invoked "persons" or "personalities" (*personae*) when alluding to individuals insofar as they laid claim to rights, titles, and prerogatives. Characters such as those of the debtor, the owner, the inheritor, and defendant, for instance, were for the Romans all "persons," in that they permitted individuals to represent themselves and their various entitlements before the law. These were legal constructions, which could be attached to living individuals according to a number of possible forms. A single "human being" could possess several "personalities" over the course of time as well as in a single moment. An individual could be, for example, in succession an owner, husband, inheritor, and testator; he could also simultaneously lay claim to the multiple personhood of substituted heir and instituted heir. Inversely, the Romans also admitted that a single "person" might be partitioned among several individuals. Thus the rights of a master could be shared among his servants, and the title to a single degree of succession divided among inheritors.[1]

When the ancient jurists alluded to humanity by employing the technical expression "human being" (*homo*), they designated what one might well consider a largely extralegal being: the material support for the attribution of all rights, or, more simply put, the physical individual to whom legal titles could be linked. As late as the sixteenth century, Hugo Donellus, faithful to this tradition, could therefore recall that "the expression *human being* [*homo*] refers to nature; *person* [*persona*] refers to civil law" (*homo naturae, persona iuris civilis vocabulum*).[2] It is no doubt also for this reason that in Roman legal discourse, the term *homo*, when used in isolation, meant simply "slave" or "servant." In the idiom of the ancient authors, the term "human being," taken on its own, designated an individual without positive rights. One might well go so far as to wager that had they employed the abstract noun "humanity" in any technical sense, the Roman jurists would have done so, therefore, to designate the specific quality of human life largely lacking in juridical qualification. "Humanity" might have been, for them, a natural element common to all individuals that must be strictly distinguished from positive legal claims and titles.

Such a usage was hardly propitious for the elaboration of a legal and political theory of humanity, at least as a doctrine of the foundation of rights and entitlements. The situation took some time to change. When it did, the architecture of the law established by the Romans acquired a new shape. Introducing their great legal system, the classical jurists had famously distinguished three varieties of codes, which they termed "natural law" (*ius naturale*), the "law of nations" (*ius gentium*), and "civil law" (*ius civile*). It is worth considering the position that "humanity" might occupy in this tripartition. The species clearly could find no place within the last of the types, which dictated the rules pertaining to one group of human beings, namely, the inhabitants of a single city. But the abstract principle of humanity could also not be easily inscribed in the order of "natural law," since that law, for the Roman jurists, was by definition indifferent to the peculiarities of human life. As Ulpian stated in the opening chapter of the *Digest*, "natural law is that which nature has taught to all animals; for it is not a law proper to the human species but is common to all animals — land animals, sea animals, and the birds as well."[3] If there was to be a domain of the law in which "humanity" might acquire some consistency, therefore, it could only be in "the law of nations." But there, the Latin authors had posited a plurality of collective subjects: "nations" (*gentes*). That term seems, by virtue of its number, to exclude the generic oneness of a species. It is as if the Roman jurists accepted that human beings might well be united as instances of a type, but only within the vast domain of natural law, whose principles long precede the foundation of cities; it is as if, in other words, the ancient lawyers believed the human species to be of real significance only from a biological or zoological perspective. Once there are cities and positive legal institutions, the Roman jurists suggested, the unity of the natural kind can no longer clearly be identified.

Then the members of the one species share above all their division into plural "nations" (*gentes*), each with its own rules and traditions.

This ancient vision came to be contested by the modern philosophers of law who aimed, in distinction to the ancients, to elaborate a properly Christian legal theory. The first among them was most likely the late Scholastic thinker Francisco Suárez. His treatise *On Laws* of 1612 announced a new and decisive departure in the law of peoples by positing a thing largely unknown to earlier Latin legal theorists: a unity of the human species, which founded, as he argued, a universal community of all men. "The human species," Suárez wrote,

> while divided in different peoples and sovereignties, always conserves a kind of unity, which is not only specific but also almost political and moral, namely, that commanded by the natural precept of mutual love and pity, a precept that applies to all, even to those who are foreigners, no matter the nation to which they belong. Therefore, although a given sovereign state, commonwealth or kingdom may constitute a perfect community in itself, consisting of its own members, nevertheless, each one of these states is also, in a certain sense, and viewed in relation to the human species, a member of that universal society; for those states when standing alone are never so self-sufficient that they do not require some mutual assistance, association, and intercourse, at times for their own greater welfare and advantage, but at other times because also of some moral necessity or need.[4]

With these words, Suárez did not go so far as to assert that "the unity of the species" immediately furnishes any positive legal principle. It is worth noting that he shied away from maintaining that the oneness of humankind is even strictly of ethical or political significance, writing cautiously that the species possesses "a *kind* of unity, which is not only specific but also *almost* political and moral" (*habet aliquam unitatem non solum specificam, sed etiam quasi politicam, & moralem*).[5] But the implications of his considerations are nonetheless quite apparent. To understand the law of nations fully, he suggested, one must refer to a principle that transcends the divisions of peoples, being founded on the unity of the kind.

Treatises of international law from the following century take one step further. They begin to lend to the "unity" conceived by Suárez the substance of a legal entity, which founds a specific set of customs and obligations. One may take as illustration Wolff's compendium of 1749. Classical in its broad outlines, Wolff's *Jus gentium* duly treats the three varieties of law known to the Romans. But in its discussion "Of the Duties of Nations Toward Each Other and the Rights Arising Therefrom," Wolff's work defines one class of obligations not enumerated by the ancient and medieval theorists. Just as every Christian individual ought to love and cherish his neighbor, the German jurist reasons, so "every nation ought to love and cherish every other as itself, even though it be an enemy."[6] It would be "inhumane" for nations to act otherwise. From this remark, Wolff proceeds to derive a new class of "duties" (*officii*), which ought to assure that peoples remain faithful to their common nature: "duties of humanity" (*officiis humanitatis*). "Since every nation ought to promote the happiness of another nation," Wolff declares, "since, moreover, the duties of humanity are those by which the happiness of another is promoted, the duties of a nation also toward other nations, by which the happiness of those nations is promoted, are duties of humanity."[7] That Wolff himself was aware that such legal "offices" were of an unusual character may be inferred from his passing comment, in a note, that such obligations, while natural, "are generally but little considered" (*vulgo parum attenduntur*).[8] He refrained, however, from saying more.

If one turns to Vattel's *Law of Nations* (*Le droit des gens*), one finds a far fuller consideration of these fledgling obligations. In the opening chapter of his book, "The Nation, Considered in Its Relation to Others," the Swiss jurist offers an extended treatment of "Common Duties, or Offices of Humanity, Between Nations."[9] As in Wolff, the analogy of the interaction of peoples to that of individuals dominates the discussion. "The *offices of humanity*," Vattel asserts, "consist in the fulfillment of the duty of mutual assistance which men owe to one another because they are men, that is to say, because they are made to live together in society, and are of necessity dependent upon one another's aid for their preservation and happiness, and for the means of a livelihood conformable to their nature." So, too, the jurist reasons, there exist "offices of humanity among Nations," which "are not less subject to the laws of nature than are individuals."[10]

Such duties demand that all peoples assist each other, since none could survive entirely on its own. Vattel does not hesitate to offer examples of instances in which such "offices" ought to be discharged. If "a powerful enemy" unjustly attacks a nation, "threatening to crush it," an obligation of humanity enjoins its neighbors to come to its aid. The natural calamities that may always befall peoples provide Vattel with similar illustrations. A nation may be struck with famine, fire, and disaster on its territory, as was the case with the earthquake in Lisbon; in such cases, it is then incumbent on more fortunate peoples to aid it.[11] Since such imperatives result not from contracts or treaties but from a common nature, they extend, Vattel specifies, even to public potentates of diverse religions. The thinker approvingly recalls how a sense of such a duty spurred on the "wise Pontiff who at present occupies the Roman See" to come in succor of "several Dutch vessels, detained at Civita Vecchia through fear of Algerian corsairs," sending papal frigates to escort them safely on their way.[12]

The precise legal status of Vattel's "duties of humanity" is tellingly ambiguous. On the one hand, the *Law of Nations* asserts that such obligations are universal, being dictated to all nations by the common nature of the human species. On the other hand, however, the treatise also specifies that the right by which peoples may lay claim to such offices must remain "imperfect." "If another nation refuses them without good reason," Vattel writes, "it offends against charity, which consists in acknowledging an imperfect right of another; but it does no injury thereby, since injury or injustice results from denying a perfect right."[13] One people might well be inconvenienced by others's neglect of the offices of humanity, but no nation could pretend to be thus harmed, since none, strictly speaking, could ever demand that they be accomplished. Universal in extension without being perfectly binding, the duties of humanity, for Vattel, occupy a curious position before the law. Their discharge is to be recommended, but not commanded; their neglect, conversely, is to be discouraged, but never condemned. One might well detect in such an account the traces of some uncertainty. The eighteenth-century jurist may have hesitated to advance his theory of the offices of the species beyond certain limits, because no matter how "natural" the status it claimed for itself, the doctrine represented, as he well knew, a decidedly novel proposition in the field of law. "These sacred precepts," Vattel observes, in conclusion, "have been for a long time unknown among nations."[14]

They were soon to become much more accepted, and by the end of the eighteenth century, the term "humanity" had acquired a central place in legal theory. As evidence, it suffices to recall the decisive importance given to the term by Vattel's slightly younger contemporary, Immanuel Kant. One may take as the single most important illustration *The Metaphysics of Morals* of 1797, which contains both "The Metaphysical First Principles of the Doctrine of Right" and "The Metaphysical First Principles of the Doctrine of Virtue." In both parts of this late work, the new legal notion plays a crucial role. But it consistently implies obscurities. Kant defines the term "humanity" (*Menschheit*) as "the capacity to set oneself an end, any end whatsoever."[15] That this "capacity" is of a curious legal and ethical status can be gleaned from the philosopher's apodictic assertion that "man has a duty [*Pflicht*] to raise himself from the crude state of his nature, from his mere animality (*quoad actum*), more and more toward humanity [*immer mehr zur Menschheit*], by which he alone is capable of setting himself ends."[16] Kant's distinction between the idea of human being and that of animal being, if not evident, is doubtless highly traditional. Far more striking is the philosopher's indication in this proposition that "humanity," while the characteristic of human beings, remains for them something always still to be achieved, that "man," in other words, must "raise himself [...] more and more" toward the very quality he must by definition possess. One might well ask how such an operation could ever be accomplished, for means and end, in such terms, necessarily grow indistinct. To move toward the ideal of "humanity," one must possess it, yet to be marked by the quality of "humanity," it seems, is only ever to approach it. The argument implies a circle that can hardly be avoided.

In his treatise on the principles of right, Kant asserts more than once that "humanity," whether considered as given or ideal, possesses for all human beings indubitable "dignity" (*Würde*).[17] As such, humanity, the philosopher claims, is deserving of the pure moral feeling that is "respect" (*Achtung*). That principle may seem a familiar moral precept, but in truth it, too, contains an unfamiliar proposition: namely, that "humanity," while inhering in human beings, may also be distinguished from them, so as to become the object of their constant ethical and juridical attention. The vision that defines this critical distinction finds its classic expression in the Kantian formula "humanity in our person" (*Meschheit in unserer Person*).[18] The philosopher appears to have held this phrase to be of decisive importance, and in one passage he even dubs it, in Latin, the very "law of right" (*lex iusti*).[19] But its exact significance cannot easily be defined. From an historical, legal perspective, it is worth noting that the formula sets in motion a striking inversion of two ancient concepts. Whereas the Roman jurists defined the "person" (*persona*) by attributing it to a "human being" (*homo*), Kant characterizes the quality of "humanity" (*Menschheit*) by locating it "in our person" (*in unserer Person*). It seems undeniable that Kant thereby intends to ground positive legal statuses or personalities in a universal principle, "humanity," which transcends them. It is all the more striking, therefore, that the syntactic structure of his formula suggests precisely the contrary, inscribing "humanity" within the very "person" that it should, in principle, enable. To conceive of the legal terms according to the exact Kantian expression, one would be obliged to imagine a relation of considerable logical complexity. According to a transcendental *proteron hysteron*, "humanity" would be a primary principle to be identified as such in a secondary institution alone. It would be locatable solely in that which it must, in all transcendental terms, precede.

Kant drew several consequences, moral and ethical, from the "right of humanity in our person." In his doctrine of virtue, he showed how the title of the kind founds the principle of external duty. Each human being is bound to others, in whose persons the figure of humanity unceasingly demands respect, thus forbidding "arrogance," "defamation," and "ridicule."[20] The right of humanity also grounds the principle of internal duty, which links each being to the higher principle within him. Acts contrary to the obligation to elevate oneself "more and more toward humanity" may then be defined, from a transcendental perspective, as vices. These are all inherent wrongs: "murdering oneself; the unnatural use of one's sexual organs; and such excessive consumption of food and drink as weakens one's capacity for making purposive use of one's powers."[21] No doubt the most well-known principle Kant derived from his conception of moral and legal humanity is the fundamental rule on which he so often insisted, and which he recorded in the *Groundwork of the Metaphysics of Morals*: "Act in such a way that you always use humanity, whether in your own person or in the person of any other, never simply as a means but always at the same time as an end."[22] Of the many striking features that mark this statement of the Kantian "minimal program" in ethics, one of the most obvious has rarely attracted attention.[23] The "categorical imperative" rests entirely on the possibility of isolating, in human beings, an abstract principle of the species, humanity, which is to be "used" in accordance with its intrinsic "worth." The formula thereby conceals a striking axiom. It is the proposition that stipulates that it is possible, and indeed necessary, to deduce the basic principles of law and ethics from a transcendental feeling for a natural kind, from a sentiment Kant, in a telling phrase, calls "respect for the species" (*Achtung für die Gattung*).[24]

One might well wonder as to the reasons for which Kant chose to identify the defining faculty of the ethical and legal agent with as obscure a thing as "the species." By what reasoning could the philosopher bind the unconditioned freedom of the will—"the capacity to set oneself an end, any end whatsoever"—to a single type of nature? Answers in Kant's works could certainly be sought. But it is likely that the thinker's choice of diction also reflects a broader historical development in moral and political terminology. In a study of the fate of the term "humanity," Reinhart Koselleck has observed that in the era of the Enlightenment, appeals to human beings as a whole and to humanity in political, social, and theological debates grew increasingly widespread. The ancient Stoic belief that rational individuals should see themselves as the inhabitants of a single "world state" (κοσμοπόλις) began to achieve some success. The critical meaning of the term "humanity," however, now simultaneously changed. Traditionally, the word referred to the entire species, in general and without distinctions among its members. By the second half of the eighteenth century, however, "humanity" became a powerful instrument of polemic, which effectively divided the collectivity it once simply seemed to designate. The generic expression now acquired "a critical, even a negating function with respect to the contrary position."[25] When employed in debate, "humanity" constituted a legitimating title, capable of contesting the various divisions of human beings imposed by class, Church, and the forms of old political association and hierarchy. "Whoever was concerned with 'humanity,'" Koselleck writes, "could claim for himself in this way the greatest degree of generality, which was contained *eo ipso* in the concept 'humanity.'"[26] Whoever opposed this abstraction consequently set himself against a fundamental enlightened principle. He risked being branded with the quality that the idea of humanity presupposed as its own negation: the quality, namely, of "inhumanity."[27]

None who lived at the close of the eighteenth century could afford to doubt the reality of that risk, since the French Revolution had staged it for all to see. After the arrest of the Bourbon king on August 10, 1792, a public trial had begun in which the legal concept of humanity played a central, if not ultimately determining, role. Summoned to court, the erstwhile sovereign was charged not only with tyranny, a political crime as old as ancient times, but also of having acted, with intent, against humanity itself. Robespierre made himself the spokesman of this radical position. In the final words of his speech in condemnation of the aristocrat on December 3, 1792, he declared: "As to Louis, I ask that the National Convention declare him, from this moment on, a traitor to the French nation, a criminal toward humanity [*traître à la nation françoise, criminel envers l'humanité*]."[28] The relation between those two iniquitous titles — "traitor to the French nation," "criminal toward humanity" — merits some reflection. At the time Robespierre invoked them, the charges may have seemed hardly distinct. Referring to the 1791 penal code, the members of the National Convention ultimately weighed in favor of the traditional accusation, judging Louis XVI guilty of treason. But in the language of the law, this first appearance of the new crime was not to prove the last.

European legal practice, however, took time to accept the Jacobin's formulation. Only in the twentieth century did the category of "crimes against humanity" acquire an accepted place in the law of nations. It is customary to date the emergence of the penal notion to the aftermath of the Second World War, when the victorious Allies tried former German National Socialist authorities for the commission of "crimes against humanity," as well as "war crimes" and "crimes against peace." But the idea that the human species constituted a legal subject that might be illegitimately assaulted predated the International Military Tribunal in Nuremberg. In an illuminating essay, Sévane Garibian has shown that the idea of crimes committed against humanity already played a notable role in the First World War, when the Allied states publicly denounced the acts of violence committed by Turkey against its Armenian civilian population. The so-called Martens Clause introduced into the preamble of the 1899 Hague Convention with Respect to the Laws and Customs of War on Land (Hague II) contained the earliest mention in modern international law of "humanity." "Populations and belligerents," the declaration read, "remain under the protection and empire of the principles of international law, as they result from the usages established between civilized nations, from the laws of humanity, and the requirements of the public conscience."[29] The first reference to "crimes against humanity" was probably intended as shorthand for crimes against such laws. It can be found in a statement issued in May 1915 by France, Britain, and Russia, in which the three world powers condemned the mass murder of Armenian civilians as "new crimes of Turkey against humanity and civilization."[30] It seems that, in drafting the statement, there was some debate among the Allied powers as to the most pertinent term for the legal subject that had been assaulted in the persons of the Armenians. Sazonov, the Russian minister of foreign affairs, had suggested that the statement denounce "new crimes against Christianity and civilization." Ultimately, however, the assembled officials decided otherwise. In consultation with the British and the French, the Russian government agreed that the word "Christianity" would be best replaced by the abstract name of the species. "Crimes against humanity" thus entered the books of the law.[31]

That penal category was to remain and become the basis of new proceedings. At the close of the First World War, in 1919, the Allied forces enjoined the Ottomans to establish an "extraordinary" martial court in Constantinople to prosecute high-ranking military officers for offenses that, "being contrary to the rules of law and humanity, [...] are of such a nature as to make the consciousness of humanity forever tremble in horror."[32] The Turkish trial that ensued broke little ground, and despite the Allies' bold declarations, the legal proceedings it involved were familiar in form. Officers were charged before military tribunals with violations of rules of internal law and, soon after the pronouncement of the sentences, most of those judged guilty either escaped detention or obtained pardon from the new régime.[33] But in retrospect, the terms with which the victors called for the courts did mark a turning point, for the international appeals established a place for humanity in positive international law. They announced the concept that would famously enter the law of nations on August 8, 1945, in article 6(c) of the Charter of the International Military Tribunal at Nuremberg. This was the concept of "crimes against humanity: namely, murder, extermination, enslavement, deportation, and other inhumane acts committed against any civilian population, before or during the war; or persecutions on political, racial or religious grounds in execution of or in connection with any crime within the jurisdiction of the Tribunal, whether or not in violation of the domestic law of the country where perpetrated."[34] That statute enabled the international court to judge the unprecedented acts of violence committed by the officials of the German National Socialist régime, not least the systematic mass murder of Jewish civilians. As Bert Röling later recalled, "persecution of a group of people, on the basis of race or religion, in occupied territory would already have been covered by the concept of the conventional war crimes."[35] But now the annihilation of German Jews could also be considered international in import. Developing the idea of illegal assaults against the single species, the Allies thus succeeding in establishing the legitimacy of what Sazonov had only a few decades earlier defined as "crimes against Christianity." Henceforth, the mass murder of Jews would be the first internationally accepted case of "crimes against humanity."[36]

In the complex history of the development of these new offenses, at least one feature of twentieth-century legal history cannot be doubted: "humanity" emerged as a technical term in the course of efforts to define atrocities with respect to which traditional categories in the law of war seemed patently inadequate. This fact may well lie at the root of the apparent paradox according to which the charge of "crimes against humanity," while in theory independent of that of "crimes of war," has proven consistently most effective when referred to deeds committed by warring states. But the extremity of the circumstances in which twentieth-century lawyers sought to inscribe the name "humanity" in the register of the law also raises the question of the nature of the now accepted juridical entity that is the species. What is the "humanity" of the law of nations, such that it appears above all as the victim of atrocious crimes? One wonders why it is that the abstract legal principle of the natural kind seems less to generate a positive right than to furnish the crucial term by which perpetrators of violent deeds against civilian masses may be judged as criminals — where, it is perhaps unnecessary to add, the judges are the victors, and the accused, of course, the vanquished. One wonders, in short, why the most defined of all relations to legal "humanity" should be that of crime or enmity, if not both.

It is certain, however, that such developments came to grant an unexpected importance to the one figure in the history of the law in whose definition "humanity" assumed the semblance of generic unity. Through the first half of the twentieth century, the pirate could largely be considered a minor figure in the law of nations. An ancient lawyer, statesman, and philosopher such as Cicero might allude to him as "the common enemy of all," in order to mark the outer limits of the domain of duties. A medieval glossator such as Bartolus could exclude him from his discussion of *ius belli* on the grounds that lawful enemies are always sovereign public persons, while the pirate, by contrast, is no more than "the enemy of the human species." Enlightened jurists, such as Wolff and Vattel, might on occasion invoke the specter of the pillager's unruly criminality, conjuring images of "wild monsters of the human species," "unworthy of the name of men," whom all must remove from their midst. But those were all references to marginal antagonists, allusions to bands of exceptional criminals and unlawful enemies who emerged, from time to time, at the edges of the sphere of European public right. That such figures could be opposed to a thing as abstract as "humanity" meant precisely that they were of relatively little importance, at least with respect to the political and legal authorities of the classical, medieval, and modern epochs, whether they held principalities or cities, kingdoms or commonwealths.

All this changed, however, with the slow but certain justifying of humanity. Once the species had achieved a place of honor in the law of nations, once the name of the natural kind was no longer the sign of a being outside the domain of right but a crucial term in the public conflicts of states, the old antagonist — criminal and enemy — stepped forth in a new and unfamiliar light. His former insignificance now concealed an unexpected relevance. On account of the indeterminate hostility that defined him as "the enemy of the human species," the pirate was suddenly the agent of the political and legal moment. The evidence suggests that this interval has yet to pass. That such a thinker as Hannah Arendt could ask in what sense Adolf Eichmann had become, by virtue of his administrative deeds, "like the pirate in traditional law, *hostis humani generis* ["enemy of the human species]"; that such a judge as Bert Röling could consider whether the law of piracy might be applied to new "criminals against humanity"; that such a jurist as M. C. Bassiouni could observe that the "universal jurisdiction" discussed in the second half of the twentieth century has its legal roots in the old status of the plunderer of the seas, whom all powers might apprehend, prosecute, and punish— these are but some of many signs that a new age has begun.[37] This is an age of legally established humanity and inhumanity, in which "the concept of piracy," as Schmitt feared, has "changed its place in the system of international law." Today, now that major legal and political deeds committed in the name of the species are increasingly not the exception but the rule, figures of the "common enemy of all" will for this reason necessarily continue to appear and reappear. Each time, the pirates of our time will confront the wishful representatives of our common kind with the same undeniable, if discomforting, reality: that of humanity irreconcilably at odds with itself.

CHAPTER FOURTEEN

Earth and Sea

It has often been observed that the law of nations accords a special place to land. In the opening pages of *Nomos of the Earth*, Carl Schmitt argued that there were good reasons why this must be so: three, to be precise, which, if one believes him, have determined the decisive position of territory in the legal tradition. Land, Schmitt noted, can be cultivated; for this reason it may become the object of exclusive claims to detention and ownership. A terrain, moreover, displays fixed and visible lines of geographical demarcation, such as ridges, faults, and rivers; all these ensure that territory may be stably partitioned among those who occupy it. Finally, Schmitt observed that land provides the "firm ground" for constructions of all kinds: "fences and containments, boundary stones, walls, houses and other buildings."[1] There are therefore good incentives to dominate it. In all these respects, Schmitt starkly contrasted the dry sections of the surface of the globe with the liquid. The seas cannot be cultivated; they lack all stable lines of division; and by nature they do not lend themselves to becoming foundations of stable architectural constructions. Hence the "old, pious horror of the seas" that one may still detect in the works of ancient literature and Biblical scripture. Virgil prophesied in the fourth *Eclogue* that "in the future, happy age, there will be no more travel by sea," and, Schmitt noted, "in a holy book of our Christian belief, in the Apocalypse of St. John, we read of a new earth, purified of sin, and we learn that there will be no sea upon it."[2] The Revelation "sent and signified" on the island of Patmos was of a world of land and nothing else: "And I saw a new heaven and a new earth: for the first heaven and the first earth were passed away; and there was no more sea."[3]

This, to be sure, was hardly an historical argument regarding the primacy of the land for the law, as Schmitt, invoking "mythic speech," implicitly acknowledged. He aimed to furnish reasons for certain incontestable facts of legal theory and history. The first could be identified with a fundamental principle in the modern doctrine of right, which thinkers of the law as diverse as Locke and Kant had variously espoused. This rule stipulated that claims to lawful dominion, whether public or private, must be referred before all else to territorial extensions. "Government," Locke asserted in chapter eight of the *Second Treatise on Government*, "has a direct jurisdiction only over the Land."[4] "The first acquisition of a thing," Kant similarly established in the theory of external ownership, "can be only acquisition of land."[5] The consequences of these propositions for the law of nations have been significant. The early modern jurists might well debate among themselves as to whether a political association, such as a kingdom or a republic, could best be said to "own," "possess," or "command" the land in which its subjects lived. Such discussions in any case presupposed one basic judgment, which no early modern thinker, as Schoenborn long ago observed, seems ever seriously to have contested: the judgment, namely, that the sovereignty of those public things that are states extends primarily to limited segments of land.[6]

The properly legal notion of "territory" is a creation of the modern age. Ancient and medieval towns, republics, and principalities had certainly conceded, in fact if not in principle, that their dominion was bounded in geographic extension. Even the Romans of the Imperial age admitted that the supremacy of their city stretched from the capital to a "frontier" (*limes*), where Latin authority grew weak. But this boundary was no border. "It was no more than a stopping point," as one scholar has written, "which was provisionally reached by the advancing legions; and even when it tended to become stable, it was not a brutal limit. It was a zone of transition, commerce, communication, between the Roman world

and the Barbarian."[7] The spaces proper to medieval cities and principalities were generally of such a kind. They were bounded not by
borderlines but by border zones, which were sufficiently wide as to
allow enclaves as well as exclaves, and in which authority, therefore,
could always be disputed. The political line of territorial demarcation in the strict sense emerged much later. As many historians have
shown, the border was an invention of the absolutist state, above all
France, whose officials availed themselves of new geodetic, typo-
graphical, and cartographical technologies to define the precise
extent of the national jurisdiction. The inception of the process has
been traced to the seventeenth century, when Richelieu developed
the doctrine according to which the territory of France could be
measured by "natural," largely linear borders, such as the Atlantic
and the Pyrenees.[8] By the early nineteenth century, the project had
been accepted as legitimate by other sovereign states. The political
authorities of Europe could be legally referred to precisely delimited
portions of the dry surfaces of the globe.

No sooner had the territorial order of states assumed an apparently definitive form, however, than the political lines that traversed
Europe began to move anew in patterns that took some time to be
understood. It was immediately evident that the Revolution of 1789
led to the drawing and redrawing of new borders both in France and
beyond it. But the aftermath of the Napoleonic Wars witnessed the
emergence of a phenomenon of considerably greater disturbance to
the law of nations than the simple fluctuation of territorial limits.
The basic tie that bound political associations to determinate sections of the earth now came into question through the appearance
of a polemical figure of dubious legitimacy: the partisan. Schmitt
was perhaps the first thinker to note the novelty that this combatant
represented in terms of the classic law of nations. In a brief study
published in 1963, *Theory of the Partisan: An Incidental Remark on the
Concept of the Political (Theorie des Partisanen: Zwischenbemerkung zum
Begriff des Politischen)*, he offered a searing analysis of the history and
theory of what he termed "the partisan problem."[9] Schmitt dated the
birth of partisan combat to the Franco-Spanish Wars of 1808–1813.

Following the defeat of the regular Spanish army by the French forces, unlicensed, civilian Iberian fighters then pursued the battle their state had officially lost, not by forming a new army in the image of the old, but by waging a host of "small" or "minor wars" (*guerillas* or *Kleinkriegen*). These battles, Schmitt argued, were to be the first to pit a regular and organized modern army against irregular and unauthorized combatants drawn from the civilian population.[10] They were certainly not the last. From the Prussian fighters who resisted Napoleon in 1813 to the Indochinese combatants who fought the French from 1946 to 1956, examples of such confrontations, Schmitt indicated, are not difficult to identify.[11]

Schmitt recalled that political thinkers as diverse as Clausewitz, Lenin, and Mao Zedong all knew to draw the strategic lessons that such confrontations contained. Schmitt's own interest in partisan warfare, however, was considerably more juridical. This self-styled last representative of "European public law" argued in *Theory of the Partisan* that the unlicensed combatants who stepped onto the scene of European politics and war to fight Napoleon brought about no less than the disintegration of three fundamental oppositions in the law of nations, which traditionally regulated the relations between sovereign states. "Even today," Schmitt wrote, there is a "*classical* martial law, and it deserves its name; for it is familiar with clear distinctions, above all between war and peace, combatant and non-combatant, and enemy and criminal. War is conducted between states by regular armies of states, between standard-bearers of a *jus belli* who respect each other at war as enemies and do not treat one another as criminals, so that a peace treaty becomes possible and even remains the normal, mutually accepted end of war."[12]

Resolutely postclassical in their legal form, *guerrilleros*, by contrast, admit no such clear distinctions. Fighting in the absence of an official and declared battle, they escape the opposition between peace and war. Civilian and yet also belligerent, they are neither combatants nor noncombatants. Finally, waging a war that does not obtain between one state and another but is also no purely civil battle, partisans cannot be considered either enemies or criminals.

But Schmitt did not limit himself to identifying the ways in which such combatants eluded the terms of the old law of nations. He also offered an account of the positive characteristics that define partisan warfare. These are, he argued, four in number. First, in distinction to the army of the modern state, partisan antagonists advance and retreat with "irregularity." Their actions, second, reveal a "heightened mobility." Fighting for a cause that no established association, such as a state, may be said officially to represent, they also display extreme "intensity in political engagement." In conclusion, Schmitt maintained that partisans could be recognized by the fact that they fight always on their own terrain; an earthly or "tellurian" character therefore defines their battle. "For the partisans who fought in 1808–13 in Spain, the Tyrol, and Russia," Schmitt wrote, "this is clear enough. But also the partisan battles of the Second World War, and what followed in Indochina and other counties that are well characterized by the names of Mao Zedong, Ho Chi Minh, and Fidel Castro, lead us to understand that the relation to the soil, together with the autochthonous population and the geographical specificity of the country—mountains, forest, jungle, or desert—remains undiminished to this day."[13]

This earthly criterion, for Schmitt, was essential. It served to separate the partisan from an older figure in the history of the law from whom the novel agent of "small wars" might otherwise be difficult, if not impossible, to distinguish. This was a combatant who had always been irregular and mobile, and who could also all too easily act in the interest and with the command of a political association, such as a state: the pirate or, as one might assert with greater precision, the "privateer." Could the partisan be no more than a pirate of the land? Schmitt was well aware of this possibility and, by insisting on the "elemental space" (*Elementarraum*) in which the post-Napoleonic combatants moved, he effectively sought to exclude it. "The partisan," Schmitt asserted, "is, and remains, different not only from the pirate, but also from the privateer in the way that land and sea are distinguished as elemental spaces of human activity and martial engagement between peoples. Land and sea have developed not only different vehicles of warfare, and not only distinctive theaters of war, but they have also developed separate concepts of war, peace and spoils."[14]

There are signs, however, that Schmitt found his arguments unconvincing. Later, in *Theory of the Partisan*, the jurist returned to the question of the partisan and the pirate, as if it were still to be resolved. Now the author conceded that he himself, in an earlier book, had failed to see the problem clearly. "If I once referred to the freebooters and pirates of the early days of capitalism as 'partisans of the sea,'" Schmitt noted, referring to *Nomos of the Earth*, which dates from 1950, "I would like to correct this terminological imprecision now."[15] The rectification implied a new account of the difference between the pirate and the partisan, which lacked all reference to the heterogeneity of earthly elements. Here Schmitt invoked a novel term as a criterion of distinction: risk. Whereas the pirate and privateer are always "highly insured" for any losses they will incur, Schmitt explained, the partisan "has an enemy and 'risks' something quite different from the blockade-breaker and the transporter of contraband."[16] This is a startling assertion, and not only because, as an addition to the distinction drawn earlier in the study, it suggests that the fundamental difference between land and sea may not suffice to separate the pirate from the partisan. On its own terms, the proposition also perplexes. An avid, if at times fantastic, philologist, Schmitt must have been well aware that his claim flew in the face of one basic fact of diction: the standard etymology derives the term "pirate" from a Greek verb, *peirao* (πειράω), which signifies the act of "wagering," "testing," and "putting to proof." By his classic name, the sea-marauder therefore corresponds exactly to the image of the partisan now drawn by Schmitt. A "pirate" is, quite literally, an individual defined by risk.

In the last pages of his essay, Schmitt returned once again to the elemental difference between the partisan and the pirate, as if finally to establish that which he had to that point solely alleged. He explained:

For the sake of concrete conceptual clarity, we shall retain the telluric-terrestrial character of the partisan, avoiding characterizing him as the privateer of the land, or even defining him in such terms. The pirate's irregularity lacks any connection whatsoever to a regularity. The privateer by contrast collects war booty at sea, and is equipped with the authorizing "letter" of a state régime. His sort of irregularity does not lack that connection to regularity in this way, and thus he was, until the Paris Peace Accord of 1856, a juridically recognized figure of European international law. It is in this respect that both the privateer of the sea war and the partisan of land war can be compared with each other. A strong resemblance and even sameness is demonstrated especially by the fact that the statements "with partisans you can only fight like a partisan" and (the other statement) "*à corsaire corsaire et demi*" [fight the privateer with one privateer and a half] amount to the same thing. Nevertheless the partisan of today is something else than a privateer of land war. The elemental contrast of land and sea is too great for that. It may very well be that the traditional distinctions between war and enemy and booty, which up until now legitimized the international opposition of land and sea, will one day be dissolved in the melting-pot of industrial–technical progress. For now, the partisan still signifies a patch of true home soil; he is one of the last sentries of the earth, as a not yet completely destroyed world-historical element.17

These lines admit what others in *Theory of the Partisan* obstinately refuse to grant. Irregular, mobile, and intensely political, the partisan, Schmitt now concedes, may legitimately "be compared" with the privateer, if not with the pirate. One may even observe between them "a strong resemblance and even sameness" (a phrase in which the conjunction "and" betrays some hesitation, suggesting both affinity and identity). Both combatants undo the good form of their lawful opponents, causing the regular agents of war to act irregularly. Both demand that they—the unequal parties—be met as equals, symmetrical, as it were, in asymmetrical and ever-shifting combat.

The author of *Theory of the Partisan* doubtless did what he could to enjoin his readers to believe that the opposition of land and sea, elementary because "elemental," sufficed to separate the irregular forces of the land from those of the sea, the age after Napoleon from that before it, modern partisans, in short, from privateers. But Schmitt also suggested, almost despite himself, that even this classical and "clear distinction" might ultimately not endure. "The partisan of today," he noted pointedly, "is something else than a privateer." That statement begged a question. What of "the partisan of tomorrow"? In 1963, Schmitt could comfort himself in calling to mind the guerillas he found most admirable: the noble and outlawed fighters who "still" signified "a patch of true home soil," being "for now" among "the last sentries of the earth," "a not yet completely destroyed world-historical element." In an age that had begun to bid farewell to the mythic unity of law and land, partisans, the newest agents of the archaic taking of the terrain, recalled one principle that Schmitt considered both primordial and unsurpassable: that political associations, such as nations, be instituted, fortified, and defended within the limits of dry earth. Despite his horror of the age in which the *ius publicum Europeum* had so declined, Schmitt retained, therefore, at least this one consolation: "the melting-pot of industrial-technical progress" had not yet brewed a thing so foul as to collapse land into the sea. But it would indeed do so shortly, at once confirming and falsifying Schmitt's disavowal. There would soon be partisans detached from all "true home soil," who moved, like sea-farers, in terrains that were not at all their own—and that were also, at times, not terrains at all.

CHAPTER FIFTEEN

Into the Air

On October 7, 1985, an Italian ship was seized off the coast of Egypt as it sailed from Alexandria towards Port Said. Four passengers were responsible. They had boarded the vessel, the *Achille Lauro*, in Genoa, where they presented themselves as tourists. It soon became apparent, however, that they acted for a political cause. They were members of the Palestinian Liberation Front, a faction of the Palestinian Liberation Organization, and upon taking control of the ship, they immediately issued a demand to the international community: Israel was to release fifty Palestinian political prisoners or the passengers aboard the vessel would be killed. Meanwhile, the guerillas declared they would direct the vessel towards the port of Tartus in Syria. Negotiations between the Egyptian government and the members of the Palestinian Liberation Front began immediately, and two days later, the ship and its hostages returned to the Egyptian coast. In exchange for the restitution of the vessel and its passengers, the Egyptian government promised the Palestinian activists immunity, putting at their disposal an aircraft with which to fly from Egypt to a place of safety. After the ship docked at the harbor, however, it became apparent that the members of the Palestinian Liberation Front had killed a citizen of the United States while at sea. The American authorities, consequently, protested the Egyptian decision to release the four individuals responsible. A U.S. airplane was dispatched to follow the vessel carrying the members of the Palestinian Liberation Front out of Egyptian air space. The guerillas were then forced to land in Sicily, at the U.S. military base in Sigonella. There the Palestinians were taken into custody before being tried at an Italian court.

American newspapers, such as the *New York Times*, public officials, such as Ronald Reagan, the president of the United States at the time, and legal entities, such as the U.S. District Court, all declared the four Palestinian militants guilty of acts of "piracy."[1] The precise meaning of that charge, however, was far from evident, if only because the members of the Liberation Front seemed not to possess the intent to commit theft. They seized the Italian ship not for the sake of private enrichment but to wage an international battle that, while not possessing the title of war, was political in its aims. They did not wish to plunder but to assert the rights of one nation against another. Irregular, mobile, and intensely political, the four individuals who took the *Achille Lauro* met each of the conditions required by Schmitt's definition of the partisan, with, of course, one considerable exception: the members of the Palestinian Liberation Front were not earth-bound, like the "tellurian" fighters Schmitt had envisaged. They were the agents of a "small war" they waged upon the open waters. They were, to put the matter simply, partisans at sea. But were they therefore pirates?

The American allegation against the Palestinian Liberation Front raised the question in no uncertain terms. The legal opinions on the subject were divided. Several courts and officials in the United States and Britain had established that any violent act at sea that lacked state authorization could be considered piracy. Lassa Oppenheim's *International Law* could be cited as justification for this view: "If a definition is desired which really covers all such acts as are in practice treated as piratical," it declared, "piracy must be defined as every unauthorized act of violence against persons or goods committed on the open sea either by a private vessel against another vessel or by the mutinous crew or passengers against their own vessel."[2] Other legal sources rendered that assertion more specific. It was recalled that in 1934, an English court, for instance, had endorsed the definition of piracy as "armed violence at sea which is not a lawful act of war."[3] And as early as 1853, a United States court had explicitly declared that insurgents who had not achieved the status of recognized belligerents could be prosecuted for piracy if they dared to act at sea:

> Wheaton defines piracy as "the offense of depredating on the high seas without being authorized by any sovereign state, or with commission from different sovereigns at war with each other." Rebels who have never obtained recognition from any other power are clearly not a sovereign state in the eye of international law, and their vessels sent out to commit violence on the high seas are therefore piratical within this definition.[4]

Not all legal authorities, however, could be cited in support of such judgments. Long before the seizing of the *Achille Lauro*, Hall argued strenuously in his *Treatise of International Law* against the belief that insurgents who fight at sea in the interest of a public association, such as a nascent state, may be legitimately treated as pirates. "It is impossible to pretend," Hall wrote in his influential compendium of 1884,

> that acts which are done for the purpose of setting up a legal state of things, and which may in fact have already succeeded in setting it up, are piratical for want of an external recognition of their validity, when the grant of that recognition is properly dependent in the main upon the existence of such a condition of affairs as can only be produced by the very acts in question [...] Primarily the pirate is a man who satisfies his personal greed or his personal vengeance by robbery or murder in places beyond the jurisdiction of the state. The man who acts within a public object may do like acts to a certain extent, but his moral attitude is different, and the acts themselves will be kept within well-marked bounds. He is not the enemy of the human race but he is the enemy solely of a particular state.[5]

The truth was that the question had arisen well before the *Achille Lauro* incident in the maritime casuistry of the century. Perhaps the most famous precedent for the capturing of the Italian ship was the taking of the Portuguese cruise liner *Santa Maria* in 1961, when a group of political dissidents led by Captain Henrique Galvão forcibly assumed control of the vessel, publicly declaring that they acted "in the name of the international junta of Liberals presided over by General Humberto Delgado, president-elect of the Portuguese Republic, fraudulently deprived of his rights by the Salazar Government."[6] Admittedly, that seizing of a vessel differed in several technical respects from the taking of the Italian ship in 1985. The perpetrators aboard the Portuguese cruise liner were themselves also of Portuguese nationality and, while stating their opposition to the government of their state, they harmed no foreign national and committed no depredation. But that capture, like the 1963 seizing of the Venezuelan cargo ship, *Anzoátegui*, by members of the Armed Forces for National Liberation, constituted a case in which violence on the high seas fell squarely between the categories of the political and the categories of the criminal. Unlike acts of war, this was not the work of an accepted belligerent; yet it also could not be considered in any sense a case of theft committed for purely private ends. Although unauthorized by any state, these maritime insurrections were acts of undeniable political engagement, and to this extent they could be compared to the events that occurred aboard the *Achille Lauro*.

If the fate of the Italian ship attracted unusual attention in 1985, it was no doubt because it called to mind a guerilla practice that was by then all too familiar. This strategic act consisted in the capturing of vessels as they traveled through the one other natural element of the globe that resembles water—at least compared to land. The people who witnessed the events aboard the *Achille Lauro* remarked upon the fact immediately: the Italian ship, they noted, had been captured in transit as if it had been a plane and not a boat. In short, it had been "hijacked." Such a designation pointed to a similarity between violence in the air and violence upon the seas that today may no longer seem so obvious. But the comparison between the two varieties of capture possesses a relatively long history. It is worth recalling again the first case of a plane seized for political purposes: as early as 1931, when revolutionaries sought control of an aircraft in Peru. But it was only at the end of the following decade, with the inception of commercial air travel, that the practice of taking planes for political causes established itself. It has been estimated that from 1948 to 1960, there were twenty-nine successful hijackings; from 1961 to 1967, a total of sixteen hijackings; and by 1968, there were no fewer than thirty such occurrences recorded in the span of a single year.[7] Soon the phenomenon had acquired a standard name. "Aerial piracy" or "air piracy," as it was called, entered the languages of the West, including the idioms employed by legal scholars. An article on aircraft piracy published in *The International Lawyer* in 1972, for instance, could preface its considerations with the following uncontroversial opening assertion: "The last decade has dramatically witnessed the emergence of the 'air pirate'—as dangerous and destructive as his prototype, the sea pirate."[8]

The terms "air," "aircraft," and "aerial piracy" were by then common usage. But a number of jurists and international lawyers quickly cautioned that such expressions were technically appropriate when used only in certain circumstances. According to Article 15 of the 1958 Geneva Convention on the High Seas, five conditions were required for an action to be termed "piratical" with precision. There was to be (1) an illegitimate act of violence, detention, or depredation; (2) it was to be committed for personal aims; (3) it was to be perpetrated against another ship or plane, or against the people or goods on board them; (4) it was to be committed at high sea or in a space outside the jurisdiction of any state; finally, (5) it was to be accomplished by people on board a private ship or plane. This full set of specifications has rarely been met. As the author of a comprehensive study of air piracy has observed, "for acts of illicit intervention in civil international aviation, conditions (3) and (5) seem until now never to have been simultaneously satisfied; what is more, conditions (2) and (5) are often not fulfilled."[9] The reasons for these facts are quite simple. In most cases of aerial hijacking, the seizure of the plane occurs soon after take-off and, therefore, before the vessel has left the air space of a state; in addition, the perpetrators generally act against the very vessel on which they travel. Such considerations have led some experts and associations to avoid all reference to piracy in the air. The Organization of International Civil Aviation (OICA), for instance, opts instead for expressions that, while hardly simple, are much more exact. This entity prefers to employ as substitutes the terms "acts of illicit capture of aircrafts" and "illicit acts committed against the safety of civil aviation."[10]

Such phrases doubtless have the merit of probity. They warn against any hasty identification of violence in the air with the depredations familiar to far older epochs. But there are good reasons to consider "sky-jacking" and "ship-jacking" to be two forms of a single type of action, which can indeed be tied historically and structurally to piracy. This action can be defined by four distinctive traits, which constitute, when conjoined, the elements of a single paradigm. First, the piratical action consists of a deed that implies a region judged exceptional with respect to ordinary jurisdiction. The high seas and international air space are examples of such regions. Second, the piratical action involves an agent who displays an antagonism that, for various possible reasons, cannot be defined as that of one individual with respect to another or, for that matter, of one political association with respect to another: an antagonism, for instance, that may not possess a single object, or that may not discriminate in its target, and which may thus appear not particular but general and even "universal." The oldest name for such an agent is no doubt the one employed by Cicero: "common enemy of all [*hostis omnium*]"; "enemy of the human species" (*hostis humani generis*) is its medieval elaboration; "enemy of humanity" is its modern incarnation. Third, the piratical action sets in motion, as a consequence of the first and second defining traits, the confusion—and, in the most extreme cases, the collapse—of the distinction between criminal and political categories. Since the agents in question act beyond the region of ordinary jurisdiction and since they are conceived as not enemies of one but "enemies of all," they cannot be considered criminals, whose place may be defined in the terms of a single civil code. But they also cannot be represented as lawful enemies, since by virtue of their enmity with respect to "all," they fail to constitute an association with which there might be peace as well as war. As the early modern jurists teach, with such antagonists there can be neither treaty nor truce. Finally, by virtue of the third defining trait, the piratical action implies a fourth consequence: a transformation in the concept of war. Since the "enemies of all" are neither criminals nor belligerents in any straightforward sense, the operations carried out against them cannot be formally identical to those employed against an enemy. They must involve the measures used in prosecuting both belligerents and criminals: procedures both of external relations and of internal security, measures of politics and of police.

Only if one takes into account this paradigm of piratical action is it possible to account for the unmistakable presence of the figure of the "enemy of all" in our time. This exceptional legal person is not simply the pirate, if one takes that appellation in its traditional sense, as referring to a private agent of illegal maritime depredations. Nor is this figure reducible to the "air pirate" baptized in the later twentieth century. The "enemy of all" can be located wherever all four elements of the paradigm may be found. Today, it would surely not be difficult to identify examples. An enumeration, analysis, and typology of the various figures of universal enmity in the present period would be of immense utility. But it would lie beyond the aims and terms of this book. For the purposes of economy, it must suffice to recall very rapidly two recent examples, in which the four distinctive traits of the paradigm may clearly be discerned.

The first belongs to the history of France in the last quarter of the twentieth century. It can be dated to 1978, when Valéry Giscard d'Estaing, the president of France, instituted a new system of national defense in response to a series of attacks committed against French civilian populations by partisans of diverse political aims.[11] The system was created to monitor the danger posed to France by distinguishing among four levels of danger, coded, in incremental severity, by gradations of color: yellow, orange, red, and scarlet. Never was it specified who exactly might pose such variously intense threats to the nation. But the creation of the measures in the wake of acts of violence committed by unrecognized belligerents implied that the agents against whom the new and exceptional measures of defense were to be taken were neither simply criminals nor, for that matter, lawful enemies; otherwise, it could be inferred, the combined efforts of the police and the army would surely have sufficed. The name of the program, in any case, suggested an answer to the question of the identity of the unnamed antagonists. With an obscure allusion to the mast up which seafarers of another epoch climbed to look out for the ships of illegal plunderers, the French authorities called their new national security system *Le Plan Vigipirate*, "The Anti-Piracy Plan," or, more literally, if inelegantly, "The Pirate Look-Out Plan."

The second example may be drawn from the more recent past of the United States. After the attacks perpetrated in the American territory by guerilla fighters aboard airplanes on September 11, 2001, the U.S. Congress allowed George W. Bush, then president of the United States, to instantiate a presidential military order for the "detention, treatment and trial of certain non-citizens." During the ensuing American invasion of Afghanistan, the U.S. military captured prisoners, some of whom the American authorities alleged belonged to the associations responsible for the non-state attacks of September 11. The U.S. military proceeded to hold these individuals outside the national territory, first mainly at the Guantánamo Bay Detention Camp. There the captives were not allowed the legal recourse granted criminals, nor were they held in accordance with the four Geneva conventions on the treatment of prisoners of war. The governmental administration justified its actions on the grounds that the detainees were neither criminals nor enemies but combatants of a third and more obscure order: "illegal enemy combatants." That the special status of such antagonists bore more than a passing resemblance to the position of the "enemy of all" in the traditional law of nations was a point explicitly suggested by an official of such prominence as John Choon Yoo, deputy assistant attorney general in the George W. Bush administration. Jane Mayer reports that in response to the bewilderment of the public after the leaking of the so-called "torture memo" of 2004, Yoo recalled that the juridical status of "illegal enemy combatant" was hardly the product of recent political and legal history. "Why is it so hard for people to understand that there is a category of behavior not covered by the legal system? He asked. What were pirates?"[12]

Such measures, statutes, and institutions will no doubt change in time, as they come to be reworked to fit the shifting political and legal necessities of the present. But one may note that one historical possibility, in any case, has now become real. The offense of piracy has been effectively loosened from any single earthly element. Not only the sea but the air, too, may be a place of piracy, if one defines that activity with reference to the four traits that mark the paradigm proper to "the enemy of all." But there is also more. As the ravaged terrain of Afghanistan has shown for all to see, land, too, may now be a place of piracy. The reason is quite simple. Today an "enemy of all" may be apprehended and held to be responsible for effectively piratical acts committed on the territory of nations as much as upon the high seas or in air space. The executive power responsible need merely declare that the nation in question, if it is foreign, constitutes a "failed" or "rogue" state; when the nation is not foreign, it will instead suffice to cite exceptional danger posed to the security of the civilian population. In either case, the place proper to piracy thereby undergoes a fundamental change. The region in which "enemies of all" commit their violent acts is consequently unbound from any single segment of the globe. It becomes structurally autonomous. In the past, a piratical act presupposed, by definition, a specific area of the earth in which exceptional legal statutes applied. For centuries, this region was that of the high seas. Subsequently, it began also to include portions of the air, once a legal theory of the earth's most elevated zones had been developed. Today, however, this classic relation has been inverted. The pirate may no longer be defined by the region in which he moves. Instead, the region of piracy may be derived from the presence of the pirate. Wherever an "enemy of all" can be found – upon the seas, in the air, or on the land – there a zone beyond the line will emerge. There, the regular statutes of the law, be they civil or martial, may not apply.

It is worth recalling, in this setting, the old legal status of the ship as a piece of "floating land" or "moving territory," in fact at sea, but in principle considered by the law as if it were firm ground. The "enemy of all" of our times presents us with an inverse phenomenon. With reference to the fiction of the ship, one might consider the contemporary pirate as an "ambulating ocean," or "moving sea," in fact perhaps on the national terrain, but viewed, nonetheless, from a legal perspective as if he crossed a no man's land. Like the wild animal according to the Roman jurists, whose body occupied an area by nature irreducible to civil law, even when it traversed the city, so, today, our "enemy of all" implies a region in which extraordinary measures may occur. Wherever today's pirate may be—in vessels of the sea or in the air, in a foreign country or even in a city in the national territory—there, the legal and political principles that regulate the just treatment of citizens and enemies, civilians and the military, may for this reason be set aside. The political and legal nature of the contemporary "enemy of all" implies no less. The least one may conclude is that the law of nations must renounce its classical relationship to the land. Dry earth is no longer a model for things that may be the objects of claims to mastery. For the land is by nature bounded, limited by the seas, which lie securely outside it. But the law, today, must bear on the total globe, a thing boundless by definition. Unlike the national territory, the globe, taken as one whole, admits of no exterior. When a region beyond the line emerges in our time—and it must—it will do so, therefore, within this new and unlimited order of the earth, in occurrences and recurrences that will be surely shifting, startling, and increasingly unruly.

CHAPTER SIXTEEN

Toward Perpetual War

Late in life, Kant conceived the idea of a single global order, which was one day to unite the many nations of the earth in a lawful condition of perpetual peace. The thought was in itself not altogether novel, since earlier writers had also imagined a world without war; the most famous of Kant's immediate predecessors was the Abbé of Saint-Pierre, whose "Project for Perpetual Peace" of 1712 attracted the attention of both Leibniz and Rousseau.[1] But it is likely that Kant was the first thinker to consider thoroughly the conditions and consequences implied by the idea of a state of everlasting peace. There can be little doubt that he shared the sentiments of those writers before him who viewed war as the expression of a primitive state, ideally to be surpassed by law. "We look with profound contempt upon the way in which savages cling to their lawless freedom," Kant observed in "Toward Perpetual Peace," which he first published in 1795.[2] "They would rather engage in incessant strife than submit to a legal constraint which they might impose on themselves, for they prefer the freedom of folly to the freedom of reason. We regard this as barbarism, coarseness, and brutish debasement of humanity."[3] There are good reasons, Kant suggested, to view the practices of warring states as no less inhumane. But the philosopher of Königsberg did not limit himself to recalling a moral condemnation of all belligerent activity as unruly, ignoble, and needlessly destructive. He also argued strenuously for the necessity of peace on altogether different grounds. These might well strike the student of transcendental philosophy as surprisingly empirical—if, that is, the shape of the earth may be judged by its inhabitants to be "empirical." Kant cited the decisive geophysical evidence more than once. At the close of his *Doctrine of Right*, he suggested that the "rational idea of a *peaceful*, even if not friendly, thoroughgoing community of all nations on the earth" could be derived from the simple fact that "Nature has enclosed all nations together within determinate limits (the spherical shape of the place they live in, a *globus terraqueus*)."[4] In "Toward Perpetual Peace," he was more explicit about the juridical repercussions of the planetary form. "On account of the spherical surface [*Kugelfläche*] of the earth," he asserted, "human beings cannot be infinitely dispersed [*ins Unendliche zerstreuen*]; rather, they must necessarily tolerate each others' company."[5]

The formal properties of Kant's *globus terraqueus* are well worth pondering. The philosopher expressly noted that the earth is not infinite; thus no matter how misanthropic they may be, human beings can only extend outwards to a certain point, after which they are, Kant claimed, bound by necessity to encounter each other again. For this reason, however, it does not suffice to assert that the globe is finite in extent. One must add that it is also unlimited in structure, since no one dwells outside it.[6] Kant himself, however, did not pause to consider the qualities of the spherical object he so blithely called to mind; nor did he justify his curious argument, which yoked the earthly aster in the unlikely service of the transcendental doctrine of objective right. The critical philosopher was more interested in deducing the legal and political consequence that the "spherical surface" implied. This was, for him, quite simple. "There is only one rational way in which states coexisting with other states," he wrote, "can emerge from the lawless condition of pure warfare. Just like individual men, they must renounce their savage and lawless freedom, adapt themselves to public coercive laws, and thus form an *international state* (*civitas gentium*), which would necessarily continue to grow until it embraced all the peoples of the earth."[7] But Kant hastened to add that this one obvious solution would most certainly fail. "Since this is not the will of the nations, according to their present conception of international right (so that they reject *in hypothesi* what is true *in thesi*), the positive ideal of a word republic cannot be realized."[8] Kant therefore proposed an alternative: "a negative substitute in the shape of an enduring and gradually expanding *federation* likely to prevent war."[9] In the *Metaphysics of Morals*, he described such an association as "a league of nations," an "alliance" among states that would be analogous, while distinct, to the union of individuals within a single civil code.[10] Such a union would entail no "sovereign authority (as in a civil constitution)," being an association founded, as Kant noted, with a telling aside, "not in order to meddle in one another's international dissensions, but to protect against attacks from without."[11]

Writing at the close of the eighteenth century, Kant was well aware, of course, that such a federation of nations also could hardly be an institution of the present. Perhaps it would arise sometime in the future, once pacific tendencies had sprouted. In the meantime, peoples remained at odds with each other and Kant, faithful to the legal tradition, provided a set of principles to regulate the relations between states. These rules defined "the Right of Nations." They were exclusively principles of war. While resolutely committed to the ideal of an eternal establishment of peace, Kant now also offered a summary treatment of the prerogatives of present sovereign states, each of which he considered, "as a moral person, as living in relation to another state in the condition of natural freedom and therefore in a condition of constant war."[12] First he enumerated the grounds by which a state may lay claim to "the right to go to war [...] if it believes it has been wronged by another state": when, for instance, it has been "actively violated," or even merely "threatened," by the other state's military "preparations, upon which is based the right of *prevention* (*ius praeventionis*), or even just the *menacing* increase in another state's power (by its acquisition of territory) (*potentia tremenda*)."[13] Next, Kant considered the rights of nations during war, which he defined as "the waging of war in accordance with principles that always leave open the possibility of leaving the state of nature among states (in external relation to one another) and entering a rightful condition."[14] Here Kant forbade various forms of belligerent activity: wars of "punishment," "extermination," and "subjugation," he argued, all contradict the peaceful ends of war and must therefore always be avoided. So, too, must the law of nations exclude any measures of a state which "would make its subjects unfit to be citizens": espionage, assassination, poisoning, and spreading false reports are of such a kind.[15] Finally, Kant specified the rights of states following the end of war. A victorious nation may not exact compensation, "since then he would have to admit that his opponent had fought an unjust war"; nor ought the triumphant state to impose a state of servitude on the vanquished, for "if it did, the war would have been a punitive war, which is self-contradictory."[16]

In the absence of a league of nations, these various rules aimed to limit the violence of armed and public confrontations. But they were to do so only to a point. After specifying the principles that were to obtain between equal and antagonistic states, Kant turned his attention in the *Metaphysics of Morals* to a different foe. "There are no limits [*keine Grenzen*] to the rights of a state against an unjust enemy," he wrote, in a single, decisive paragraph, explaining, in parentheses: "(no limits with respect to quantity or degree, though there are limits with respect to quality); that is to say, an injured state may not use *any* means *whatsoever* but may use those means that are allowable to any degree that it is able to, in order to maintain what belongs to it."[17]

An apparent exception to the restriction of legal war, Kant's "unjust enemy" naturally drew the notice of Carl Schmitt. In a central section of *Nomos of the Earth*, Schmitt recalled how by the eighteenth century, modern European public law had in principle excluded the "punitive war," the "war of extermination," and the "war of subjugation" as legitimate forms of belligerency. But with Kant's doctrine of right, Schmitt argued, that early modern juridical achievement began to come undone. In the place of the classic modern doctrine of the "just war," whose legality lies in its outer form, Kant, herald of a new age, set a war that admits of "just" and "unjust enemies." Schmitt recalled Kant's self-explanation:

What is an *unjust enemy* in terms of the concepts of the Right of
Nations? It is an enemy whose publicly expressed will (whether by
word or deed) reveals a maxim by which, if it were made a universal
rule, any condition of peace among nations would be impossible and,
instead, a state of nature would be perpetuated. Violation of public
contracts is an expression of this sort. Since this can be assumed to be a
matter of concern to all nations whose freedom is threatened by it, they
are called upon to unite against such misconduct in order to deprive
the state of its power to do it.[18]

Schmitt barely concealed his horror before this definition: "It
suffices," he exclaimed, "for there to be a *publicly* expressed will,
and it suffices, for this expression *to reveal a maxim*, in order to
justify the action of those who feel themselves threatened in their
freedom! A preventative war against such an enemy would be more
than a just war. It would be a crusade."[19] In guise of elaborating a
doctrine of right suited to the federation of peaceful states, Kant
would thus have cleared the way for a battle of a kind long surpassed
in European right. "Closer to the theologians than to the jurists,"
the enlightened writer would have formulated his doctrine of martial law as did the Scholastic thinkers, who conceived war to be just
not in its form (*justa forma*) but in its final cause (*justa causa*). Unwit-
tingly, Kant would have thus conceived, in the name of peace, a war
of the most extreme violence, at once novel in scope and medieval
in doctrinal justification: a battle which pitted the bearers of civilized humanity against a criminal antagonist, with respect to whom
"there are no limits to the right of a state."[20]

On this point, Schmitt's sensitivity in reading exceeded his acu-
ity in analysis. He clearly flagged the central figure of the exception
in the Kantian law of nations, but he mistook the exact terms of its
definition. Schmitt overlooked one technical but crucial fact. The
lack of limitation invoked in the *Metaphysics of Morals* was most
expressly limited. Against an unjust enemy, "there are no limits with
respect to quantity or degree," the critical philosopher stipulated,
with precision, before adding: "though there are limits with respect

to quality."[21] This is a point of doctrine, which involves one categorial distinction that Kant considered by definition unsurpassable: the distinction, namely, between quantity and quality.[22] The philosopher clearly specified the terms by which the conceptual pair was to be applied to the state at war. In waging war on an "unjust enemy," he argued, a legitimate public association may avail itself of any legal means of battle, which it may deploy with infinite intensity. But it may avail itself of such means alone. As the philosopher continued after declaring that "there are no limits to the rights of a state against an unjust enemy," "that is to say, an injured state may not use *any* means *whatever* but may use those means that are allowable to any degree that it is able to, in order to maintain what belongs to it."[23] Unlimited quantity of force may therefore be expended in the battle against the illegitimate opponent; but the quality of belligerency must remain limited. Kant did not hesitate to offer examples. Confronted with evidence of a violation of a contract, be it actual or merely threatened, "all nations," he observed, "are called upon to unite against such misconduct in order to deprive the state of its power to do it." The just may act without regard to degree in their response to the illegal opponent. "But they are not called upon to *divide its territory among themselves* and to make the state, as it were, disappear from the earth, since that would be an injustice against its people, which cannot lose its original right to unite into a commonwealth."[24] Political and military pressures of a different sort ought instead, in such cases, to be envisaged. Kant offered only one example: an offending state, he reasoned, "can be allowed to adopt a new constitution that by its nature will be unfavorable to the inclination to war."[25]

Kant's theory of the unjust enemy lends itself to more than a single reading. Suspended between the restriction of quality and the non-restriction of quantity, between limitation in kind and non-limitation in degree, it is structurally ambiguous. One would be justified in interpreting it as imposing an implacable barrier to the violent means of battle, since it dictates that no partitioning of a territory, no extermination of a people, and no destruction of a nation may ever be judged as legal. But one might also draw a different conclusion from the exceptional martial clause. One might argue that its distinction between quantity and quality provides the basis for a battle of new and obscure variety. Unlike old wars of conquest, the armed endeavor against an unjust enemy described by Kant cannot end with military defeat. More is required. The offending nation must renounce its iniquitous inclinations toward other peoples, and it must do so by an official change in politico-legal form: by the adoption of a constitution, likely one in keeping with Kant's republican ideal.[26] At least in this chapter of his doctrine of right, if not elsewhere, the philosopher of the self-determining freedom of the will seems hardly to doubt that a sovereign state may be forced, in such a way, into a position of liberty, coerced, so to speak, into deeds that, despite their dire and necessitating cause, still express a principle of spontaneity. The grammar of Kant's statement is to this degree significant. It stipulates that, while it is not permitted to annex the territory of the unjust enemy, to destroy its people, or to annihilate its state, the breaker of international contracts nevertheless "can be allowed to adopt a new constitution that by its nature will be unfavorable to the inclination to war." It is difficult not to perceive a note of euphemism in this "allowance" (*lassen*). What exactly could it mean to wage a war upon a state in order to "*allow it to adopt a new constitution that by its nature will be unfavorable to the inclination to war*"? Kant's formulation clears a legal space for wars declared with the express aim of obligating antagonists to renounce all war, where "renunciation" may be in truth a name for a new variety of subjection: acquiescence before the victorious armies of peace.

This much, in any case, is certain: when confronted with an enemy "whose publicly expressed will (whether by word or deed) reveals a maxim by which, if it were made a universal rule, any condition of peace among nations would be impossible," a war without limits of degree is not so much permitted as demanded. On this point, Kant's statement is unequivocal. In the restricted case of the unjust enemy—one presumes it is only in this case—a just state must act without restriction in the quantity of its military efforts, while still continuing to restrict their qualities. Before the breaker of the oath, the guardians of contracts, representatives of the universality of the law, must not allow themselves to be swayed: with all their might, they must enter the throes of battle, not to take a terrain or to assassinate its people, but to "allow," by military motions, the criminal state "to adopt a new constitution." Then the battle for peace, a war against all war, simultaneously with and without the limits that define the confrontation of states, cannot be avoided. Kant maintains that such an operation is the surest means of anticipating an everlasting global order.

But there is more. To understand the sense of the Kantian imperative in all its implications, it is necessary to recall one fundamental rule in the critical philosophy. It may be simply formulated. Because of the absolutely unconditioned freedom of their will, human beings can always, in every condition, fail to keep their word. Were it otherwise, promises, pledges, and contracts would be not commitments but natural laws, physical and logical necessities shorn of ethical and moral significance. They might be true, even compelling; but they would not be the deeds of free agents. The only morally binding engagement, Kant taught, is the one that can be renounced. Of course, such a commitment need not be betrayed; it may always also be respected. But the possibility of the breaking of a contract—the possibility of the breaking of all contracts—cannot be set aside. A being of utterly bad faith may never be excluded. This elementary principle is of great consequence for the idea of a single global order. It dictates that the project for eternal peace be, in truth, a project for the perpetual preparation for peace through war. As long as human beings are liable to lie, as long as a state may always declare a "maxim by which, if it were made a universal rule, any condition of peace among nations would be impossible," warfare remains imminent. Vigilance towards the virtual infraction of treaties must be constant. Anywhere where there are contracts, anywhere where there are international conventions, treaties and alliances, an unjust enemy may always suddenly emerge. Then the battle for peace, unbounded in quantity but not in quality, must commence. It cannot end, for its aims are neither local in space nor discrete in the course of time. In this war, by definition, no single defeat—not even one involving the "allowance of a new constitution"—can ever last; no one victory may be considered permanent. Unlike the old, armed, and public conflicts of states, the modern confrontation against the enemy of all must each time, in each place, begin anew. Infinitely intense, preparatory, and provisional, it admits of no regions such as the high seas or the air, which would constitute stable exceptions to its rule; planetary in scope, it refuses to concede that there are elements of nature that lie beyond the line of the law of nations. A perpetual war in the name of a peace that cannot be, it is familiar only with mobile zones of transitory violence, their borders incessantly drawn and redrawn across the "spherical surface of the earth."

Notes

NOTE ON TRANSLATIONS

Wherever possible, I have indicated English translations of works cited in the notes and made use of them in quotations. On occasion, I have, however, silently modified published versions in accordance with the originals.

Unless otherwise noted, all translations are my own.

CHAPTER ONE: BEYOND THE LINE

1. Marcus Tullius Cicero, *De officiis* 1.4; an English translation can be found in *On Duties*, ed. and trans. M. T. Griffin and E. M. Atkins (Cambridge, UK: Cambridge University Press, 1991), p. 3. Neither the term "obligation" nor the word "duty" exactly fit the Latin *officium*, but there are no others that suit the ancient expression better. Joseph Hellegouarc'h has defined it as referring to "a set of acts and obligations in the domain of social relations." See *Le vocabulaire latin des relations et des partis politiques sous la république* (Paris: Les Belles Lettres, 1963), p. 152. The Roman term appears to have corresponded to the Greek expression τὸ καθῆκον, especially as it was employed by the Stoics, see Pliny, *Nat. Hist.* praef. 22; Aulus Gellius, *Noctes atticae* 13.28; Cicero, *Att.* 6.4. On the senses of *officium* see Hellegouarc'h, *Le vocabulaire latin*, pp. 152–63. See also *Thesaurus Linguae Latinae*, vol. 9, pp. 518–27.

2. See E. M. Atkins, "Cicero," in Christopher Rowe and Malcolm Schofield (eds.), *The Cambridge History of Greek and Roman Political Thought* (Cambridge, UK: Cambridge University Press, 2000), pp. 477–516 and 505.

3. Cicero, *De officiis* 1.4; *On Duties*, p. 3.

4. *Ibid.* See also, *De officiis* 1.53; *On Duties*, p. 22: "Gradus autem plures sunt societatis hominum" (There are indeed several degrees of fellowship among men).

5. Cicero, *De officiis* 1.54; *On Duties*, p. 23.

6. Cicero, *De officiis* 1.55; *On Duties*, p. 23.

7. Cicero, *De officiis* 1.53; *On Duties*, pp. 22–23.

8. Cicero, *De officiis* 1.33; *On Duties*, p. 14.

9. Cicero, *De officiis* 1.53; *On Duties*, p. 22.

10. Cicero, *De officiis* 1.53; *On Duties*, p. 23.

11. Cicero, *De officiis* 1.50; *On Duties*, p. 21.

12. Cicero, *De officiis* 1.51; *On Duties*, p. 22.

13. Cicero, *De officiis* 1.39; *On Duties*, pp. 17–18. On Cicero and war, see Jonathan Barnes, "Cicéron et la guerre juste," *Bulletin de la Société Française de Philosophie* 80 (1984), pp. 37–80.

14. Cicero, *De officiis* 3.107; *On Duties*, p. 141.

15. Cicero, *De officiis* 1. 23; *On Duties*, p. 10.

16. *Ibid.* Cicero accepts the unlikely etymology that ties the term *fidem* to *fiat*.

CHAPTER TWO: RUMORS OF DEMISE

1. Cited in Gérard A. Jaeger, *Pirates, filibustiers et corsairs: Histoire et légendes d'une société d'exception* (Avignon: Aubanel, 1987), pp. 157–58.

2. *Ibid.*

3. As Alfred T. Rubin notes, although the exact textual source of the phrase *hostis generis humani* "has not been found," it can be traced to Sir Edward Coke's *Commentaries on the Laws of England* (1628, first published in 1644), which states "pirata est hostis humani generis." Rubin comments that "the form, as a Latin insertion in an English text, makes it look like a stock phrase Coke was borrowing from another source." See "The Law of Piracy," *Denver Journal of International Law and Piracy* 15.2–3 (1987), p. 17 n.61 and 113. Rubin also suggests that a possible classical source for Coke's phrase may be found in a passage from Sallust 81.1, where Jugurtha calls the Romans "men with no sense of justice and of insatiable greed, common enemies of all mankind" (*Romanos iniustos, profunda avaritia communis omnium hostis esse*). See *The Jugurthine War: The Conspiracy of Catiline*, trans. S. A. Handford (London: Penguin Classics, 1964), p. 113. Centuries before Coke, however, the phrase appears in Bartolus of Saxoferrato. See "De captivis et postliminio reversis rubrica," *Apostilla Domini Bartoli De Saxoferato Super Secunda Parte Digesti Novi* (Milan: Johannes Antoni de Donato, 1486).

4. On the slave trade and its abolition in the nineteenth century, see Robin Blackburn, *The Overthrow of Colonial Slavery, 1776–1848* (London: Verso, 1988).

5. See the remarks on the assumed end of piracy in Corinne Touret, *La piraterie au vingtième siècle: Piraterie maritime et aérienne* (Paris: Éditions Montchrestien, 1998), pp. 11–12.

6. Edwin D. Dickinson, "Is the Crime of Piracy Obsolete?" *Harvard Law Review* 360 (1924–1925), pp. 334–60.

7. Philip Gosse, *The History of Piracy* (London: Longmans, Green & Co., 1932), p. 297.

8. *Ibid.*, pp. 297–98.

9. *Ibid.*, p. 298.

10. Charles Glass, "The New Piracy," *London Review of Books* 25.24 (2003), p. 2.

11. *Ibid.* See also the older account in Jack A. Gottschalk and Brian P. Flanagan, *Jolly Roger with an Uzi: The Rise and Threat of Modern Piracy* (Annapolis, MD: U.S. Naval Institute Press, 2000), pp. 85–94.

12. Roger Villar, *Piracy Today: Robbery and Violence at Sea since 1980* (Portsmouth: Carmichael and Sweet, 1985), p. 10.

13. P. W. Birnie, "Piracy Past, Present and Future," in Eric Ellen (ed.), *Piracy at Sea* (Paris: International Maritime Bureau, 1989), pp. 131–58 and 131–32.

14. See "Annex 5" and "Yearly Statistics of Incidents which Occurred since 1984 (Worldwide)" in International Maritime Organization, *Piracy and Armed Robbery Against Ships: Annual Report — 2006*.

15. ICC International Maritime Bureau, *Piracy and Armed Robbery Against Ships: Annual Report — 2007*, p. 24.

16. One may take as preliminary evidence the spectacular seizing of a Ukrainian vessel containing considerable arms (among which were thirty-three tanks) in September 2008.

17. For an overview of the growth of such cases, see the table in Jacques de Watteville *La piraterie aérienne: Étude de droit international et de droit suisse* (Lausanne: Imprimerie Vaudoise, 1978), p. 20 n.4.

18. On the terminology of the crimes, see Wayne Glowka, "Yachtjacking, Boatnapping, or Getting Seajacked by Ship-Jackers," *American Speech* 62.2 (1987), pp. 181–82 and Sidney I. Landau, "More on *Skyjack* and *Skyjacker*," *American Speech* 47.3/4 (1972), p. 307.

CHAPTER THREE: ALONG LIQUID PATHS

1. Henry A. Ormerod, *Piracy in the Ancient World: An Essay on Mediterranean History* (Liverpool: Liverpool University Press, 1924), p. 13.

2. Philip de Souza, *Piracy in the Graeco-Roman World* (Cambridge, UK: Cambridge University Press, 1999), p. 2.

3. Homer, *Odyssey* 15.427.

4. *Ibid.*, 3.71–74; 9.252–55. Cf. 17.425, in which Odysseus, disguised as the Cretan Kastor, claims that he has been raiding in Egypt. See also the *Homeric Hymn to Apollo*, vv. 452–55, at which pirates appear. On the figure of "liquid paths" or, as they have often been rendered, the "watr'y ways," see Parry, "The Traditional Metaphor in Homer," *Classical Philology* 28.1 (1933), pp. 30–43, esp. pp. 37–38.

5. Thucydides, *History* 1.5, in *The Peloponnesan War: The Complete Hobbes Translation*, ed. David Grene (Chicago: University of Chicago Press, 1989), pp. 3–4. On this passage, see MacDonald, "*Ahisteia* and *Lhizomai* in Thucydides and in *IG* I (3rd ed.) 41, 67 and 75," *The American Journal of Philology* 105 (1984), pp. 77–84 and Claudio Ferone, *Lesteia: Forme di predazione nell'Egeo in età classica* (Naples: G. Procaccini, 1997), pp. 165–70.

6. Montesquieu, *De l'esprit des lois*, bk. 21, ch. 7: "Les premiers grecs étaient tous pirates."

7. Amidst the large critical literature, see above all the four books devoted to ancient piracy as a single phenomenon: Sestier, *La piraterie dans l'antiquité* (Paris: A. Marescq Ainé, 1880); Ormerod, *Piracy in the Ancient World*; Ziehbarth, *Beiträge zur Geschichte des Seeraubes und Seehandels im alten Griechenland* (Hamburg: De Gruyter, 1929); de Souza, *Piracy in the Graeco-Roman World*.

8. Sestier, *La piraterie dans l'antiquité*, p. 1.

9. Ormerod, *Piracy in the Ancient World*, p. 13.

10. Coleman Phillipson, *The International Law and Custom of Ancient Greece and Rome*, vol. 2 (London: Macmillan, 1911), p. 370.

11. Lionel Casson, *The Ancient Mariners: Seafarers and Sea Fighters of the Mediterranean in Ancient Times* (New York: Macmillan, 1959), p. 198.

12. Auguste Jardé, *La formation du people grec*, pp. 302–303. For a different view of Homeric raiding, see Alastar Jackson, "War and Raids for Booty in the World of Odysseus," in John Rich and Graham Shipley (eds.), *War and Society in the Greek World* (London: Routledge, 1993), pp. 64–76.

13. Jardé, *La formation du people grec*, p. 302.

14. *Ibid.*

15. Yvon Garlan, *La guerre dans l'antiquité* (Paris: Fernand Nathan, 1972), p. 19.

16. Sestier, *La piraterie dans l'antiquité*, p. vii.

17. For overviews of the classical terminology of piracy, see Ormerod, *Piracy in the Ancient World*, pp. 59–74; de Souza, *Piracy in the Graeco-Roman World*, pp. 2–13; Rubin, *The Law of Piracy*, 2nd ed. (Irvington-on-Hudson: Transnational Publishers, Inc., 1998), pp. 1–6; Ferone, *Lesteia*, pp. 43–67.

18. See nn. 3 and 4 above.

19. See de Souza, *Piracy in the Graeco-Roman World*, p. 3.

20. *Ibid.*, pp. 3–5.

21. See, for example, the note on *peiran* in Georg Autenrieth's *A Homeric Dictionary, for Schools and Colleges, Based Upon the German of Dr. Georg Autenrieth*, trans. Robert P. Keep (New York: Harper & Brothers, 1887), p. 252.

22. See the entries in George Liddell and Robert Scott, *A Greek-English Lexicon*, 9th ed. (Oxford, UK: Clarendon Press, 1996), pp. 1354–55.

23. De Souza, *Piracy in the Graeco-Roman World*, p. 12.

24. See "latro" and "latrocinium" in P. G. W. Glare (ed.), *Oxford Latin Dictionary* (Oxford, UK: Clarendon Press, 1983), pp. 1007–1008.

25. Cicero, *De officiis* 3.107; *On Duties*, p. 141.

26. De Souza, *Piracy in the Graeco-Roman World,* p. 9.

27. *Ibid.*, p. 13.

28. Yvon Garlan, "Signification historique de la piraterie grecque," *Dialogues d'histoire ancienne* 4 (1978), p. 2.

29. Plutarch, *Life of Kimon* 8.3–5. On this passage, see Brulé, *La piraterie crétoise hellénistique*, pp. 121–22; de Souza, *Piracy in the Graeco-Latin World*, pp. 29–30.

30. See Polybius, *Histories* 4.68; Diodorus Siculus, *History* 20.97.5. On pirate peoples more generally, see Yvon Garlan, "Les pirates," in *Guerre et économie en Grèce ancienne* (Paris: La Découverte, 1989), pp. 180–85.

31. Livy, *History of Rome* 37.11.6–7. On Livy's diction, see Alessandro Milan, "Ricerche sul *Latrocinium* in Livio I: *Latro* nelle fonti preaugustee," *Atti dell'Istituto veneto di scienze, lettere ed arti, Classe di scienze morali e lettere* 138 (1979–1980), pp. 171–97. The term *archipirata* can also be found in Diodorus Siculus, who attributes the title to Timocles, captured by the Rhodians in 304 (*History* 20.97.5).

32. Rubin, *The Law of Piracy*, pp. 11–12.

33. See, on this subject, Brulé, *La piraterie crétoise hellénistique*, esp. pp. 117–40.

34. Thucydides, *History* 1.5, in *The Pelaponnesan War*, pp. 3–4.

35. Franz Kafka, "A Page from an Old Document," in Stanley Corngold (ed. and trans.), *Kafka's Selected Stories* (New York: Norton, 2007), p. 110.

CHAPTER FOUR: CAPTURES

1. Thucydides, *History* 1.4, in *The Pelaponnesan War*, p.3.

2. Χαλκηδόνιοι δέ, ξένων ἐν τῇ πόλει συχνῶν παρ' αὐτοῖς γινομένων, ὀφείλοντες αὐτοῖς μισθὸν οὐκ ἠδύναντο διαλῦσαι. ἀνήγγειλαν οὖν, εἴ τις τῶν πολιτῶν ἢ μετοίκων σῦλον ἔχει κατὰ πόλεως ἢ ἰδιώτου καὶ βούλεται λαβεῖν, ἀπογράψασθαι. ἀπογραψαμένων δὲ συχνῶν, τὰ πλοῖα τὰ πλέοντα εἰς τὸν Πόντον ἐσύλων μετὰ προφάσεως εὐλόγου. ἔταξαν δὲ χρόνον ἐν ᾧ λόγον ὑπὲρ αὐτῶν ἔφασαν ποιήσασθαι. συλλεγέντων δὲ χρημάτων συχνῶν, τοὺς μὲν στρατιώτας ἀπήλλαξαν, ὑπὲρ δὲ τῶν σύλων διεδικάσαντο. τοῖς δὲ μὴ δικαίως συληθεῖσιν ἡ πόλις ἀπὸ τῶν προσόδων ἀπεδίδου. Aristotle, *1347b 20*, *Metaphysics 2: Books 10–14. Oeconomia. Magna Moralia* (Loeb Classical Library no.287), trans. G. Cyril Armstrong (Cambridge, MA: Harvard University Press, 1958), pp. 358–59.

3. On *sylan*, see Rodolphe Dareste, "Le droit des représailles," *Nouvelles études d'histoire du droit* (Paris: Larose, 1902), pp. 38–54; Bernard Haussoullier, *Traité entre Delphes et Pellana. Étude de droit grec* (Paris: Champion, 1917), pp. 20–25; Charles-Albert Lécrivain, "Le droit de se faire justice soi-même et les représailles dans les relations internationales de la Grèce," *Mémoires de l'académie des sciences de Toulouse* 9 (1897), pp. 277–90; A. Wilhelm, "Die lokrische Mädcheninschrift," *Jahreshefte der österreichischen archäologischen Instututs in Wien* 14 (1911), pp. 198–201; Louis Gernet, *Recherches sur le développement de la pensée morale et juridique en Grèce* (Paris: Albin Michel, 2001), pp. 267–76; Kurt Latte, "Συλᾶν," in *Kleine Schriften zu Religion, Recht, Literatur und Sprache der Griechen und Römer*, ed. Olof Gigon, Wolfgang Buchwald and Wolfgang Kunkel (Munich: Beck, 1968), pp. 416–19; Yvon Garlan, "Étude d'histoire militaire et diplomatique II: Sur le règlement des droits de représailles," *Bulletin de correspondence hellénique* 89 (1965), pp. 338–39; Philippe Gauthier, *Symbola: Les étrangers et la justice dans les cités grecques*, Annales de l'est, mémoire, 42 (Nancy: Université de Nancy II, 1972), pp. 209–59; Benedetto Bravo, "Sulân: Représailles et justice privée contres des étrangers dans les cités grecques (étude du vocabulaire et des institutions)," *Annali della scuola normale superiore di Pisa* X.3 (1980), pp. 705–49; Kendrick W. Pritchett, *The Greek State at War*, part 5 (Berkeley: University of California Press, 1991), pp. 73–132.

4. Gauthier, *Symbola*, p. 210.

5. See *Iliad* 4.466; 6.28; 71; 10.343; 387; 13.640; 15.428; 16.500; 17.60. On the history of the term, see Gernet, *Recherches*, pp. 267–76. Later texts, especially by scholiasts, employ the verb σκυλεύειν for this act. The two terms may be etymologically related, as suggested long ago by several philologists. See Gernet, *Recherches*, p. 272; Bravo, *Sulân*, pp. 723–26; Pritchett, *The Greek State at War*, pp. 132–47.

6. See Gauthier, *Symbola*, pp. 210–19. A more elaborate classification can be found in Bravo, *Sulân*, pp. 721–22.

7. Gauthier, *Symbola*, p. 211.

8. τὰ ἱρὰ συλήσαντες ἐνέπρησαν, ἀποτινύμενοι τῶν ἐν Σάρδισι κατακαυθέντων ἱρῶν. Herodotus, *History* 6.101.3.

9. See Gauthier, *Symbola*, pp. 212–15, who notes that many texts employ for the capture of individuals the form ἄγειν, for that of goods, by contrast, φέρειν. On ἀνδροληψία or the seizing of persons, see Bravo, "Androlêpsíai: La 'Prise d'hommes' comme vengeance d'un meurtre commis dans une cité étrangère," in Joseph Modrzejewski and Detlef Liebs (eds.), *Symposion 1977: Vorträge zur Griechischen und Hellenistischen Rechtsgeschichte* (Cologne and Vienna: Böhlau, 1981), pp. 131–56.

10. In this respect, the meaning of συλᾶν comes close to that of ῥυσιάζειν, and σῦλαι close to ῥύσια; scholars have written in this sense both of *gage* and *Pfändernehmen*. See the effective summary in Gauthier, *Symbola*, pp. 215–16; cf. Bravo, *Sulân*, pp. 750–91; Pritchett, *The Greek State at War*, Part 5, pp. 86–115.

11. Gauthier, *Symbola*, pp. 217–19.

12. Gernet, *Recherches*, pp. 267–76.

13. *Ibid.*, p. 276.

14. Gauthier, *Symbola*, p. 212.

15. ἐπειδὰν γάρ τις μισθωσάμενος τριηραρχίαν ἐκπλεύσῃ, πάντας ἀνθρώπους ἄγει καὶ φέρει, καὶ τὰς μὲν ὠφελίας ἰδίᾳ καρποῦται, τὰς δὲ δίκας τούτων ὁ τυχὼν δίδωσιν ὑμῶν, καὶ μόνοις ὑμῖν οὐδαμόσε ἔστιν ἄνευ κηρυκείου βαδίσαι διὰ τὰς ὑπὸ τούτων ἀνδροληψίας καὶ σύλας κατεσκευασμένας. Demosthenes, *De cor. Trier.*, 51.13 in *Demosthenes: Private Orations, L–LVIII, in Neaeram LIX*, vol. 6, trans. A. T. Murray (Cambridge, MA: Harvard University Press, 1956), pp. 61–63. On the trireme, see Jean Taillardat, "La trière athénienne et la guerre sur mer aux Ve et IVe siècle," in Jean-Pierre Vernant (ed.), *Problèmes de la guerre en Grèce ancienne* (Paris–The Hague: Mouton, 1968), pp. 183–205; M. Amit, *Athens and the Sea* (Louvain:

Latomus, 1965), pp. 99–116.

16. On Greek *symbola*, see the monumental work by Gauthier, *Symbola*, and his article "Les saisies licites aux dépens des étrangers dans les cités grecques," *Revue historique de droit français et étranger* 60 (1982), pp. 553–76.

17. On Greek asylum, see Eilhard Schlesinger, *Die griechische Asylie* (Göttingen: W. F. Kaestner, 1933); E. Szanto, "Asylia," in Georg Wissowa (ed.), *Paulys Real-Encyclopädie der Classischen Altertumswissenschaft*. vol. 4 (Stuttgart: Mtezler, 1896), pp. 1879–81; Lécrivain, "Le droit de se faire justice soi-même," pp. 285–90; Gauthier, *Symbola*, pp. 219–59; and, most recently and comprehensively, Kent Rigsby, *Asylia: Territorial Inviolability in the Hellenistic World* (Berkeley: University of California Press, 1996).

18. Dareste, *Nouvelles études d'histoire du droit*, p. 39.

CHAPTER FIVE: GREATER EMPIRE

1. Thucydides, *History* 1.4.

2. Herodotus, *History* 1.171.

3. Thucydides, *History* 1.4.

4. Plutarch, *Life of Theseus* 19.5.

5. Herodotus, *History* 2.152.

6. See Xenophon, *Hellenics* 6.1.1; Pierre Brulé, *La piraterie crétoise*, Centre de Recherches d'Histoire Ancienne, vol. 27 (Besançon: Université de Besançon, 1978), pp. 128–29; G. T. Griffith, *The Mercenaries of the Hellenistic World* 2nd ed. (Cambridge, UK: Cambridge University Press, 1968), p. 4.

7. Griffith, *The Mercenaries of the Hellenistic World*, p. 7.

8. See Ormerod, *Piracy in the Ancient World*, pp. 123–24. Cf. Janice J. Gabbert, "Piracy in the Early Hellenistic Period: A Career Open to Talents," *Greece and Rome* 33 (1986), pp. 158–59.

9. See Ormerod, *Piracy in the Ancient World*, p. 161.

10. ληισταί Τυρσηνοί. Homer, *Hymn to Dionysus* 7.8; Ovid, *Metamorphoses* 3.582–700. Ormerod has collected numerous testimonies of the Greek fear of the Tyrrhenian sea. Cf. *Piracy in the Ancient World*, pp. 152–55.

11. Maurice Holleaux, "The Romans in Illyria," in F. E. Adcock, S. A. Cook, and M. P. Charlesworth (eds.), *The Cambridge Ancient History: The Hellenistic Monarchies and the Rise of Rome,* vol. 6 (Cambridge, UK: Cambridge University Press, 1928), p. 824; cf. the author's original statement in *Études d'épigraphe et d'histoire*

grecques: Rome, la Macédoine et l'orient grec, première partie, vol. 4 (Paris: Librairie d'Amérique et d'Orient Adrien-Maisonneuve, 1952), pp. 76–114.

12. Ormerod, *Piracy in the Ancient World*, p. 166.

13. See H. J. Dell, "The Origin and Nature of Illyrian Piracy," *Historia* 16 (1967), pp. 344–54.

14. See Dell, "The Origin and Nature of Illyrian Piracy" and "Demetrius of Pharus and the Istrian War," *Historia* 19 (1970). See also, de Souza, *Piracy in the Graeco-Roman World*, pp. 76–80.

15. οὐ γὰρ τισὶν, ἀλλὰ πᾶσι, τότε κοινοὺς ἐχθροὺς εἶναι συνέβαινε τοὺς Ἰλλυριούς. Polybius 2.12.6.

16. See Ormerod, *Piracy in the Ancient World*, pp. 151–89; de Souza, *Piracy in the Graeco-Roman World*, pp. 80–96.

17. On Cilicia, see Ronald Syme "Observations on the Province of Cilicia," in W. M. Calder and Josef Keil (eds.), *Anatolian Studies Presented to W. H. Buckler* (Manchester: Manchester University Press, 1939), pp. 299–322.

18. See de Souza, *Piracy in the Graeco-Roman World*, p. 98.

19. Strabo, *Geography* 4.5.2.

20. *Ibid*. On the slave market on Delos, see Maróti, "Der Sklavenmarkt auf Delos und die Piraterie," *Helikon* 9–10 (1969–70), pp. 24–42.

21. Garlan, *Guerre et économie en Grèce ancienne*, p. 193.

22. See Ormerod, *Piracy in the Ancient World*, pp. 203–207; cf. de Souza, *Piracy in the Graeco-Roman World*, pp. 98–102.

23. "Marcus Antonius praetor in Ciliciam maritimos praedones id est piratas persecutus est." Livy, *Epistle* 68. Few sources remain bearing witness to this project; in addition to Livy, one may read of the campaign in Julius Obsequens 104 and Trogus, *Prol.*, 39. See Ormerod, *Piracy in the Ancient World*, pp. 208–209; de Souza, *Piracy in the Graeco-Roman World*, pp. 102–108. The nature of Marcus Antonius' title has been debated; he may have been assigned not only the province of Cilicia but also Asia. The exact dating of the first Roman campaigns against the pirates in Cilicia is also uncertain. Jean-Louis Ferrary has argued it may have begun as early as 103 AD. See Ferrary, "Recherches sur la législation de Saturninus et de Glaucia," *Mélanges d'archéologie de l'école française de Rome* 89.1 (1977), pp. 619–60.

24. The famous law has generally been dated to the period between 101 and 99. For a summary and analysis of the scholarship on the subject, see de Souza, *Piracy in the Graeco-Roman World*, pp. 108–16. Cf. Adalberto Giovannini and Erhard

Grzybek, "La *lex de piratis persequendis*," *Museum Helveticum* 35 (1978), pp. 33–47; Mark Hassall, Michael Crawford, and Joyce Reynolds, "Rome and the Eastern Provinces at the End of the Second Century BC: The So-Called Piracy Law and a New Inscription from Cnidos," *The Journal of Roman Studies* 64 (1974), pp. 195–220; Andrew W. Lintott, "Notes on the Roman Law Inscribed at Delphi and Cnido," *Zeitschrift für Papyrologie und Epigraphik* 20 (1976), pp. 65–82; Max Radin, "The Roman Law of Delphi and the Lex Gabinia," *The Classical Journal* 23.9 (1928), pp. 678–82; Lucia Monaco, *Persecutio Piratarum: Battaglie ambigue e svolte costituzionali nella Roma repubblicana* (Naples: Casa Editrice Dott. Eugenio Jovene, 1996); and Hartel Pohl, *Die römische Politik und die Piraterie im östlichen Mittelmeer vom 3. bis zum 1. Jh. V. Chr.*, Untersuchungen Zur Antiken Literatur Und Geschichte, vol. 42 (Berlin: de Gruyter, 1993), esp. pp. 208–82.

25. See Maróti, "Ho Koinos Polemos," *Klio* 40 (1962), pp. 124–27.; cf. Marcel Benabou, "Rome et la police des mers au Ier siècle avant J.-C.: La répression de la piraterie cilicienne," in Micheline Galley and Leïla Ladjimi Sebai (eds.), *L'homme méditerranéen et la mer: Actes du troisième Congrès International d'Études des Cultures de la Méditerranée Occidentale, 1981* (Jerba, 1985), pp. 60–69.

26. Plutarch, *Life of Pompey* 24.

27. On piracy and Mithraditic wars, see Maróti "Die Rolle der Seeräuber in der Zeit des Mithridatischen Krieges," in Luigi de Rosa (ed.), *Ricerche Storiche ed Economiche in Memora de Corrado Barbagallo*, vol. 1 (Naples: Edizioni scientifiche italiane, 1970), pp. 479–93 and "Die Rolle der Seeräuber unter den Anhängern des Sextus Pompeius," in H. Diesner et al. (eds.), *Sozialökonomische Verhältnisse im alten Orient und klassischen Altertum* (Berlin: Akademie-Verlag, 1961); de Souza, *Piracy in the Graeco-Roman World*, pp. 116–18; Ormerod, *Piracy in the Ancient World*, pp. 209–12.

28. See Suetonius, *Life of Caesar* 4; Plutarch, *Life of Caesar* 1–2; Val. Max. 6.9.15. Cf. A. M. Ward "Caesar and the Pirates," *American Journal of Ancient History* 2 (1977), pp. 27–36.

29. Plutarch, *Life of Pompey* 24.

30. Dio Cassius 36.20–21.

31. Appian, *Mithraditic Wars* 93.

32. Cicero, *Pro Lege Manilia* 11.31–33 and 18.55. On Delos, see H. B. Mattingly, "M. Anotonius, C. Verres and the Sack of Delos by the Pirates," in M. J. Fontana (ed.), *Philias Charin: Miscellanea di studi classici in onore di Eugenio Manni*, vol. 4

(Rome: Bretschneider, 1980), pp. 1489–515.

33. Cicero, *Pro Lege Manilia* 18.55.

34. Appian, *Mithraditic Wars* 93; Livy, *Per.* 99.

35. Dio Cassius 36.24.

36. Plutarch, *Life of Pompey* 25.3.

37. *Ibid.*

38. οὕτω Πομπήιος τὴν ἡγεμονίαν τῆς θαλάσσης τῶν τε νήσων καὶ τῆς ἡπείρου ἐς τετρακοσίους σταδίους ἀπὸ τῆς θαλάσσης ἄνω εἰλήφει. Dio Cassius 36.36a.

39. Appian, *Mithraditic Wars* 94.

40. Plutarch, *Life of Pompey* 25.2–3.

41. "Imperium aequum in omnibus provinciis cum procunsulibus usque ad quinquagesinum miliarium a mari." Velleius 2.31.2. See Hugh Last, "*Imperium Maius*: A Note," *The Journal of Roman Studies* 37.1/2 (1947), pp. 160–62. The question of the legal status of Pompey's command is vexed. In addition to Last, see W. R. Loader, "Pompey's Command under the Lex Gabinia," *The Classical Review* 54.3 (1940), pp. 134–36; Shelach Jameson, "Pompey's *Imperium* in 67: Some Constitutional Fictions," *Historia* 19 (1970), pp. 539–60; J. P. V. D. Baldson, "Roman History, 58–56 BC: Three Ciceronian Problems," *The Journal of Roman Studies* 47.1/2 (1957); J. Béranger, "À propos d'un *imperium infinitum*: Histoire et stylistique," in *Mélanges de philologie, de littérature et d'histoire anciennes, offerts à J. Marouzeau par ses collègues et élèves étrangers* (Paris: Les Belles Lettres, 1948), pp. 19–27; Victor Ehrenberg, "Imperium Maius in the Roman Republic," *The American Journal of Philology* 74.2 (1953), pp. 113–36.

42. See in particular Jameson: "If it were not for Velleius' apparent statement to the contrary, it would probably never have been doubted that Pompey was granted *imperium maius*." "Pompey's *Imperium* in 67," p. 545. Prone to hyperbole, Cicero suggests, apparently for polemical reasons, that the campaign against the pirates in Rome could usher in an *infinitum imperium*. See Maróti, "On the Problem of M. Antonius Creticus' *Imperium Infinitum*"; Béranger, "À propos d'un *imperium infinitum*: Histoire et stylistique."

43. See Ormerod, *Piracy in the Ancient World*, pp. 208–209; de Souza, *Piracy in the Graeco-Roman World*, pp. 141–48.

44. Hugh Last, "The Breakdown of the Sullan System and the Rise of Pompey," in J. A. Crook, Andrew Lintott, and Elizabeth Rawson (eds.), *Cambridge Ancient History: The Last Age of the Roman Republic*, pp. 313–49 and 347.

45. *Ibid.*

46. See in particular Livy, *Per.* 99; Appian, *Mithraditic Wars* 95; Florus 3.6.16.

47. Ormerod, *Piracy in the Ancient World*, p. 239.

48. De Souza, *Piracy in the Graeco-Roman World*, p. 168.

49. Dio Cassius 36.37.4.

50. Plutarch, *Life of Pompey* 28.2.

51. *Ibid.*

52. Cicero, *Pro Lege Manilia* 12.35.

53. Maróti, "Die Rolle der Seeräuber unter den Anhängern des Sextus Pompeius," p. 214.

54. *Ibid.*, p. 347; see also Last, "The Breakdown of the Sullan System and the Rise of Pompey," p. 349.

55. On Pompey's having "paved the way" for the Principate, see Wilhelmina Mary Feemster Jashemski, *The Origins and History of the Pro-Consular and the Propraetorian Imperium to 27* BC (Chicago: University of Chicago Press, 1950), esp. pp. 95–99. The definition of the Principate is from A. E. R Boak. See "The Extraordinary Commands from 80 to 48 BC: A Study in the Origins of the Principate," *The American Historical Review* 24.1 (1918), p. 1. The first formulation of the argument, as both scholars note, can be found in Theodor Mommsen's *Römisches Staatsrecht*, vol. 2, pp. 635–36. Cf. Brian Croke, "Mommsen's Pompey," *Quaderni di Storia* 11 (1985), pp. 137–49.

56. "Remota itaque iustitia quid sunt regna nisi magna latrocinia? *quia et latrocinia quid sunt nisi parva regna? Manus et ipsa hominum est, imperio principis regitur, pacto societatis astringitur, placiti lege praeda dividitur. Hoc malum si in tantum perditorum hominum accessibus crescit, ut et loca teneat sedes constituat, civitates occupet populos subiuget, evidentius regni nomen adsumit, quod ei iam in manifesto confert non dempta cupiditas, sed addita impunitas. Eleganter enim et veraciter Alexandro illi Magno quidam comprehensus pirata respondit. Nam cum idem rex hominem interrogaret, quid ei videretur, ut mare haberet infestum, ille libera contumacia: *Quod tibi*, inquit, *ut orbem terrarum; sed quia <id> ego exiguo navigio facio, latro vocor; quia tu magna classe, imperator.*" Augustine, *De civitate dei* 6.3.15.

CHAPTER SIX: CROSSINGS

1. See Jonathan Ziskind, "The International Legal Status of the Sea in

Antiquity," *Acta Orientalia* 35 (1973), pp. 35–49.

2. James Bennett Pritchard, (ed.), *Ancient Near Eastern Texts Relating to the Old Testament* (Princeton, NJ: Princeton University Press, 1955), p. 27. Ziskind quotes this declaration in "The International Legal Status of the Sea in Antiquity," p. 36.

3. Ziskind, "The International Legal Status of the Sea in Antiquity," pp. 38–40.

4. *Ibid.*, p. 40.

5. The sources discussed by Ziskind do not always lend themselves to his unequivocal conclusions. See in particular, "The International Legal Status of the Sea in Antiquity," pp. 40–43.

6. See Ludovic Beauchet, *Histoire du droit privé de la république athénienne: Le droit de propriété*, vol. 3 (Paris: Chevalier–Marescq & cie, 1897), pp. 45–57, esp. p. 53. Max Kaser has argued that the Roman idea of ownership was itself a relatively late invention. See "Der römische Eigentumsbegriff," in Hans Dölle (ed.), *Deutsche Landesreferate zum VI. internationalen Kongreß für Rechtsvergleichung in Hamburg 1962* (Berlin: De Gruyter, 1962), pp. 19–38 and "The Concept of Roman Ownership," *Tydskrif vir hedendaagse Romeins-Hollandse Reg.* 27 (1964), pp. 5–19.

7. For a summary of some recent views, see the articles collected in Peter Birks (ed.), *New Perspectives in the Roman Law of Property: Essays for Barry Nichols* (Oxford, UK: Clarendon Press, 1989).

8. There is no lack of such summaries. See, for instance, Pasquale Voci, *Piccolo manuale di diritto romano* (Milano: Giuffrè, 1979), pp. 261–76; David Deroussin, "Personnes, choses, corps," in Emmanuel Dockès and Gilles Lhuilier (eds.), *Le corps et ses représentations*, vol. 1 (Paris: Litec, 2001), pp. 87–90; Alan Watson, *The Law of Property in the Later Roman Republic* (Oxford, UK: Clarendon Press, 1968), pp. 1–15.

9. The fullest account of things *extra patrimonium* may still be that of Gisueppe Branca, "Le cose extra patrimonium humani iuris," *Annali Triestini di diritto economia Annali Triestini di diritto economia e politica* 12 (1941).

10. See Gaius, *Inst.* 2.4; Marcianus, *Inst.* 3.3.2–8.

11. Gaius, *Inst.* 2.4.

12. On *res sanctae*, see Gaius, *Inst.* 2.4; Justinian, *Inst.* 2.1.10; *Dig* 1.8.8; 9. 3–4, 11; Isidore, *Origines* 15. 4.2. On Remus, see *Dig* 1.8.11, where the source is Pomponius, 2 ex var. lect.

13. See the effective analysis in Voci, *Piccolo manuale*, pp. 263–64.

14. Justinian, *Institutes* 2.1.6; *Dig* 50. 16.15.

15. On the Roman juridical notion of natural law, see the fundamental paper by Yan Thomas, "*Imago Naturae*: Note sur l'institutionnalité de la nature à Rome," *Théologie et droit dans la science politique de l'état moderne: Actes de la table ronde organisée par l'École française de Rome avec le concours du CNRS, 12–14 Novembre 1987* (Rome: École française de Rome, 1991), pp. 201–27.

16. *Dig* 1.8.2pr and *Dig* 1.8.2.1 (Marcianus 3 inst). Cf. the strikingly similar terms in Justinian's *Institutes*, 2.1 pr. and 1. On Marcianus's definition and the Roman legal conception of the sea more generally, see Percy Thomas Fenn, "Justinian and the Freedom of the Sea," *The American Journal of International Law* 19 (1923), pp. 716–29; Aldo Dell'Oro, "Le *res communes omnium* dell'elenco di Marciano e il problema del loro fondamento giuridico"; Biondo Biondi, "Condizione giuridica e del mare e del litus maris," *Studi in onore di Silvio Perozzi nel XI anno del suo insegnamento* (Palermo: Castiglia, 1925), pp. 269–80; Fulvio Maroi, "Sulla condizione giuridica del mare e delle sue rive in diritto romano," *Rivista italiana per le scienze* 62 (1919), pp. 151–70; Nicole Charbonnel and Marcel Morabito, "Les rivages de la mer: Droit romain et glossateurs," *Revue de l'histoire du droit* 65.1 (1987), pp. 23–44; George Klingenberg, "*Maris Proprium* in D. 47, 10, 14," *The Legal History Review* 72.1–2 (2004), pp. 37–60.

17. *Dig* 43.8.3pr.

18. See Charbonnel and Morabito, "Les rivages de la mer," pp. 26–27.

19. *Dig* 41.1.3.45pr (Pampinaus 10 resp.); *Dig* 18.1.51 (Paulus 21 ad ed.).

20. See Charbonnel and Morabito, "Les rivages de la mer," pp. 24–25.

21. See Pampaloni, "Sulla condizione giuridica delle rive del mare in diritto romano e odierno." Cf. the differing views represented by Biondi, "Condizione giuridica del mare e del litus maris"; Dell'Oro, "Le *res communes omnium* dell'elenco di Marciano e il problema del loro fondamento giuridico"; Charbonnel and Morabito, "Les rivages de la mer."

22. Justinian, *Institutes* 2.1.3.

23. "[S]olebat Aquilius [. . .] quid esset litus ita definire: qua fluctus eluderet." Cicero, *Topica* 7.32. Cf. "[I]dque Marcum Tullium aiunt cum arbiter esset primum constituisse." *Dig* 50.16.96pr (Celsus 25 *Dig*).

24. See Jean Dufau, *Le domaine public* (Paris: Éditions du Moniteur, 1977), pp. 164–71.

25. See Charbonnel and Morabito, "Les rivages de la mer," p. 25.

26. "[Q]uod in mare aedificatum sit, fieret privatum." *Dig* 1.8.10 (Pomponius

6 ex plaut).

27. "Si pilas in mare iactaverim et supra eas inaedificaverim, continuo aedificium meum fit." *Dig* 41.1.30.4 (Pomponius 34 ad sab.). Cf. *Dig* 41.1.50 (Pomponius 6 ex plaut.); *Dig* 39.1.1. 18 (Ulpianus 52 ad ed.).

28. Neratius (Nerva 5 membr.); "*Quod in litore quis aedificaverit, eius erit.*" *Dig* 41.1.14pr. (Nerva 5 membr.).

29. "Quod si quis in mare vel in litore aedificet, licet in suo non aedificet, [...] tamen [...] suum facit." Ulpian, *Dig* 39.1.1.18 (Ulpianus 52 ad ed.). Cf. *Dig* 1.8.5.1 (Gaius 2 rer. cott.); *Dig* 41.3.45pr. (Papinianus 10 resp.).

30. On the shore as a *res nullius*, see *Dig* 41.1.30.4 (Pomponius 34 ad ed.); *Dig* 41.1. 14pr. (Nerva 5 membr.); Cf. the related question of the *res inventae in litore*, *Dig* 1.8.3 (Florentinus 6 inst.), as well as that of the island, *Dig* 4.1.1.7.3 (Gaius 2 rer. cott.). For a discussion of the shore and the *res nullius*, see Gennaro Franciosi, "Res nullius e occupatio," *Atti dell'accademia di scienze morali e politiche di Napoli* 75 (1964), pp. 237–52. On the *res nullius* more generally, see Ubaldo Robbe, *La differenza sostantiale fra "res nullius" e "res nullius in bonis" e la distinzione delle "res" pseudo-marcianea "che non ha capo nè coda,"* vol. 1 (Milan: A. Giuffrè Editore, 1979); A. Mieli, "'Res Publica', 'Res Communis Omnium', 'Res Nullius': Grozio e le fonti romane sul diritto del mare," *Index* 26 (1998), pp. 383–87.

31. On the capture of wild animals, see David Daube, "Doves and Bees," in *Droits de l'antiquité et sociologie juridique: Mélanges Henri Lévy-Bruhl* (Paris: Sirey, 1959), pp. 63–75; Grant McLeod, "Wild and Tame Animals and Birds in Roman Law," in Peter Birks (ed.), *New Perspectives in the Roman Law of Property*, pp. 169–76.

32. See *Dig* 41.2.1.1 (Paulus 54 ad ed.). See Thomas, "*Imago naturae*," pp. 213–19.

33. "Illud videndum est, sublato aedificio, quod in litore positum erat, cuius condicionis is locus sit, hoc est utrum maneat eius cuius fuit aedificium, an rursus in pristinam causam reccidit perindeque publicus sit, ac si numquam in eo aedificatum fuisset. quod propius est, ut existimari debeat, si modo recipit pristinam litoris speciem." Neratius, *Dig* 41.1.14.1 (Nerva 5 membr.).

34. "In tantum, ut et soli domini constituantur qui ibi aedificant, sed quamdiu aedificium manet: alioquin aedificio dilapso quasi iure postliminii revertitur locus in pristinam causam, et si alius in eodem loco aedificaverit, eius fiet." Marcianus, *Institutes* 3, *Dig* 1.8.6pr.

35. Less often, rights of *postliminium* could be granted in peace as well as war, see Ferdinando Bona, "Postliminium in pace," *Studia et documenta iuris* 21 (1955), pp. 249–75.

CHAPTER SEVEN: AFLOAT

1. See Walter Ashburner, *The Rhodian Sea-Law* (Oxford, UK: Oxford University Press, 1909), p. cxliii. He cites Strabo, Epictetus, and Pliny, while noting the attention given to wreckers in the *Digest*, esp. *Dig* 47.9.

2. Seneca the Elder, *Controversiae* 1.6 in *Declamations*.

3. *Ibid.*, 3.3.

4. *Ibid.*, 7.1.

5. *Ibid.*, 1.2.

6. *Ibid.*

7. *Ibid.*

8. On piracy in classical literature, see Ormerod, *Piracy in the Ancient World*; de Souza, *Piracy in the Graeco-Roman World*; Sestier, *La piraterie dans l'antiquité*. For Euripides, *Hypsipyla*, ed. G. Italie (Berlin: A. Ebering, 1923).

9. P. A. Mackay, "Klephtika: The Tradition of the Tales of Banditry in Apuleius," *Greece and Rome*, 10.2 (1963), p. 149.

10. The dating of the romance has been much debated; the philologists of the early modern period attributed it the mid second century AD, but twentieth-century scholars have assigned it to the first century BC. See Albin Lesky, *Geschichte der griechischen Literatur*, 3rd ed. (Bern/Munich, 1971), pp. 957–72; B.P. Reardon, "Theme, Structure and Narrative in Chariton," *Yale Classical Studies* 27 (1982), esp. pp. 1–2. Cf. C. Ruíz-Montero, "Una obserrvación para la cronología de Caritón de Afrodisias," *Estudios classicos* 24 (1980), pp. 63–69.

11. English translation in Reardon, *Collected Ancient Greek Novels*, p. 22; Georges Molinié (ed.), *Le roman de Chairéas et Callirhoé* 1.1–2.

12. Reardon, *Collected Ancient Greek Novels*, p. 29; Molinié, *Le roman de Chairéas et Callirhoé* 1.7.

13. Reardon, *Collected Ancient Greek Novels*, p. 30; Molinié, *Le roman de Chairéas et Callirhoé* 1.8.

14. Reardon, *Collected Ancient Greek Novels*, p. 34; Molinié, *Le roman de Chairéas et Callirhoé* 1.12.

15. Reardon, *Collected Ancient Greek Novels*, p. 56; Molinié, *Le roman de Chairéas*

et Callirhoé 3.4.

16. Reardon, *Collected Ancient Greek Novels*, pp. 57–68; Molinié, *Le roman de Chairéas et Callirhoé* 3.4.

17. B. E. Perry, "Chariton and His Romance from a Literary-Historical Point of View," *American Journal of Philology* 51 (1930), p. 113. On the scene, see also E. Karabélias, "Le roman de Cariton d'Aphrodisias et le droit: Renversements de situation et exploitation des ambiguïtés juridiques," in G. Nenci and G. Thür (eds.), *Symposium* (Cologne and Vienna: Böhlau, 1988), pp. 391–96; Saundra Schwartz, "The Trial Scene in the Greek Novels and in Acts," in T. Penner and C. Stichelle (eds.), *Contextualizing Acts: Lukan Narrative and Graeco-Roman Discourse* (Atlanta: Society of Biblical Literature Symposium Series, 2003), pp. 111–17.

18. Reardon, *Collected Ancient Novels*, p. 85; Molinié, *Le Roman de Chairéas et Callirhoé* 5.8.

19. See Bartolus, *Dig* 49.15.19 and 24. The principle is restated by many of the founders of modern international law. See B. A. Wortley, "*Pirata Non Mutat Dominium*," *British Yearbook of International Law* 24 (1947), pp. 258–72.

20. *Ibid.*

21. Giovanni Bocaccio, *Il Decamerone*, ed. Vittore Branca, 2 vols. (Turin: Einaudi, 1980), p. 305.

22. *Ibid.*, p. 307.

23. *Ibid.*, p. 311.

24. *Ibid.*, p. 314.

CHAPTER EIGHT: DIALECTIC OF THE SEA DOGS

1. *Odyssey* 3.71–4; 9.252–5.

2. *Odyssey* 14.222–234.

3. Cf. *Odyssey* 17.424–433.

4. De Souza, *Piracy in the Graeco-Roman World*, p. 21. On piracy in Homer, cf. Bravo, *Sulân*, pp. 975–77; Werner Nowag, *Raub und Beute in der archaischen Zeit der Griechen* (Frankfurt am Main: Haag/Herchen, 1983), see chs. 2 and 3; Jackson, "War and Raids for Booty in the World of Odysseus" and "Privateers in the Ancient Greek World," in M. R. D. Foot (ed.), *War and Society: Historical Studies in Honour and Memory of J. R. Western, 1928–1971* (London: Paul Elek, 1973), pp. 214–53.

5. Goethe, *Faust*, pt. 2, act 5. On the relations between trade and piracy in the

Hellenistic world, see Vincent Gabrielson, "Economic Activity, Maritime Trade and Piracy in the Hellenistic Aegean," *Revue des études anciennes* 103.1–2 (2001), pp. 219–40.

6. Eugène Cauchy, *Le droit maritime international considérée dans ses origines*, vol. 1 (Paris: Guillaumin et Compagnie, 1862), p.343

7. See Cauchy, *Le droit maritime international*, p. 344.

8. On the history of the corsair lexicon, see Du Cange, "*Glossarium ad Scriptores mediae et infimae Graecitatis*," in Walter Ashburner, *The Rhodian Sea-Law*, pp. cxliv–cxlv.

9. Boccaccio, *Decamerone*, vol. 1, p. 306.

10. *Ibid.*, p. 168.

11. Henry Brongniart, *Les corsaires et la guerre maritime* (Paris: Augustin Challamel, 1904), p. 5 (italics mine).

12. William Edward Hall, *Treatise of International Law*, 8th ed. (Oxford, UK: Clarendon Press, 1924), pp. 620–21.

13. *Ibid.*, p. 310.

14. James G. Lydon, *Pirates, Privateers, and Profits* (Upper Saddle, NJ: Gregg Press, 1970), p. 25.

15. Kenneth R. Andrews, *Elizabethan Privateering: English Privateering During the Spanish War, 1585–1603* (Cambridge, UK: Cambridge University Press, 1966), p. 5.

16. See Ashburner, *The Rhodian Sea-Law*, pp. cxliv–cxlv.

17. Ashburner, *The Rhodian Sea-Law*, p. cxlv.

18. Frederic L. Cheyette, "The Sovereign and the Pirates, 1332," *Speculum* 45.1 (1970), p. 48.

19. *Ibid.*

20. See above chapter four, "Captures."

21. On the development of the *lettre de marque*, see René de Mas Latrie, *Du droit de marque, ou droit de représailles au Moyen Âge* (Paris: A. Franck, 1883); Pierre-Clément Timbal, "Les lettres de marque dans le droit de la France Médiévale," *Recueils de la société Jean Bodin* 10.2 (1958), pp. 109–38; Francis Raymond Stark, "The Abolition of Privateering and the Declaration of Paris," *Studies in History, Economics and Public Law* 8.3 (1897), esp. 49–60.

22. See Rubin, *The Law of Piracy*, p. 31 n. 102.

23. On the etymology of the term "marque," see Stark, "The Abolition of

Privateering," pp. 52–53. Cf. Rubin, *The Law of Piracy*, pp. 31–32 n.103, who, basing himself on *The American Heritage Dictionary* (1969), refers to the Indo-European root **merg-*: "boundary, border."

24. Jean Merrien, *Histoire des corsaires*, p. 30.

25. See Mas Latrie, *Du droit de marque*, p. 11. Cf. Timbal, "Les lettres de marque."

26. Griffith, *Hellenistic Mercenaries*, p. 262.

27. See ch. 48, Ólafur Halldórsson (ed.), *Foeringa Saga* (Reykjavík: Stofnun Árna Magnússonar á Íslandi, 1987); and ch. 45, *The Tale of Thrond of Gate: Commonly called Foereyinga saga*, trans. Frederick York Powell (London: D. Nutt, 1896), p. 65.

28. Cauchy, *Le droit maritime international*, p. 64.

29. There have been two editions of the Old French text: Wendelin Foerster and Johan Trost (eds.), *Wistasse Le Moine. Altfranzösischer Abenteuerroman des XIII. Jahrhunderts nach der einzingen Pariser Handschrift* (Halle: Niemeyer, 1891) and, more recently, Denis Joseph Conlon (ed.), *Li Romans de Witasse le moine, Roman du treizième siècle, édité d'après le manuscrit, fonds français 1553, de la Bibliothèque Nationale, Paris* (Chapel Hill: University of North Carolina Press, 1972). An English translation can be found in Glyn S. Burgess (ed.), *Two Medieval Outlaws: Eustace the Monk and Fouke Fitz Waryn* (Cambridge, UK: D. S. Brewer, 1997), pp. 51–78.

30. On the dating of the romance, see Burgess, *Two Medieval Outlaws*, p. 4. He also notes that various archival sources, such as patents and charters, mention Eustace, albeit "tersely." Fourteenth and fifteenth century chroniclers, such as Roger of Wendover and Matthew of Paris, discuss him at more length.

31. Conlon, *Li Romans de Witasse le Moine*, vv. 1–16; Burgess, *Two Medieval Outlaws*, p. 50.

32. Conlon, *Li Romans de Witasse le Moine*, vv. 37–38; Burgess, *Two Medieval Outlaws*, p. 50.

33. Cheyette, "The Sovereign and the Pirate," p. 56.

34. *Ibid.*

35. *Ibid.*, p. 65.

36. *Ibid.*, p. 56.

37. There is a vast scholarly literature on privateers from the end of the Middle Ages through the eighteenth century. Among many others, see Andrews, "Sir Robert Cecil and Mediterranean Plunder" and *Elizabethan Privateering*; Lydon, *Pirates,*

Privateers and Profits; Mollat, "De la piraterie sauvage à la course réglementée (XIVe–XVe siècle)," *Mélanges de l'école française de Rome* 87 (1975), pp. 7–25 and "Essai d'orientation pour l'étude de la guerre de la course et la piraterie (XIIIe–XVe siècles)," *Annuario de estudios medievales* 10 (1980), pp. 743–49; Hugh F. Rankin, *The Golden Age of Piracy* (Williamsburg, Virginia: Colonial Williamsburg, 1969); Marcus Rediker, *Between the Devil and the Deep Blue Sea: Merchant Seamen, Pirates and the Anglo-American Maritime World 1700–1750* (Cambridge, UK: Cambridge University Press, 1987); Violet Barbour, "Privateers and Pirates of the West Indies," *The American Historical Review* 16.3 (1911), pp. 529–66; Jacqueline Guiral-Hadziiosif, "Course et piraterie à Valence de 1410 à 1430," *Anuario de estudios medieavles* 10 (1980), pp. 759–65 and *Valence, port méditerranéen au XVe siècle* (Paris: Publications de la Sorbonne, 1986); Evandro Putzulu, "Pirati e corsari nei mari della Sardegna durante la prima metà del secolo XV," in *IV Congreso De historia de la corona d'Aragón: Actas y communicaciones*, vol. 1 (Palma de Mallorca, 1959), pp. 155–79; Irene B. Katele, "Piracy and the Venetian State: The Dilemma of Maritime Defense in the Fourteenth Century," *Speculum* 63.4 (1988), pp. 865–89; Anna Unali, *Mariners, Pirates i corsaris catalans a l'època medieval*, trans. Maria Teresa Ferrer i Mallol and Maria Antònia Oliver (Barcelona: Edicions de la Magrana, 1986); María Teresa Ferrer i Mallol, "Productes de commerç catalano-portuguès segons una reclamació per pirateria," *Miscellània de Textos Medievals* 6 (1992), pp. 137–63 and *Corsarios castellanos y vascos en el mediterráneo medieval* (Barcelona: Consejo Superior de Investigaciones Científicas, Institución Milá y Fontanals, Departamento de Estudios Medievales, 2000); Anne Merlin-Chazelas, "Ordonnance inédite de François Ier pour la répression de la piraterie," *Bulletin philologique et historique (jusqu'à 1610) du comité des travaux historiques et scientifiques* 1966, vol. I, pp. 87–93; Philippe Rigaud, (ed.), *Pirates et corsaires dans les mers de la Provence, XVe–XVIe siècles: Letras de la costiera* (Paris: Éditions de la CTHS, 2006) and "Pirates et corsaires sur le bas-Rhône: IVXe–XVe siècles"; Alberto Tenenti, "I corsari in mediterraneo all'inizio del cinquecento," *Rivista Storica Italiana* 72 (1960), pp. 234–87, "Venezia e la pirateria nel levante: 1300 c. –1460 c.," in Agostino Pertusi (ed.), *Venezia e il Levante fino al secolo XV* (Florence: Olschki, 1973), pp. 705–71, and *Venezia e i corsari, 1680–1615* (Bari: Laterza, 1961); Michel Fontenay and Alberto Tenenti, "Course et piraterie méditerranéennes de la fin du Moyen Âge au début du XIXe siècle," in M. Mallot (ed.), *Course et piraterie: Études*, pp. 78–136; Anne Pérotin-Dumon, "The Pirate and the Emperor: Power and the Law of the Sea, 1450–1850," in James

Tracy (ed.), *The Political Economy of Merchant Empires* (Cambridge, UK: Cambridge University Press, 1991), pp. 196–227; the articles collected in Michel Mollat (ed.), *Course et piraterie: Études présentées à la commission internationale d'histoire maritime à l'occasion de son XVe colloque internationale pendant le XIVe congrès international des sciences historiques*, 3 vols. (San Francisco: Institut de Recherche et d'Histoire des Textes, Centre National de Recherche Scientifique, 1975).

38. Francisco de Vitoria, *On the Law of War*, §13, in *Political Writings*, ed. Anthony Pagden and Jeremy Lawrence (Cambridge, UK: Cambridge University Press, 1991), p. 303.

39. "Evenit autem interdum, ut occasione belli publici nascatur bellum privatum, puta si quis in hostes inciderit, et vitae aut rerum adeat periculum." Hugo Grotius, *De Jure Belli Ac Pacis Libri Tres, in Quibus Jus Naturae & Gentium, Item Juris Publici Praecipua Explicantur*, 3.18 (Washington, D.C.: Carnegie Endowment for International Peace, 1946), p. 565.

40. On the Barbary "wars," see, among many others, Peter Earle, *Corsairs of Malta and Barbary* (London: Sidgwick and Jackson, 1970); Godfrey Fisher, *Barbary Legend: War, Trade and Piracy in North Africa, 1415–1830* (Oxford, UK: Clarendon Press, 1957); Jacques Heers, *Les barbaresques: La course et la guerre en Méditteranée, XIVe-XVIe siècle (Paris: Perrin, 2001)*; Salvatore Bono, *Les corsaires en Méditteranée* trans. Ahmed Somaï (Paris: Paris-Méditteranée, 1998); John B. Wolf, *The Barbary Coast: Algiers under the Turks* (New York: Norton, 1979); Luca Lo Basso, *In traccia de' legni nemici: corsari europei nel mediterraneo del settecento* (Ventimiglia: Philobiblon, 2002); Fernand Braudel, *La méditerrannée et le monde méditerranéen à l'époque de Philippe II*, vol. 2, pp. 190–212.

41. Earle, *Corsairs of Malta and Barbary*, p. 3.

42. Fontenay and Tenenti, "Course et piraterie méditerranéennes de la fin du Moyen Âge au début du XIXe siècle," p. 79.

43. Peter Earle, *Corsairs of Malta and Barbary*, pp. 30–31.

44. *Ibid.*, p. 34.

45. *Ibid.*, pp. 115–20.

46. On the English privateers and "sea dogs," see, among others, Andrews, *Elizabethan Privateering*; Harry Kelsey, *Sir Francis Drake: The Queen's Pirate* (New Haven, CT: Yale University Press, 2000), and the works mentioned above in n.35.

47. See Peter Earle, *The Pirate Wars* (London: Methuen, 2003).

48. See Robert C. Ritchie, *Captain Kidd and the War against the Pirates*

(Cambridge, MA: Harvard University Press, 1986).

49. Janice E. Thomson, *Mercenaries, Pirates, and Sovereigns: Extraterritorial Violence in Early Modern Europe* (Princeton, NJ: Princeton University Press, 1994), p. 54.

50. See the famous terms of "Politik als Beruf," in Max Weber, *Gesammelte politische Schriften*, vol. 5, ed. Johannes Winckelmann (Tübingen: Mohr, 1988), pp. 505–60 and p. 506.

51. Thomson, *Mercenaries, Pirates and Sovereigns*, p. 70.

52. *Ibid.*

53. Reprinted in Edward Hertslet, *The Map of Europe by Treaty*, vol. 2. (London: Butterworths, 1875), pp. 1282–283. On the *Declaration* more generally, see Francis Piggott, *The Declaration of Paris, 1856: A Study* (London: University of London, 1919).

54. "Second Marcy Note" (Mr Marcy to Count Sartiges, July 28, 1856), in Piggott, *Declaration of Paris*, p. 395.

55. Thomson, *Mercenaries, Pirates and Sovereigns*, p. 177 n.16.

56. *Ibid.*, p. 187.

57. *Ibid.*, p. 190.

58. The effort failed. See Thomson, *Mercenaries, Pirates and Sovereigns*, p. 76.

59. Stark, *The Abolition of Privateering*, p. 12.

60. Piggott, *Declaration of Paris*, p. 438 quoted in Thomson, *Mercenaries, Pirates and Sovereigns*, p. 178 n.36.

CHAPTER NINE: ELDER FOES

1. Christian Wolff, *The Law of Nations Treated According to a Scientific Method*, trans. Joseph H. Drake (Washington: Carnegie Endowment for International Peace, 1934), vol. 6, §722, p. 373; *Jus gentium methodo scientifica pertractatum*, in Jean École et al. (ed.) *Gesammelte Werke*, vol. 25 (Hildesheim, New York: Georg Olms, 1962), p. 586.

2. *Ibid.*

3. Emerich de Vattel, *The Law of Nations or the Principles of Natural Law Applied to the Conduct and to the Affairs of Nations and of Sovereigns*, trans. Charles G. Fenwick (Washington: Carnegie Institution of Washington, 1916), 3.5, §31, p. 259; *Le droit des gens, ou Principes de la loi naturelle* (Amsterdam: E. van Harreveld, 1758) p. 15.

4. *Ibid.*

5. *Ibid.*

6. *Ibid.*

7. Wolff, *The Law of Nations Treated According to a Scientific Method*, vol. 6, §722, pp. 733–34; *Jus gentium*, pp. 586–87.

8. Vattel, *The Law of Nations*, 3.5, §31, p. 259; *Le droit des gens*, p. 15.

9. Wolff, *The Law of Nations Treated According to a Scientific Method*, vol. 6, §722, p. 373. "Per inconstantiam tamen loquendi, quam methodus scientifica minime sert, contingit, qui hostes sunt, eos etiam inimicos appellari." Wolff, *Jus gentium*, p. 586.

10. Ibid.

11. Vattel, *The Law of Nations*, 3.5, §31, p. 259; *Le droit des gens*, p. 15.

12. On the term *inimicus*, see Moreno Morani, "Il 'nemico' nelle lingue indeuropee," in Miglio, Gianfranco, Moreno Morani, Pier Paolo Portinaro, and Alessandro Vitale, *Amicus (Inimicus) Hostis: Le radici concettuali della conflittualita privata e della conflittualita politica* (Milano: Giuffrè, 1992), pp. 9–83, esp. pp. 17–18.

13. See Plaut. *Tri* 654: "cives [...] quos tu inimicos habes"; Acc. 192 R: "hostem ut profugiens inimici invadam in manus?;" Cicero *Manil.* 28: "saepius cum hoste conflixit quam quisquam cum inimico concertavit;" Liv. 5.8.11: "ne quam opem ab inimico videretur petisse, vinci ab hoste quam vincere per civem maluit;" Seneca *Ep* 91.5: "ex amico inimicus, hostis ex socio." Cf. Maurizio Bettini and Alberto Borghini, "La guerra e lo scambio: hostis, perduellis, inimicus," in Gruppo di Lecce della Società di Linguistica Italiana (ed.), *Linguistica e antropologia, Atti del XIV Congresso Internazionale di Studi. Lecce 23–25 maggio 1980* (Lecce: Bulzoni, 1980), pp. 311–12.

14. See P. Jal, "*Hostis (Publicus)* dans la littérature latine de la fin de la république," *Revue des études anciennes* 65 (1963), pp. 54–59. See in particular Jal's discussion of Ael. Spart. Sev. 14.5 and 9 on p. 55.

15. On *inimicus*, see the evidence collected in Jal, "*Hostis (Publicus)*," pp. 63–64.

16. On the meaning of *hostis* and the impossibility of distinguishing strictly between *hostes* and *inimicus*, see Jal, "*Hostis (Publicus)*"; Morani, "Il 'nemico' nelle lingue indeuropee," esp. 25–32; Bettini and Borghini, "La guerra e lo scambio," p. 311 n.21.

17. Cf., for example, Livy 35.50.2 (*hostes*) and 37.1.5 (*inimici*). See also Loretana de Libero, "'*Ut eosdem quos populos romanus amicos atque hostes habeant:*' Die

Freund-Feind-Klausel in den Beziehungen Roms zu griechischen und italienischen Staaten," *Historia* (1997), pp. 270–305.

18. On *adversarius*, see Jal, "*Hostis (Publicus)*," pp. 64–65; Morani, "Il 'nemico' nelle lingue indeuropee," p. 52. On *perduellio*, see Theodor Mommsen, *Römisches Staatsrecht*, 2 vols., 3rd ed. (Leipzig: S. Hirzel, 1877), pp. 537–38; André Magde-lain, "Remarques sur la perduellio," *Historia* 22 (1973), pp. 405–22; C. H. Brecht, *Zur Abgrenzung des Begriffes Perduellio von den verwandten Verbrechensbegriffen im römischen Strafrecht bis zum Ausgang der Republik* (Munich: Beck, 1938); and David Daube, "Review of Brecht, *Zur Abgrenzung des Begriffes Perduellio*," *The Journal of Roman Studies* 31 (1941), pp. 180–84. On *rebellis, usurpator* and *tyrannus*, see R. MacMullen, "The Roman Concept Robber-Pretender," *Revue internationale des droits de l'antiquité* 10 (1963), pp. 221–25.

19. "Hostis apud antiquos peregrinus dicebatur, et qui nunc hostis, perduellio." Festus, *De verborum significatione* 8.

20. See Peter Haggenmacher, *Grotius et la doctrine de la guerre juste* (Paris: Presses universitaires de France, 1983), p. 101.

21. "Hostes hi sunt, qui nobis aut quibus nos publice bellum decrevimus: ceteri latrones aut praedones sunt." *Dig* 50.16.118 (Pomponius, *Quintus maius*).

22. "Hostes sunt, quibus bellum publice populus Romanus decrevit vel ipse populo Romano: ceteri latrunculi vel praedones appellantur. Et ideo qui a latroni-bus captus est, servus latronum non est, nec postliminium illi necessarium est: ab hostibus autem captus, ut puta a Germanis et Parthis, et servus est hostium et postliminio statum pristinum recuperat." *Dig* 4.15.24 (Ulpian, *Institutes*).

23. See Carl Georg Bruns' discussion of the "Lex duodecim tabularum" in *Fontes iuris Romani Antiqui*, vol. 1 (Tübingen: Mohr, 1909). See Émile Benveniste, *Le vocabulaire des institutions indo-européennes*, vol. 1 (Paris: Éditions de Minuit, 1969), pp. 92–93.

24. Benveniste, *Le vocabulaire*, vol. 1, p. 93.

25. See Gauthier, "Notes sur l'étranger et l'hospitalité en Grèce et à Rome," *Ancient Society* 4 (1973), pp. 3–13.

26. See Benveniste, *Le vocabulaire*, vol. 1, p. 95.

27. See Benveniste, *Le vocabulaire*, vol. 1, pp. 92–96, and Gauthier's pertinent remarks on the limits of the legal "equality" shown the *hostis* in "L'étranger et l'hospitalité en Grèce et à Rome," pp. 1–21.

28. Haggenmacher, *Grotius et la doctrine de la guerre juste*, p. 100.

29. Gabriele Steinmayr, "Sviluppi semantici della base *latro* in Grecia e in Roma," *Atti e mernorie dell'Academia di Verona* (1955–1956), p. 161.

30. See Bartolus, *Dig* 49.15.19 and 24; Paulus, *Dig* 44.15.19 pr. 2.

31. Brent D. Shaw, "Bandits in the Roman Empire," *Past and Present* 105 (1984), p. 23.

32. Shaw, "Bandits in the Roman Empire," p. 22.

33. "Ovandi ac non triumphandi causa est, cum aut bella non rite indicta neque cum iusto hoste gesta sunt aut hostium nomen humile et non idoneum est, ut piratarumque, aut deditione repente facta inpulverea, ut dici solet, incruentaque victoria obvenit." Aulus Gellius, *Noctes atticae* 5.6.21. On the *ius triumphandi* more generally, see H. S. Versnel, *Triumphus: An Inquiry into the Origin, Development and Meaning of the Roman Triumph* (Leiden: Brill, 1970), pp. 164–95.

34. "Ac maioribus quidem vestris, Quirites, cum eo hoste res erat, qui haberet rem publicam, curiam, aerarium, consensum et concordiam civium, rationem aliquam, si ita res tulisset, pacis et foederis; hic vester hostis vestram rem publicam oppugnat, ipse habet nulla; senatum, id est orbis terrae consilium, delere gestit, ipse consilium publicum nullum habet; aerarium vestrum exhausit, suum non habet. Nam concordiam civium qui habere potest, nullum habet civitatem? Pacis vero quae potest esse cum eo ratio, in quo est incredibilis crudelitas, fides nulla?" Cicero, *Philippic* 4.14–15. Cf. Rodomontes Galligani, "*Cicero Infesissimus Antoni Hosti*," *Latinas* 44.2 (1996), pp. 115–38. Ian Baucom has also examined this passage from a different perspective in an unpublished paper, "Cicero's Ghost: The Atlantic, the Enemy, and the Laws of War."

35. See Galligani, "*Cicero Infensissimus Antoni Hostis*."

36. Cicero, *De Officiis* 3.107.

37. Rubin, *The Law of Piracy*, p. 15.

38. Cicero, *De Officiis* 3.107. See Grotius, *On the Law of War and Peace*, 2.13–15, pp. 373–74; *De Iure Belli ac Pacis*, p. 248.

CHAPTER TEN: YOUNGER ANTAGONISTS

1. Azzo of Bologna, *Supra Cod.* 1; *de just. et jure*, discussed in Bruno Paradisi, "International Law and Social Structure in the Middle Ages," *The Indian Year Book of International Affairs* 2 (1964), p. 156.

2. See Paradisi, "International Law and Social Structure," pp. 154–61.

3. Bartolus of Saxoferrato, "De Captivis et Postliminio Reversis Rubrica,"

in *Apostilla domini Bartoli de Saxoferato super secunda parte Digesti novi* (Milan: Johannes Antoni de Donato, 1486).

4. See the materials discussed in B. A. Whatley, "Historical Sketch of the Law of Piracy," *Law Magazine and Review* 3 (1874), pp. 538–43. Cf. the remarks on pirates in "The Black Book of the Admiralty," in Sir Travers Twiss (ed.), *Monumenta Juridica*, vol. 1 (London: Longman & Co., 1873), pp. 148–49 and "La Tabula de Amalfi" ("The Amalfian Table") in Sir Travers Twiss (ed.), *Monumenta Juridica*, vol. 4 (London: Longman & Co., 1873), pp. 12–13 and pp. 26–27.

5. Pierino Belli, *A Treatise On Military Matters and Warfare in Eleven Parts*, trans. Herbet C. Nutting (Washington: Carnegie Institute, 1936), 2.9, 1–2, p. 83. Cf. the later remark on pirates in 2.12, 6, p. 85, which restates Bartolus' thesis in D. 49.19.2.

6. Balthazar de Ayala, *De Jure et Officiis Bellicis et Disciplina Militari Libri III*, 1.2, 14, p. 10; *Three Books on the Law of War and on the Duties Connected with War and on Military Discipline*, vol. 1, ed. John Westlake (Washington: Carnegie Institution of Washington, 1912), p. 11.

7. Ayala, *Three Books on the Law of War and on the Duties Connected with War and on Military Discipline,* 1.2, pp. 11–12. The published English translation appears to be based on the edition of 1597.

8. The 1589 title was *De Jure Belli Commentationes Tres*; the edition of 1612 bears the title by which the treatise has been called ever since, *De Iure Belli Libri Tres*.

9. Rubin, *The Law of Piracy*, p. 28.

10. Alberico Gentili, *Three Books on the Law of War*, trans. John C. Rolfe (Washington: Carnegie Endowment for International Peace, 1933), 1.3, p. 15; *De Iure Belli Libri Tres* (Hanau: Apud Haeredes Guilielmi Antonii, 1612), p. 22.

11. Gentili, *Three Books on the Law of War*, 1.3, p. 15; *De Iure Belli Libri Tres*, p. 22.

12. Gentili, *Three Books on the Law of War*, 1.3, p. 20; *De Iure Belli Libri Tres*, p. 32.

13. Gentili, *Three Books on the Law of War*, 1.3, p. 15; *De Iure Belli Libri Tres*, p. 23.

14. Gentili, *Three Books on the Law of War*, 1.3, p. 22; *De Iure Belli Libri Tres*, p. 36.

15. *Ibid.*

16. *Ibid.*

17. Gentili, *Three Books on the Law of War*, 1.4, p. 22; *De Iure Belli Libri Tres*, p. 35.

18. Gentili, *Three Books on the Law of War*, 1.4, p. 24; *De Iure Belli Libri Tres*, p. 39.

19. *Ibid.*

20. Gentili, *Three Books on the Law of War*, 1.4, p. 25; *De Iure Belli Libri Tres*, p. 40.

21. *Ibid.*

22. *Ibid.*

23. Gentili, *Three Books on the Law of War*, 1.4, p. 25; *De Iure Belli Libri Tres*, p. 41.

24. Rubin, *The Law of Piracy*, p. 29.

25. Gentili, *Three Books on the Law of War*, 1.4, p. 26; *De Iure Belli Libri Tres*, p. 40.

26. Gentili, *Three Books on the Law of War*, 1.4, p. 26; *De Iure Belli Libri Tres*, pp. 41–42.

27. Rubin, *The Law of Piracy*, p. 30.

28. *Ibid.*

29. For the collection of the jurist's writings to that end, see Alberico Gentili, *Hispanicae Advocationis Libri Duo* (Amsterdam: Johannes Ravenstein, 1661); *The Two Books of the Pleas of a Spanish Advocate of Alberico Gentili, Jurisconsult*, trans. Frank Frost Abbott (Washington, D.C.: Carnegie Endowment for International Peace, 1921).

30. The French king Henri IV appears to have graced the fifteen-year old Grotius with the title "miracle of Holland," exclaiming, upon meeting the young Dutchman in 1598, "Voilà le miracle de Hollande!" See Edward Dumbauld, *The Life and Legal Writings of Hugo Grotius* (Norman, Oklahoma: University of Oklahoma Press, 1969), p. 56 n.165.

31. Grotius, *The Law of War and Peace, in Three Books, Wherein Are Set Forth the Law of Nature and of Nations Also the Principles of Public Law*, trans. Francis W. Kelsey (Washington, D.C.: Carnegie Endowment for International Peace, 1925), 3.2, p. 630; *De Jure Belli ac Pacis*, p. 449.

32. *Ibid.* On the terminology of "pirate" in Grotius, cf. Rubin, *The Law of Piracy*, pp. 38–39.

33. Grotius, *The Law of War and Peace*, 3.2, pp. 631–32; *De Jure Belli ac Pacis*, pp. 449–50.

34. Cornelius van Bynkershoek, *Quaestionum Juris Publici Libri Duo* (Lugduni Batavorum: Apud Joannem van Kerckhem, 1737), p. 124; *Two Books of Questions of Public Law*, trans. Tenney Frank (Washington, D.C.: Carnegie Endowment for

International Peace, 1930), p. 99.

35. Grotius, *The Law of War and Peace*, 3.3, pp. 632–33; *De Jure Belli ac Pacis*, p. 450.

36. Richard Zouche, *An Exposition of Fecial Law and Procedure, or of Law between Nations, and Questions concerning the Same*, trans. J. L. Brierly (Washington, D.C.: Carnegie Endowment for International Peace, 1911), 1.7, pp. 34–38; *Iuris et Iudicii Fecialis, Sive, Iuris Inter Gentes, et Quaestionum de Eodem Explicatio* (Oxford, UK: T. Robinson, 1650), pp. 31–35.

37. Zouche, *An Exposition of Fecial Law and Procedure*, 1.7, p. 38; *Iuris et Iudicii Fecialis, Sive, Iuris Inter*, p. 35.

38. Molloy, *A Treatise of Affaires Maritime and of Commerce in Three Books*, pp. 29–30. Cf. William Blackstone, *Commentaries on the Laws of England*, vol. 4 (Oxford, UK: Clarendon Press, 1765–68), p. 71: "The crime of *piracy*, or robbery and depredation upon the high seas, is an offense against the universal law of society; a pirate being, according to Sir Edward Coke, *hostis humani generis*." Cf. Sir Edward Coke, *The Third Part of the Institutes of the Laws of England Concerning High Treason, and Other Pleas of the Crown, and Criminall Causes* (London: M. Flesher, for W. Lee, and D. Pakeman, 1644), p. 113.

39. William Wynn, *The Life of Sir Leoline Jenkins* (London: Joseph Downing; William Taylor; William and John Innys; and John Osborn, 1724), p. lxxxvi.

40. Vattel, *The Law of Nations*, 3.12, §190, p. 305; *Le droit des gens*, 3, p. 91.

41. Stephen C. Neff, *War and the Law of Nations: A General History* (Cambridge, UK: Cambridge University Press, 2005), p. 88.

42. Carl Schmitt, *Der Nomos Der Erde Im Völkerrecht Des Jus Publicum Europaeum*, 4th ed. (Berlin: Duncker & Humblot, 1997), esp. pp. 136–40.

43. Wolff, *The Law of Nations Treated According to a Scientific Method*, 7, §778, p. 402; *Jus gentium*, p. 632.

44. Wolff, *The Law of Nations Treated According to a Scientific Method*, 6, §627 p. 319; *Jus gentium*, pp. 498–99. The phrase "monster of the human species" (*generis humani monstrum*) appears twice in the note. Cf. 6, §652, which addresses the related question of the "disturber of public security" (*turbator securitatis publicae*). Cf. Locke's claim in the *Second Treatise on Government* that he who breaks to pieces governments "is justly to be esteemed the common enemy and pest of mankind" (*Second Treatise*, 19, § 230).

45. Vattel, *The Law of Nations*, 3.3, §34, p. 246; *Le droit des gens*, 3, p. 15. On

"the enemy of the human species," see *The Law of Nations* 3.8, §155, pp. 279–89. On violators of the law of nations in Vattel more generally, see Dan Edelstein, "War and Terror: The Law of Nations from Grotius to the French Revolution," *French Historical Studies* 31.2 (2008), pp. 241–44.

46. Vattel, *The Law of Nations*, 3.8, §155, p. 293; *Le droit des gens*, 3, pp. 76–77.

47. Vattel, *The Law of Nations*, 3.4, § 68, p. 258; *Le droit des gens*, 3, p. 31. The conception of pirates living in a state of "savagery" is, of course, not exclusive to Vattel; see, for instance, Blackstone's account, in different but related terms: "As therefore he [the pirate] has renounced the benefits of society and government, and has reduced himself to the savage state of nature, by declaring war against all mankind, all mankind must declare war against him." Blackstone, *Commentaries on the Law of England*, p. 71.

48. Wolff, *The Law of Nations Treated According to a Scientific Method*, 6, §627, p. 319; *Jus gentium*, p. 499. The marginal note in the treatise refers to *De Jure Belli ac Pacis.*, 3, 22, § 2 *sq.*

CHAPTER ELEVEN: LAW OF THE SEA CAMELS

1. See Gilbert Gidel, *Le droit international public de la mer* (Chateauroux: Les Établissements Mellottée, 1932–1934), p. 157; Thomas Wemyss Fulton, *The Sovereignty of the Sea, an Historical Account of the Claims of England to the Dominion of the British Seas, and of the Evolution of the Territorial Waters: With Special Reference to the Rights of Fishing and the Naval Salute* (Edinburgh and London: William Blackwood and Sons, 1911), p. 4.

2. See Fulton, *The Sovereignty of the Sea*, p. 4 n.1.

3. *Mare Liberum Sive de Jure quod Batavis Competiti ad Indicana Commercia Dissertatio.* The *Mare Liberum* appeared anonymously in 1609; Grotius was not identified as its author until the edition of 1618. As late as 1617, Welwood could allude to "a book called *Mare Liberum*" by "an unknown author." See Fulton, *The Sovereignty of the Sea*, p. 342 n.1.

4. Suarez, *The Sovereignty of the Sea*, p. 338.

5. Grotius, *The Freedom of the Seas, or the Right Which Belongs to the Dutch to Take Part in the East Indian Trade,* ed. James Brown Scott, Carnegie Endowment for International Peace, Division of International Law (New York: Oxford University Press, 1916), vol. 1, p. 6 (*iure gentium quibusvis ad quovis liberam esse navigationis*).

6. Alfonso de Castro, *De Potestate Legis Poenalis* (Lyon, 1566); Fernando

Vázquez de Menchaca, *Illustrium Controversiarum Aliorumque usu Frequentium Libri Tres* (Venice, 1564).

7. As Fulton notes in *The Sovereignty of the Seas*, p. 349, this claim contains the "germ" of the principle according to which territorial sovereignty ends *ubi finitur armorum vis*, which Bynkershoek famously advanced. See n. 20 below.

8. The treaty was signed in the spring of 1609. See Fulton's reference to Jean Dumont, *Le corps diplomatique*, in *The Sovereignty of the Seas*, p. 350.

9. See the various treatises listed in Fulton, *The Sovereignty of the Sea*, p. 351 n.1.

10. Seraphin de Freitas, *De Iusto Iperii Lusitanorum Imperio Asiatico Adversus Grotii Mare Liberum* (Valladolid, 1625).

11. See William Welwood, *An Abridgement of All Sea-Lawes*, vol. 27 (London: T. Man, 1613), pp. 199–236. On Grotius and Welwood, see Fulton, *The Sovereignty of the Sea*, pp. 352–58; Ernest Nys, *Les origines du droit international* (Bruxelles: A. Castaigne, 1894), pp. 385–86; Samuel Muller, *Mare Clausum, Bijdrage Tot de Geschiedenis der Rivaliteit van Engeland en Nederland in de Zeventiende Eeuw* (Amsterdam: F. Muller, 1872), pp. 76–85.

12. William Welwood, *De Dominio Maris, Iuribusque ad Dominium Praecipe Spectantibus Assertio Brevis* (Cosmpoli: G. Fonti-Filuius, 1615).

13. John Selden, *Mare Clausum, Seu De Dominio Maris Libri Duo* (London: Will. Stensbeii pro Richardo Meighen, 1636).

14. On Grotius and Selden, see, among others, Ernest Nys, "Une bataille de livres: Épisode de l'histoire littéraire du droit international," in *Études de droit international et de politique* (Paris: A. Fontemoing, 1901), pp. 261–72; Fulton, *The Sovereignty of the Seas*, pp. 336–77; Ziskind, "The International Legal Status of the Sea in Antiquity," pp. 35–49; Pitman B. Potter, *The Freedom of the Seas in History, Law, and Politics* (New York: Longmans, Green & Co., 1924), pp. 57–80.

15. See Grotius's *Defensio capitis quinti Maris liberi oppugnati a Gulielmo Welwodo juris civilis professore* in Muller, *Mare clausum*, pp. 331–60.

16. The work was titled *Maris liberi vindicaei adversus virum clarissimum Johannem Seldenum*. See Nys, "Une bataille de livres," p. 269.

17. Nys, "Une bataille de livres," pp. 261–72.

18. *Ibid.*, pp. 271–72.

19. Samuel Pufendorf, *Of the Law of Nature and Nations*, 3rd ed., trans. Basil Kennet (London: R. Sare et al., 1717), 4.5, pp. 167–68; *De Jure Naturae Et Gentium Libri Octo* (London: Sumtibus Adami Junghans iprimebat Vitus Haberegger, 1672),

pp. 386–87.

20. See Bynkershoek, *De Dominio Maris Dissertatio*, in *Opera Minora* (Lugduni Batavorum: Joannem van Kerckhem, 1744), vol. 2, p. 364; *On the Sovereignty of the Seas*, trans. Ralph van Deman Magoffin (Washington: Carnegie Endowment for International Peace, 1923), pp. 44–45. Bynkershoek later reaffirmed the view in his *Quaestionum Juris Publici Libri Duo* (Lugduni Batavorum: Apud Joannem van Kerckhem, 1737). On Bynkershoek and the principle of *armorum vis*, see Wyndham L. Walker, "Territorial Waters: The Canon Shot Rule," *British Yearbook of International Law* 22 (1945), pp. 210–31.

21. Wolff, *The Law of Nations Treated According to a Scientific Method*, vol. 1, §127, p. 71; *Jus gentium*, p. 103.

22. Vattel, *The Law of Nations*, vol. 1, xxiii, §279, p. 106; *Le droit des gens*, vol. 1, pp. 243–44.

23. Vattel, *The Law of Nations*, vol. 1, xxiii, §279, p. 106; *Le droit des gens*, vol. 1, p. 245.

24. C. John Colombos, *The International Law of the Seas*, 6th ed. (New York: David McKay Company Inc., 1967), p. 47.

25. Vattel, *The Law of Nations*, vol. 1, xxiii, §289, p. 108; *Le droit des gens*, vol. 1, p. 249.

26. Fulton, *The Sovereignty of the Sea*, p. 539.

27. Wilhelm G. Grewe, *Epochen der Völkerrechtsgeschichte* (Baden-Baden: Nomos Verlagsgesellschaft, 1984) p. 383. On the history of the demarcation of the high seas more generally, see Grewe, *Epochen der Völkerrechtsgeschichte*, pp. 374–87; Fulton, *The Sovereignty of the Sea*, pp. 537–603.

28. Though the rule is most often identified with Bynkershoek, it long predated him. Thus a document of the Dutch Embassy from 1610 stipulates, "For it is by the Law of nacions, no prince can Challenge further into the Sea then he can Command with a Cannon." See Fulton, *The Sovereignty of the Sea*, p. 156 n.1.

29. See Fernando Galiani, *De' Doveri de' principi neutrali verso i pirncipi guerreggianti, e di questi verso i neutrali* (Naples, 1782), p. 432. On Galiani, see Walker, "Territorial Waters," pp. 228–30.

30. See Colombos, *International Law of the Sea*, p. 47.

31. "Perpetual Peace: A Philosophical Sketch," in H. S. Reiss (ed.), *Kant: Political Writings* (Cambridge, UK: Cambridge University Press, 1991), p. 106; Immanuel Kant, "Zum Ewigen Frieden," in *Gesammelte Schriften*, vol. 8 (Berlin:

de Gruyter, 1983), p. 358.

32. For *herrenlos* in Kant as a translation of *res nullius*, see, most famously, the wording of the juridical postulate in *Die Metaphysik der Sitten*, in *Werke: Akademie-Textausgabe*, vol. 6 (Berlin: De Gruyter, 1968), p. 246. On the legal use of the term in German, cf. Johannes Krüger, *Zum Begriffe "Herrenlos" im bürgerlichen Gesetzbuch* (Leipzig: Robert Noske, 1905).

33. "Perpetual Peace: A Philosophical Sketch," in H.S. Reiss (ed.), *Kant: Political Writings* (Cambridge, UK: Cambridge University Press, 1991), p. 106; Kant, "Zum Ewigen Frieden," p. 358.

34. *Ibid.*

35. Vattel, *The Law of Nations*, 1.19, §216, p. 88; *Le droit des gens*, vol. 2, p. 16.

36. Gilbert Gidel, *Le droit international public de la mer,* p. 248; Alexander Müller, *Die Piraterie im Völkerrecht unter besonderer Berüksichtigung des Entwurfes der Völkerbundskommission* (Grünberg: Hch. Ritter, 1929), p. 7.

37. Baldus on *Code* 9. 2.7; Cinus on *CJ.* 4.19.16. Cf. the illuminating discussion in Yan Thomas, *"Fictio Legis:* L'empire de la fiction romaine et ses limites médiévales," *Droit* 21 (1995), p. 17.

38. *Ibid.*, p. 17.

39. William Edward Hall, *A Treatise on International Law*, 8th ed. (Oxford, UK: Clarendon Press, 1924), pp. 217–18.

40. *Ibid.*

41. United Nations, *Convention on the High Seas, Treaty Series*, no. 6465, vol. 450 (Geneva, 1958), art. 8.

42. Colombos, *International Law of the Sea*, p. 259.

43. Fulton, *The Sovereignty of the Sea*, p. 262.

44. Baron Ferdinand de Cournot Cussy, *Phases et causes célèbres du droit maritime des nations*, vol. 2 (Leipzig: F. A. Brockhaus, 1856), p. 147. Cf. the very similar terms invoked earlier by General Dupin before the Cour de Cassation as described by Cussy on p. 89.

45. See Colombos, *International Law of the Sea*, pp. 273–76.

46. Gidel, *Le droit international public de la mer*, p. 251 n.2.

47. Colombos, *International Law of the Sea*, p. 285.

48. *Ibid.*, pp. 286–87.

49. Henri Walther, *L'affaire du "Lotus"; ou, De l'abordage hauturier en droit pénal international* (Paris: Les Éditions Internationales, 1928), p. 187.

50. On the legal status of the merchant vessel, see A. Pearce Higgens, "Le régime juridique des navires de commerce en haute mer en temps de paix," *Académie de droit international, Recueil de Cours*, vol. 30 (1929), pp. 5–77; and, for a more historical overview (with a discussion of Hübner and Lampredi), Eugène Cauchy, *Le droit maritime international*, vol. 2, pp. 153–57 and pp. 274–76.

51. Hall, *A Treatise on International Law*, p. 310.

52. *Ibid.*, pp. 310–11.

53. Colombos, *International Law of the Sea*, p. 288.

54. *Ibid.*, p. 446. Cf. Gerhard Schlikker, *Die völkerrechtliche Lehre von der Piraterie und den ihr gleichgestellten Verbrechen* (Borna-Leipzig: Robert Noske, 1907), pp. 8–11; Paul Stiel, *Der Tatbestand der Piraterie nach geltendem Völkerrecht*, Staats- und völkerrechtliche Abhandlungen, vol. 2.4 (Leipzig: Duncker & Humblot, 1905), pp. 5–10.

55. Müller, *Die Piraterie im Völkerrecht*, p. 7.

CHAPTER TWELVE: OF IRON CAGES AND *U-BOOTS*

1. Herman Melville, "Benito Cereno," in *Billy Budd and Other Stories*, ed. Frederick Busch (New York: Penguin, 1986), pp. 221–22.

2. Edgar Allan Poe, *The Narrative of Arthur Gordon Pym*, ed. Richard Kopley (New York: Penguin, 1994), p. 101.

3. Lucian, *Lucian: Phalaris. Hippias or the Bath. Dionysus. Heracles. Amber or the Swans. The Fly. Nigrinus. Demonax. The Hall. My Native Land. Octogenarians. A True Story. Slander. the Consonants at Law. The Carousel (Symposium) or the Lapiths*, vol. 1, trans. M. A. Harmon (Cambridge, MA: Harvard University Press, 1913), pp. 342–45.

4. Richard Stoneman, *The Greek Alexander Romance* (London: Penguin Books, 1991), p. 118.

5. On the literary and iconographical traditions of Alexander beneath the seas, see the chapter "Alexander and the Faithless Lady" in David J. Ross, *Studies in the Alexander Romance* (London: Pindar Press, 1985), pp. 382–403.

6. Stoneman, *The Greek Alexander Romance*, pp. 118–19.

7. See the Latin and Old French texts in Alfons Hilka, *Der altfranzösische Prosa-Alexander-Roman nach der Berliner Bilderhandschrift, nebst dem lateinischen Original der Historia de Preliis* (Halle: Niemeyer, 1920), pp. 231–33.

8. Alexander of Paris, *Le roman d'Alexandre*, ed. E. C. Armstrong et al., trans.

Laurence Harf-Lancner (Paris: Le Livre de Poche, 1994), pp. 320–21.

9. Alexander of Paris, *Le roman d'Alexandre*, pp. 316–17.

10. See Llewellyn Atherly-Jones, "The Deutschland," *Papers Read before the Grotius Society in the Year 1917* 3 (1917), p. 39.

11. See Colombos, *International Law of the Sea*, p. 511. On the *jeune école*'s theories of the submarine, see Arne Røksund, *The Jeune École: The Strategy of the Weak* (Leiden: Brill, 2007), pp. 177–244.

12. Colombos, *International Law of the Sea*, p. 511.

13. Jules Verne, *Vingt mille lieues sous les mers,* ed. Jacques Noiray (Paris: Folio Gallimard, 2005), p. 118.

14. James Wilford Garner, *International Law and the World War*, vol. 1 (London: Longmans, Green and Co., 1920), p. 357.

15. See Max Fleischmann, (ed.), "Der Lusitania Fall im Urteile von deutschen Gelehrten," *Zeitschrift für Völkerrecht* 9 (1916), p. 159. Garner refers to this phrase in *International Law and the World War*, vol. 1, p. 375.

16. Ernst Zitelmann, "The War and International Law," trans. Mitchell Kennerly, *Modern Germany in Relation to the Great War, by Various German Authors* (New York, 1916), p. 609. This passage is also quoted in Garner, *International Law and the World War*, pp. 375–76.

17. Garner, *International Law and the World War*, vol. 1, p. 370.

18. Raphael Semmes, *Memories of Service Afloat During the War Between the States* (Baltimore, MD: Kelly, Piet & Co., 1869), p. 131. Garner quotes this passage in *International Law and the World War*, pp. 370–71.

19. Garner, *International Law and the World War*, pp. 373–74.

20. *Ibid.*, p. 374.

21. On the Washington Conference, see Ronald Roxburgh. "Submarines at the Washington Conference," *British Yearbook of International Law* 3 (1922–1923), pp. 150–58; H. W. Malkin, "The Washington Conference (November 12, 1921–February 6, 1922)," *British Yearbook of International Law* 3 (1922–1923), pp. 179–82.

22. See London Naval Treaty in Dietrich Schindler and Jiří Toman, *The Laws of Armed Conflicts: A Collection of Conventions, Resolutions, and Other Documents*, 3rd ed. (Dorchecht: Nijhoff, 2004), pp. 881–82. That restriction of underwater warfare subsequently came to be incorporated into the London Protocol of November 6th, 1936. See the *procès-verbal* relating to the Rules of Submarine Warfare in Schindler and Toman, *The Laws of Armed Conflicts*, pp. 883–84.

23. George A. Finch, "Piracy in the Mediterranean," *The American Journal of International Law* 31.4 (1937), p. 659.

24. From the preamble of the Nyon Arrangement drafted at the Nyon Conference on the Prevention of Piratical Acts in the Mediterranean and Turkey. For the full text of the agreement, see Schindler and Toman, *The Laws of Armed Conflicts*, pp. 887–89.

25. *Ibid.*

26. Anonymous, "The Nyon Arrangements: Piracy by Treaty?" *British Yearbook of International Law* 19 (1938), p. 199. Finch observes, moreover, that seeds of the full-fledged formula may be found in Woodrow Wilson's statement before the U.S. Congress of April 2, 1917, that "the present German submarine warfare is a warfare against mankind. It is a war against all nations." Finch, "Piracy in the Mediterranean," p. 665.

27. Anonymous, "The Nyon Arrangements," p. 199.

28. See Anonymous,"The Nyon Arrangements"; Finch, "Piracy in the Mediterranean"; and Raoul Genet, "The Charge of Piracy in the Spanish Civil War," *The American Journal of International Law* 32.2 (1938), pp. 253–63. In his discussion of the Nyon Arrangement, Rubin stresses the fact that the references to "piracy" appear only in the preamble, concluding: "[T]he clauses in which they appear both look like late additions to the text and seem to reflect British positions trying to turn the political use of the word 'piracy' to some legal rule [....] It seems clear from the silence of the operative texts concluded at Nyon that not all of the countries represented there agreed that the word 'piratical' had any place in the legal rationale for their concurrences." Rubin, *The Law of Piracy*, pp. 319–20.

29. Anonymous, "The Nyon Arrangements," p. 198.

30. *Ibid.*, p. 199.

31. *Ibid.*, p. 208; cf. Finch, "Piracy in the Mediterranean," p. 644.

32. Anonymous, "The Nyon Arrangements," p. 208.

33. From a different perspective, cf. Finch, "Piracy in the Mediterranean," pp. 664–65.

34. Genet, "The Charge of Piracy," p. 254. Cf. "La qualification de 'pirates' et le dilemme de la guerre civile," *Revue internationale française du droit des gens* 3 (1937), pp. 13–25.

35. *Ibid.*, p. 256.

36. *Ibid.*, pp. 256–57.

37. *Ibid.*, p. 257.

38. Schmitt's paper appeared first in *Völkerbund und Völkerrecht* 4: 6–7 (September-October, 1937), pp. 351–54. It is reprinted in Schmitt, *Frieden oder Pazifismus? Arbeiten zum Völkerrecht und zur Internationalen Politik, 1924–1978*, ed. Günther Maschke (Berlin: Duncker & Humblot, 2005), pp. 509–11. After the war, Schmitt once again considered the historical significance of the submarine, see *Nomos der Erde*, pp. 290–93.

39. See Schmitt, "Il concetto della pirateria," *La vita italiana* 26 (1938), pp. 189–94.

40. Schmitt, "Letter to Jünger, November 14, 1937," in Helmuth Kiesel (ed.), *Briefe 1930–1983: Ernst Jünger, Carl Schmitt* (Stuttgart: Klett–Cotta, 1999), pp. 69–70. As Masckhe's notes to Schmitt's article indicate, Schmitt promptly mailed a copy of his essay to the *Oberkommando* of the German Marine, whose office duly responded with appreciation. See *Frieden oder Pazifismus*, p. 517.

41. Stiel, *Der Tatbestand der Piraterie*, p. 80. Schmitt quotes this phrase in *Frieden oder Pazifismus*, p. 508.

42. *Ibid.*

43. *Ibid.*, p. 509.

44. *Ibid.*, p. 508.

45. *Ibid.*

46. *Ibid.*

47. Schmitt, *Land und Meer: Eine weltgeschichtliche Betrachtung*, 4th ed. (Stuttgart: Klett–Cotta, 2001), pp. 43–44.

48. Schmitt, *Frieden oder Pazifismus?*, p. 510.

49. *Ibid.*

50. *Ibid.*, p. 508.

51. Schmitt, "Der Führer shützt das Reich. Zur Reichstagsrede Adolf Hitlers vom 13. Juli 1934," first published in *Deutsche Juristenzeitung* 39 (1934), pp. 945–50. It is reprinted in *Positionen und Begriffe im Kampf mit Wiemar* (Berlin: Duncker & Humblot, 1994), pp. 199–203.

52. Schmitt, *Frieden oder Pazifismus?*, p. 508.

53. Schmitt, *Positionen und Begriffe*, p. 200. Numerous texts bearing witness to Schmitt's sympathy with, and deference to, National Socialist doctrines of race could also be mentioned here. See in particular the report Schmitt published regarding the conference he organized in October 3–4, 1936 on the subject of

"German Juridical Science in Combat with the Jewish Spirit." This text has not been recently reprinted. See "Die Deutsche Rechtswissenschaft im Kampf gegen den Jüdischen Geist," *Deutsche Juristen–Zeitung* 40.20 (1936), pp. 1193–99.

54. Schmitt, *Frieden oder Pazifismus?*, p. 509.

CHAPTER THIRTEEN: JUSTIFYING HUMANITY

1. See Yan Thomas, "Brève histoire de la notion juridique de la personne," in Yan Thomas and Olivier Cayla, *Du droit de ne pas naître, À propos de l'affaire Perruche* (Paris: Gallimard, 2002), esp. pp. 126–27. Cf. Yan Thomas, "Le sujet du droit, la personne et la nature: Sur la critique contemporaine du sujet de droit," *Le débat* 100 (1998), pp. 85–107.

2. Hugo Donnellus, *Commentaria Iuri Civilis*, vol. 1 (Naples, 1763), p. 65. There is a discussion of Donnellus's distinction in Thomas and Cayla, *Du droit de ne pas naître*, p. 130 n.1.

3. "Ius naturale est, quod natura omnia animalia docuit: nam ius istud non humani generis proprium, sed omnium animalium, quae in terra, quae in mari nascuntur, avium quoque commune est." Ulpian, *Institutes* 1, in *Dig* 1.1.3.

4. *Selections from Three Works of Francisco Suárez, S. J.: De Legibus, ac Deo legislatore 1612; Defensio fidei catholicae, et apostolicae adversus anglicanae sectae errors, 1613; De triplici virtute theologica, fide, spe, et charitate, 1612*, trans. Gwladys L. Williams, Ammi Brown and John Waldron, rev. Henry Davis, S. J. and an introduction by James Brown Scott (Oxford, UK: The Clarendon Press, 1944), vol. 2, pp. 348–49; *De Legibus*, in *Selections from Three Works of Francisco Suárez*, vol. 1, pp. 190–91. On the passage, see James Brown Scott, *The Catholic Conception of International Law: Francisco De Vitoria, Founder of the Modern Law of Nations, Francisco Suárez, Founder of the Modern Philosophy of Law in General and in Particular of the Law of Nations, a Critical Examination and a Justified Appreciation* (Washington, D.C.: Georgetown University Press, 1934), pp. 483–94. Cf. Jean–François Courtine, *Nature et empire de la loi: Études suáreziennes* (Paris: Vrin, 1999), pp. 115–61 and esp. 155–61.

5. *Selections from Three Works of Francisco Suárez*, vol. 2, pp. 348–49; *Selections from Three Works of Francisco Suárez*, vol. 1, p. 190 (italics mine).

6. Wolff, *The Law of Nations Treated According to a Scientific Method*, vol. 2, §161, p. 86; *Jus gentium*, p. 168.

7. Wolff, *The Law of Nations Treated According to a Scientific Method*, vol. 2, §161 p. 87; *Jus gentium*, p. 129.

8. Wolff, *The Law of Nations Treated According to a Scientific Method*, vol. 2, §164, p. 88; *Jus gentium*, p. 129.

9. Vattel, *The Law of Nations*, vol. 2, 1, §1–20, pp. 113–20; *Le droit des gens*, vol. 1, pp. 145–55.

10. Vattel, *The Law of Nations*, vol. 2, 1, §2, p. 114; *Le droit des gens*, vol. 1, p. 146.

11. Vattel, *The Law of Nations*,vol. 2, 1, §5, p. 115.

12. *Ibid.*

13. *Ibid.*

14. Vattel, *The Law of Nations*, vol. 2, 1, §20, p. 120 ; *Le droit des gens*, p. 155.

15. Kant, *The Metaphysics of Morals*, trans. Mary Gregor (Cambridge, UK: Cambridge University Press, 1991), p. 195; *Gesammelte Schriften*, vol. 6, p. 392. Cf. the different definitions in *Kritik der Urteilskraft*, §60 and *Religion innerhalb der Grenzen der bloßen Vernunft*, in *Gesammelte Schriften*, vol. 6, pp. 21 and 26.

16. Kant, *The Metaphysics of Morals*, p.191; *Gesammelte Schriften*, vol. 6, p. 387.

17. Kant, *The Metaphysics of Morals*, pp. 216 and 225; *Gesammelte Schriften*, vol. 6, pp. 420 and 429.

18. For references in the *Metaphysik der Sitten* alone, see Kant, *The Metaphysics of Morals*, pp. 62, 97, 185n, 219, 225, 230, 236; *Gesammelte Schriften*, vol. 6, pp. 236, 278, 379n, 423, 429, 435, 441.

19. Kant, *Metaphysics of Morals*, p. 62; *Gesammelte Schriften*, vol. 6, p. 236. On the formula *lex iusti*, see Byrd, Sharon B. and Joachim Hruschka, "Lex iusti, lex iuridica und lex iustitiae in Kants Rechtslehre," *Archiv für Rechts-und Sozialphilosophie* 91.4 (2005), pp. 484–500.

20. See "The Metaphysical First Principles of the Doctrine of Virtue," in Kant, *The Metaphysics of Morals*, pp. 254–59; *Gesammelte Schriften*, vol. 6, pp. 462–68.

21. Kant, *The Metaphysics of Morals*, p. 216; *Gesammelte Schriften*, vol. 6, p. 420.

22. Kant, *The Metaphysics of Morals*, p. 96; *Gesammelte Schriften*, vol. 6, p. 429.

23. The term is Walter Benjamin's. See *Zur Kritik der Gewalt* in *Gesammelte Schriften*, p. 187.

24. Kant, *The Metaphysics of Morals*, p. 168; *Gesammelte Schriften*, vol. 6, pp. 362–63. On Kantian "humanity," see Thomas E. Hill, "Humanity as an End in Itself," *Ethics* 91.1 (1980), pp. 84–99.

25. Reinhart Koselleck, "The Historical-Political Semantics of Asymmetric Counterconcepts," in *Futures Past: On the Semantics of Historical Time*, trans. Keith Tribe (Cambridge, MA: The MIT Press, 1985), pp. 159–97 and 189.

26. *Ibid.*

27. Koselleck notes that "among the Stoics, where *genus humanum* can be addressed most honestly as a political entity, the adjective *inhumanum* already appears as a means of defining the boundary at which a person ceases to be a member of universal human society." *Futures Past*, p. 187.

28. Michael Walzer (ed.), *Regicide and Revolution: Speeches at the Trial of Louis XVI* (New York: Columbia University Press, 1993), p. 138.

29. The clause can be found in the Preamble to the 1899 Second Convention, in F. Stoerk (ed.), *Nouveau recueil général de traités*, vol. 26 (Leipzig: Librairie Dieterich, 1902), as well as in the Fourth Convention of 1907, in H. Triepel (ed.), *Nouveau recueil general de traités*, vol. 3 (Leipzig: Librairie Dieterich), p. 323.

30. See Sévane Garibian, "Génocide arménien et conceptualization du crime contre l'humanité. De l'intervention pour cause d'humanité à l'intervention pour violation des lois de l'humanité," *Revue d'Histoire de la Shoah* 177–178 (2003), p. 278.

31. See the discussion of the terms in Garibian, "Génocide arménien," p. 279.

32. Garibian, "Génocide arménien," p. 266. The Treaty of Sèvres of 1922, by contrast, appears to have omitted all reference to any abstract principle of the species; instead it introduced a distinction between breaches of the law of war, on the one hand, and "massacres," where that term seems to extend to acts contrary to the laws of humanity. The general statements issued by the Allied powers against the Central Empires in the Preliminary Peace Conference of 1919 also included references to violations of "customs of war and the elementary laws of humanity," though not "crimes against humanity." Cf. Egon Schwelb, "Crimes against Humanity," *British Yearbook of International Law* 23 (1946), pp. 178–226 and esp. 180–83.

33. See the summary in Garibian, "Génocide arménien," pp. 286–87.

34. *Charter of the International Military Tribunal, Nuremberg Trial Proceedings*, vol. 1 (1945). On article 6 (c), see Schwelb, "Crimes against Humanity," pp. 188–97.

35. V. A. Röling, "The Nuremberg and Tokyo Trial in Retrospect," in M. Chérif Bassiouni and Ved P. Nanda (eds.), *A Treatise on International Criminal Law* (Springfield, IL: Thomas, 1973), p. 592. Cf. Röling and Cassese's incisive remarks in *The Tokyo Trial and Beyond: Reflections of a Peacemonger* (Cambridge, MA: Polity Press, 1993), pp. 55–56.

36. Three years later, in 1948, an international convention adopted by the United Nations General Assembly confirmed that motion: "[A]cts committed

with intent to destroy, in whole or in part, a national, ethnical, racial or religious group," now officially termed "genocide"—or literally, "the killing of a kind"—were pronounced "a crime under international law." The term "humanity" does not appear in the text of the Convention (see *Convention on the Prevention and Punishment of the Crime of Genocide*, article 1). One might well wonder whether, and to what extent, the notion of "crimes against humanity" is indeed compatible with the idea of "genocide." The form of the first term insists on the unity of the species, grasped as one legal subject; the second term instead intends a "genus" that coincides with a single nation. The question of whether the murder of the Jews is better considered a "crime against humanity" or an act of "genocide," therefore, is far from trivial.

37. Hannah Arendt, *Eichmann in Jerusalem: A Report on the Banality of Evil* (London: Penguin Books, 1994), pp. 261–62; Röling and Cassese, *The Tokyo Trial and Beyond*, pp. 96–97; M. Chérif Bassiouni, "The History of Universal Jurisdiction and Its Place in International Law," in Stephen Macedo (ed.), *Universal Jurisdiction: National Courts and the Prosecution of Serious Crimes under International Law* (Philadelphia: University of Pennsylvania Press, 2003), pp. 39–63.

CHAPTER FOURTEEN: EARTH AND SEA

1. Schmitt, *Der Nomos der Erde*, p. 13.

2. *Ibid.*, p. 12

3. Revelations 21:1.

4. John Locke, *Second Treatise*, ch. 8, §121.

5. Kant, *The Metaphysics of Morals*, vol. 1, §12; cf. vol. 1, §16.

6. See W. Schoenborn, "La nature juridique du territoire," *Recueil des cours de l'Académie de Droit International de La Haye* (1929), vol. 30, pp. 101–102.

7. Claude Blumann, "Frontières et limites," in *La frontière: colloque de Poitiers de la société française de droit international 1979* (Paris: SFDI, 1980), p. 4.

8. See Grewe, *Epochen der Völkerrechtsgeschichte*, pp. 374–81.

9. Schmitt, "The Theory of the Partisan: A Commentary/Remark on the Concept of the Political," trans. A. C. Goodson, *The New Centennial Review* 4.3 (2004), p. 3; *Theorie des Partisanen: Zwischenbemerkung zum Begriff des Politischen*, 4th ed. (Berlin: Duncker & Humblot, 1995), p. 11. A considerable body of scholarly literature on Schmitt's theory of the partisan exists. See, among others, Julien Freund, "Der Partisan oder der kriegerische Friede," in Helmut Quaritsch (ed.),

Complexio Oppositorum: Über Carl Schmitt (Berlin: Duncker & Humblot, 1988), pp. 387–91; Raymond Aron, *Penser la guerre, Clausewitz* (Paris: Gallimard, 1976), vol. 2, pp. 210–22; Jacques Derrida, *Politiques de l'amitié* (Paris: Galilée, 1994), pp. 162–71; Ernesto Laclau, "On 'Real' and 'Absolute' Enemies," *The New Centennial Review* 5.1 (2005), pp. 1–12; Rodolphe Gasché, "The Partisan and the Philosopher," *New Centennial Review* 4.3 (2004), pp. 9–34; Herfried Münkler, *Über den Krieg: Stationen der Kriegsgeschichte im Spiegel ihrer theoretischen Reflexion* (Weilerswist: Velbrück Wissenschaft, 2002), pp. 179–82. More material on Schmitt's theory may be found in Joachim Schickel, *Gespräche mit Carl Schmitt* (Berlin: Merve, 1983).

10. Schmitt, "The Theory of the Partisan," pp. 3–6; *Theorie des Partisanen*, pp. 11–17.

11. Schmitt's inventory of examples and the omissions it implies would be in itself worthy of investigation.

12. Schmitt, "Theory of the Partisan," p. 6; *Theorie des Partisanen*, p. 16.

13. Schmitt, "Theory of the Partisan," p. 13; *Theorie des Partisanen*, p. 26.

14. Schmitt, "Theory of the Partisan," pp. 13–14; *Theorie des Partisanen*, pp. 26–27.

15. Schmitt, "Theory of the Partisan," p. 20; *Theorie des Partisanen*, p. 35.

16. *Ibid.*

17. Schmitt, "Theory of the Partisan," pp. 49–50; *Theorie des Partisanen*, pp. 73–74.

CHAPTER FIFTEEN: INTO THE AIR

1. See Attachment to Warrant for Arrest issued by the U.S. District Court, District of Columbia, October 12, 1985, which alleged "piracy as defined by the law of nations," 24 ILM 1554 (1985); Malvina Halberstam, "Terrorism on the High Seas: The Achille Lauro, Piracy and the Imo Convention on Maritime Safety," *The American Journal of International Law* 82.2 (1988), p. 270 n.7; and L. C. Green, "Terrorism and the Law of the Sea," in Yoram and Mala Tabori Dinstein (eds.), *International Law at a Time of Perplexity: Essays in Honor of Shabtai Rosenne* (Dordrecht: Martinus Nijhoff, 1989), p. 263 n.70.

2. Lassa Oppenheim, *International Law: A Treatise*, ed. H. Lauterpacht, 8th ed. (London: Longmans, 1955), pp. 608–609.

3. Halberstam, "Terrorism on the High Seas," p. 273 n.16, citing *In Re Piracy Jure Gentium* (1934), App. Cas. 586, 598.

4. Halberstam, "Terrorism on the High Seas," p. 274 n.20, citing *United States v. The Ambrose Light*, 25 F. 408, 412–13 (S.D.N.Y., 1885).

5. Hall, *A Treatise on International Law*, p. 312.

6. See L. C. Green, "The *Santa Maria*: Rebels or Pirates," *British Yearbook of International Law* 37 (1961), p. 496.

7. Paul Stephen Dempsey, "Aerial Piracy and Terrorism: Unilateral and Multilateral Responses to Aircraft Hijacking," *Connecticut Journal of International Law* 2 (1986–1987), p. 429.

8. Celine Y. November, "Aircraft Piracy: The Hague Hijacking Convention," *The International Lawyer* 6.3 (1972), p. 642. On "air piracy," see also, among others, E. du Pontavice, "La piraterie aérienne: Notion et effets," *Revue générale de l'air et de l'espace* 32.3 (1969), pp. 276–339; John B. Rhinelander, "The International Law of Aerial Piracy: New Proposals for the New Dimension," in McWhinney, *Aerial Piracy and International Law* (Dobbs Ferry, NY: Oceana Publications, 1971), pp. 59–71; Rubin, "Terrorism and Piracy: A Legal View," *Studies in Conflict and Terrorism* 3.1–2 (1980), pp. 117–30; Jacon W. F. Sundberg, "Piracy: Air and Sea," *De Paul Law Review* 20 (1971), pp. 337–435.

9. De Watteville, *La piraterie aérienne*, p. 16.

10. De Watteville, *La piraterie aérienne*, p. 16. Cf. Jacobson, "From High Seas to High Air." Despite the technical imprecision of the expression, it remains in use in works of art, particularly in French. See Touret, *La piraterie au vingtième siècle: Piraterie maritime et aérienne*; McWhinney, (ed.), *Aerial Piracy and International Law*; Paul De la Pradelle, "La piraterie aérienne," *Annuaire de droit maritime et aérien* (1974), pp. 197–206; and De Watteville, *La piraterie aérienne*.

11. See T. Chetrit, "Le plan vigipirate," *Droit et défense* 4 (1995), pp. 57–60.

12. Jane Mayer, *The Dark Side: The Inside Story of How the War on Terror Turned into a War on American Ideals* (New York: Doubleday, 2008), p. 153. The literature on the notion of the "illegal enemy combatant" is already abundant. See, among many others, the contributions to Karen J. Greenberg (ed.), *The Torture Debate in America* (Cambridge, UK: Cambridge University Press, 2005).

CHAPTER SIXTEEN: TOWARD PERPETUAL WAR

1. For an effective summary, see Alexis Philonenko, "Kant et le problème de la paix," in *Essais sur la philosophie de la guerre* (Paris: Vrin, 1976), pp. 4–20 and 26–27. A vast body of scholarly literature has been devoted to Kant's late project

for perpetual peace. An exceptionally illuminating treatment can be found in Peter Fenves's chapter "Under the Sign of Failure," in *Late Kant: Towards Another Law of the Earth* (London: Routledge, 2003), pp. 92–113.

2. Kant, "Perpetual Peace: A Philosophical Sketch," p. 102; "Zum ewigen Frieden," *Werke*, vol. 8, p. 354.

3. Kant, "Perpetual Peace: A Philosophical Sketch," pp. 102–103; "Zum ewigen Frieden," *Werke*, vol. 8, p. 354.

4. Kant, *The Metaphysics of Morals*, p. 158; "Zum ewigen Frieden," *Werke*, vol. 6, p. 352.

5. Kant, "Perpetual Peace: A Philosophical Sketch," p. 106; "Zum ewigen Frieden," *Werke*, vol. 6, p. 358.

6. As Jean-Claude Milner has recently recalled, "limited does not mean finite; unlimited does not mean infinite. The set of possible values for the variable x in the function $1/x$ is infinite; but it is limited, since there is a value of x for which the function is not satisfied, namely $x=0$." Milner, *Les penchants criminels de l'Europe démocratique* (Paris: Verdier, 2003), pp. 19–20. Conversely, one might well imagine a world, such as that conceived by more than one medieval philosopher, in which God created a finite set of beings; the transcendental terms, such as "being," would then apply to all created things without limitation, though these terms would be finite in extension.

7. Kant, "Perpetual Peace: A Philosophical Sketch," p. 105; "Zum ewigen Frieden," *Werke*, vol. 8, p. 357.

8. *Ibid.*

9. *Ibid.*

10. Kant, *The Metaphysics of Morals*, p. 151; *Werke*, vol. 6, p. 344.

11. *Ibid.*

12. Kant, *The Metaphysics of Morals*, p. 150; *Werke*, vol. 6, p. 343.

13. Kant, *The Metaphysics of Morals*, pp. 152–53; *Werke*, vol. 6, p. 346.

14. Kant, *The Metaphysics of Morals*, p. 153; *Werke*, vol. 6, p. 347.

15. Kant, *The Metaphysics of Morals*, p. 154; *Werke*, vol. 6, p. 347.

16. Kant, *The Metaphysics of Morals*, p. 154; *Werke*, vol. 6, p. 348.

17. Kant, *The Metaphysics of Morals*, p. 155; *Werke*, vol. 6, p. 349.

18. *Ibid.*

19. Schmitt, *Nomos der Erde*, p. 141. On Schmitt, Kant, and the "unjust enemy," see, Jürgen Habermas, "Kants Idee des Ewigen Friedens—aus dem historischen

Abstand von 200 Jahren," *Kritische Justiz* 28 (1995), esp. pp. 294 n.2 and 309–19; Heinz-Gerd Schmitz, "Kants Lehre von *hostis iniustus* und Carl Schmitts Kritik dieser Konzeption," *Archiv für Rechts-und Sozialphilosophie* 89.3 (2003), pp. 399–417.

20. Schmitt, *Nomos der Erde*, p. 141.

21. Kant, *The Metaphysics of Morals*, p. 151; *Werke*, vol. 6, p. 344.

22. For the classic presentation of the categories, see Kant's discussion "On the Pure Concepts of the Understanding, or Categories" in the "Transcendental Analytic" of *The Critique of Pure Reason*. See Kant, *Werke*, vol. 4, pp. 63–67. On the distinction in Kant between quantity and quality, see Anneliese Maier, *Kants Qualitätskategorien*, Kant-Studien 65 (Pan-Verlag, Kurt Metzner: Berlin, 1930).

23. Kant, *The Metaphysics of Morals*, p. 155; *Werke*, vol. 6, p. 349.

24. Kant, *The Metaphysics of Morals*, pp. 155–56; *Werke*, vol. 6, p. 349.

25. Kant, *The Metaphysics of Morals*, p. 156; *Werke*, vol. 6, p. 349.

26. For Kant's account of the republican constitution, see "Perpetual Peace: A Philosophical Sketch," pp. 99–102; "Zum ewigen Frieden," *Werke*, vol. 8, pp. 357–60.

Bibliography

Albrecht, A. R, "War Reprisals in the War Crimes Trials and in the Geneva Conventions of 1949," *The American Journal of International Law* 47.4 (1953), pp. 590–614.

Amit, M., *Athens and the Sea: A Study in Athenian Sea-Power* (Louvain: Latomus, 1965).

Andrews, Kenneth R., *Elizabethan Privateering: English Privateering during the Spanish War, 1585–1603* (Cambridge: Cambridge University Press, 1966).

———, *Drake's Voyages: A Re-Assessment of Their Place in Elizabethan Maritime Expansion* (New York: Scribners, 1967).

———, "Sir Robert Cecil and Mediterranean Plunder," *The English Historical Review* 87.344 (1972), pp. 513–32.

Anonymous, "The Nyon Arrangements: Piracy by Treaty?" *British Yearbook of International Law* 19 (1938), pp. 198–208.

Arendt, Hannah, *Eichmann in Jerusalem: A Report on the Banality of Evil* (London: Penguin Books, 1994).

Aristotle, *Metaphysics 2: Books 10–14. Oeconomia. Magna Moralia* (Loeb Classical Library no. 287), trans. G. Cyril Armstrong (Cambridge, MA: Harvard University Press, 1958).

Aron, Raymond, *Penser la guerre: Clausewitz*, 2 vols. (Paris: Gallimard, 1976).

Ashburner, Walter, *The Rhodian Sea-Law* (Oxford: Oxford University Press, 1909).

Atherly-Jones, Llewellyn, "The Deutschland," *Papers Read before the Grotius Society in the Year 1917* 3 (1917), pp. 37–41.

Atkins, E. M, "Cicero," in Christopher Rowe and Malcolm Schofield (eds.), *The Cambridge History of Greek and Roman Political Thought* (Cambridge, UK:

Cambridge University Press, 2005), pp. 477–516.

Augustine, *City of God*, trans. Philip Schaff (New York: Christian Literature Publishing Company, 1890).

Autenrieth, Georg, *A Homeric Dictionary, for Schools and Colleges, Based Upon the German of Dr. Georg Autenrieth*, trans. Robert P. Keep (New York: Harper & Brothers, 1887).

Ayala, Balthazar de, *De Jure et Officiis Bellicis et Disciplina Militari Libri III* (Antwerp, 1582).

——, *Three Books on the Law of War and on the Duties Connected with War and on Military Discipline*, vol. 1, ed. John Westlake (Washington, D.C.: Carnegie Institution of Washington, 1912).

Bacquet, Jehan, *Des biens qui n'appartiennent à personne (res nullius) et des biens dont l'usage est commun à tous les hommes (res communes)* (Paris: Librairie Générale de Droit et de Jurisprudence, 1921).

Baldson, J. P. V. D, "Roman History, 58–56 BC: Three Ciceronian Problems," *The Journal of Roman Studies* 47.1/2 (1957), pp. 15–20.

Barbour, Violet, "Privateers and Pirates of the West Indies," *The American Historical Review* 16.3 (1911), pp. 529–66.

Barnes, Jonathan, "Cicéron et la guerre juste," *Bulletin de la société française de philosophie* 80 (1984), pp. 37–80.

Beauchet, Ludovic, *Histoire du droit privé de la république athénienne*, 4 vols. (Paris: Chevalier-Marescq & cie, 1897).

Belli, Pierino, *De Re Militari et Bello Tractatus* (Venice: Francesco di Portonari, 1563).

——, *A Treatise on Military Matters and Warfare in Eleven Parts*, trans. Herbert C. Nutting (Washington, D.C.: Carnegie Institute, 1936).

Benabou, Marcel, "Rome et la police des mers au Ier siècle avant J.-C.: La répression de la piraterie cilicienne," in Micheline Galley and Leïla Ladjimi Sebai (eds.), *L'homme méditerranéen et la mer: Actes du troisième Congrès International d'Études des Cultures de la Méditerranée Occidentale, 1981* (Jerba: Les Editions Salammbô, 1985), pp. 60–69.

Benjamin, Walter. *Gesammelte Schriften*, 7 vols., eds. Rolf Tiedemann and Hermann Schweppenhauser (Frankfurt-am-Main: Suhrkampf-Verlag, 1972–1989).

Benveniste, Émile, *Le vocabulaire des institutions indo-européennes*, 2 vols. (Paris: Éditions de Minuit, 1969).

Béranger, J., "À propos d'un *Imperium Infinitum*: Histoire et stylistique," in *Mélanges de philologie, de littérature et d'histoire anciennes, offerts à J. Marouzeau par ses collègues et élèves étrangers* (Paris: Les Belles Lettres, 1948), pp. 19–27.

Berber, Friedrich, "Von der Piraterie in der Antike," in Hans Peter Ipsen and Karl-Hartmann Necker (eds.), *Recht über See, Festschrift Rolf Stödter Zum 70. Gerburtstag* (Hamburg: Decker, 1979), pp. 147–53.

Bettini, Maurizio and Alberto Borghini, "La guerra e lo scambio: hostis, perduellis, inimicus," in Gruppo di Lecce della Società di Linguistica Italiana (ed.), *Linguistica e antropologia, Atti del XIV Congresso Internazionale di Studi. Lecce 23–25 maggio 1980* (Lecce: Bulzoni, 1980), pp. 303–12.

Biondi, Biondo, "Condizione giuridica del mare e del litus maris," *Studi in onore di Silvio Perozzi nel XI anno del suo insegnamento* (Palermo: Castiglia, 1925), pp. 269–80.

Biraghi, Gioietta, "La pirateria greca in Tucidide," *Acme* 5 (1952), pp. 471–77.

Peter Birks (ed.), *New Perspectives in the Roman Law of Property: Essays for Barry Nichols* (Oxford: Clarendon Press, 1989).

Blackburn, Robin, *The Overthrow of Colonial Slavery, 1776–1848* (London: Verso, 1988).

Blackstone, William, *Commentaries on the Laws of England*, 4 vols. (Oxford: Clarendon Press, 1765–1768).

Blumann, Claude, "Frontières et limites," in *La frontière: Colloque de Poitiers de la société française de droit international 1979* (Paris: SFDI, 1980), pp. 3–33.

Boak, A. E. R, "The Extraordinary Commands from 80 to 48 BC: A Study in the Origins of the Principate," *The American Historical Review* 24.1 (1918), pp. 1–25.

Boccaccio, Giovanni, *Il Decamerone*, ed. Vittore Branca, 2 vols. (Turin: Einaudi, 1980).

Bohman, James, "Punishment as a Political Obligation: Crimes against Humanity and the Enforceable Right to Membership," *Buffalo Criminal Law Review* 5 (2001–2002), pp. 551–90.

Bona, Ferdinando, "Postliminium in pace," *Studia et documenta iuris* 21 (1955), pp. 249–75.

———, "Preda di guerra e occupazione privata di 'res hostium'," *Studia et documenta iuris* 25 (1959), pp. 309–70.

Bono, Salvatore, *Les corsaires en Méditteranée*, trans. Ahmed Somaï (Paris: Paris-Méditteranée, 1998).

Boulton, J. W., "Maritime Order and the Development of the International Law of Piracy," *International Relations* 7.5 (1983), pp. 2335–350.

———, "The Modern International Law of Piracy: Content and Contemporary Relevance," *International Relations* 7.6 (1983), pp. 2493–551.

Branca, Giuseppe, "Le cose extra patrimonium humani iuris," *Annali Triestini di diritto economia Annali Triestini di diritto economia e politica* 2 (1941).

Braudel, Fernand, *La méditerrannée et le monde méditerranéen à l'époque de Philippe II* (Paris: A. Colin, 1966).

Bravo, Benedetto, "Sulân: Représailles et justice privée contres les étrangers dans les cités grecques (étude du vocabulaire et des institutions)," *Annali della scuola normale superiore di Pisa X.3* (1980), pp. 675–987.

———, "Androlêpsíai: La prise d'hommes comme vengeance d'un meurtre dans une cité étrangère," in Joseph Modrzejewski and Detlef Liebs (eds.), *Symposion 1977: Vorträge zur griechischen und hellenistischen Rechtsgeschichte* (Cologne and Vienna: Böhlau, 1981), pp. 131–56.

Brecht, C. H., *Zur Abgrenzung des Begriffes Perduellio von den verwandten Verbrechensbegriffen im römischen Strafrecht bis zum Ausgang der Republik* (Munich: Beck, 1938).

Brongniart, Henry, *Les corsaires et la guerre maritime* (Paris: Augustin Challamel, 1904).

Brulé, Pierre, *La piraterie crétoise hellénistique*, Centre de Recherches d'Histoire Ancienne, vol. 27 (Besançon: Université de Besançon, 1978).

Bruns, Carl Georg, *Fontes Iuris Romani Antiqui,* 2 vols. (Tübingen: Mohr, 1909).

Burgess, Glyn S. (ed.), *Two Medieval Outlaws: Eustace the Monk and Fouke Fitz Waryn* (Cambridge: D. S. Brewer, 1997).

Bynkershoek, Cornelius van, *Quaestionum Juris Publici Libri Duo* (Lugduni Batavorum: Apud Joannem van Kerckhem, 1737).

———, *Opera Minora, Olim Separatim, Nunc Conjunctim Edita, Recensuit Et Nonnulla Addidit Auctor,* 2nd ed. (Lugduni Batavorum: Joannem van Kerckhem, 1744).

———, *De Dominio Maris Dissertatio*, in *Opera Minora* (Lugduni Batavorum: Joannem van Kerckhem, 1744), pp. 352–425.

———, *On the Sovereignty of the Seas*, trans. Ralph van Deman Magoffin (Washington, D.C.: Carnegie Endowment for International Peace, 1923).

———, *Two Books of Questions of Public Law*, trans. Tenney Frank (Washington, D.C.: Carnegie Endowment for International Peace, 1930).

Byrd, Sharon B. and Joachim Hruschka, "Lex iusti, lex iuridica und lex iusti-tiae in Kants Rechtslehre," *Archiv für Rechts-und Sozialphilosophie* 91.4 (2005), pp. 484–500.

Casson, Lionel, *The Ancient Mariners: Seafarers and Sea Fighters of the Mediterranean in Ancient Times* (New York: Macmillan, 1959).

Castro, Alfonso de, *De Potestate Legis Poenalis* (Lyon, 1566).

Cauchy, Eugène, *Le droit maritime international considérée dans ses origines*, 2 vols. (Paris: Guillaumin et Compagnie, 1862).

Cavallar, Georg, *Kant and the Theory and Practice of International Right* (Cardiff: University of Wales, 1999).

Charbonnel, Nicole and Marcel Morabito, "Les rivages de la mer: Droit romain et glossateurs," *Revue de l'histoire du droit* 65.1 (1987), pp. 23–44.

Charteris, A.H., "The Legal Position of Merchantmen in Foreign Ports and National Waters," *British Yearbook of International Law* 45 (1920–1921), pp. 45–96.

Chetrit, T., "Le plan vigipirate," *Droit et défense* 4 (1995), pp. 57–60.

Cheyette, Frederic L.,"The Sovereign and the Pirates, 1332," *Speculum* 45.1 (1970), pp. 45–68.

Coke, Sir Edward, *The Third Part of the Institutes of the Laws of England Concerning High Treason, and Other Pleas of the Crown, and Criminall Causes* (London: M. Flesher, for W. Lee, and D. Pakeman, 1644).

Colombos, C. John, *The International Law of the Sea*, 6th ed. (New York: David McKay Company Inc., 1967).

Conlon, Denis Joseph (ed.), *Li Romans de Witasse le moine, Roman du treizième siècle, édité d'après le manuscrit, fonds français 1553, de la Bibliothèque Nationale, Paris* (Chapel Hill: The University of North Carolina Press, 1972).

Corngold, Stanley (ed. and trans.), *Kafka's Selected Stories* (New York: Norton, 2007).

Costa, Emilio, *Le acque nel diritto romano* (Bologna, 1918).

Courtine, Jean-François, *Nature et empire de la loi: Études suáreziennes* (Paris: Vrin, 1999).

Crawford, Michael, "Aut Sacrom Aut Publicom," in Peter Birks (ed.), *New Perspectives in the Roman Law of Property: Essays for Barry Nicholas* (Oxford: Clarendon Press, 1989), pp. 91–8.

Crockett, Clyde H., "Towards a Revision of the International Law of Piracy," *De Paul Law Review* 26 (1976), pp. 78–99.

Croix, Robert de la, *Histoire de la piraterie* (Paris: Éditions France, 1974).

Croke, Brian, "Mommsen's Pompey," *Quaderni di Storia* 11 (1985), pp. 137–49.

Crook, J. A., Andrew Lintott, and Elizabeth Rawson, *Cambridge Ancient History, Vol. 9 : The Last Age of the Roman Republic, 146–43 BC* (Cambridge, UK: Cambridge University Press, 1994).

Cussy, Baron Ferdinand de Cournot, *Phases et causes célèbres du droit maritime des nations*, 2 vols. (Leipzig: F. A. Brockhaus, 1856).

Dareste, Rodolphe, *Nouvelles études d'histoire du droit* (Paris: Larose, 1902).

Daube, David, Review of Brecht, *Zur Abgrenzung des Begriffes Perduellio*, *The Journal of Roman Studies* 31 (1941), pp. 180–84.

———, "Doves and Bees," in *Droits de l'antiquité et sociologie juridique: Mélanges Henri Lévy-Bruhl* (Paris: Sirey, 1959), pp. 63–75.

De la Pradelle, Paul, "La piraterie aérienne," *Annuaire de droit maritime et aérien* (1974), pp. 197–206.

De Souza, Philip, *Piracy in the Graeco-Roman World* (Cambridge, UK: Cambridge University Press, 1999).

Dell, H. J., "The Origin and Nature of Illyrian Piracy," *Historia* 16 (1967), pp. 344–58.

———, "Demetrius of Pharus and the Istrian War," *Historia* 19 (1970), pp. 30–38.

Dell'Oro, Aldo, "Le *res communes omnium* dell'elenco di Marciano e il problema del loro fondamento giuridico," *Studi urbinati di scienze giuridiche ed economiche* 30 (1962–1963), pp. 237–90.

Demosthenes, *Demosthenes: Private Orations, L–LVIII, in Neaeram LIX*, vol. 6, trans. A. T. Murray (Cambridge, MA: Harvard University Press, 1956).

Dempsey, Paul Stephen, "Aerial Piracy and Terrorism: Unilateral and Multilateral Responses to Aircraft Hijacking," *Connecticut Journal of International Law* 2 (1986–1987), pp. 427–62.

Deroussin, David, "Personnes, choses, corps," in Emmanuel Dockès and Gilles Lhuilier (eds.), *Le corps et ses représentations*, vol. 1 (Paris: Litec, 2001), pp. 79–146.

Derow, P. S., "Kleemporos," *Phoenix* 27 (1973), pp. 118–34.

Derrida, Jacques, *Politiques de l'amitié* (Paris: Galilée, 1994).

Días Borrás, Andrés, *Los orígines de la piratería islámica en Valencia: la ofensiva musulmana trecentista y la reacción cristiana* (Barcelona: Consejo Superior de Investigaciones científicas, 1993).

Dickinson, Edwin D.,"The Analogy between Natural Persons and International Persons in the Law of Nations," *The Yale Law Journal* 26.7 (1917), pp. 564–91.

———, "Is the Crime of Piracy Obsolete?" *Harvard Law Review* 360 (1924–1925), pp. 334–60.

Doni, Anton Francesco, *I Marmi*, 4 vols. (Venice: Francesco Marcolini, 1552).

Donnellus, Hugo, *Commentaria Iuri Civilis*, vol. 1 (Naples, 1763).

Dreizehnter, Alois, "Pompeius als Städtegründer," *Chiron* 5 (1975), pp. 213–46.

Dubner, Barry Hart, *The Law of International Sea Piracy* (The Hague; Boston; London: Martinus Nijhoff, 1980).

———, "Piracy in Contemporary National and International Law," *California Western International Law Journal* 21 (1990–1991), pp. 139–49.

———, "Recent Developments in the International Law of the Sea," *The International Lawyer* 36 (2002), pp. 721–32.

Dufau, Jean, *Le domaine public* (Paris: Éditions du Moniteur, 1977).

Dumbauld, Edward, *The Life and Legal Writings of Hugo Grotius* (Norman, Oklahoma: University of Oklahoma Press, 1969).

Dyck, Andrew R., *A Commentary on Cicero, De Officiis* (Ann Arbor: The University of Michigan Press, 1997).

Earle, Peter, *Corsairs of Malta and Barbary* (London: Sidgwick and Jackson, 1970).

———, *The Pirate Wars* (London: Methuen, 2003).

Edelstein, Dan, "Hostis Humani Generis: Devils, Natural Right, and Terror in the French Revolution," *Telos* 141 (2007), pp. 57–81.

———, "War and Terror: The Law of Nations from Grotius to the French Revolution," *French Historical Studies* 31.2 (2008), pp. 229–62.

Ehrenberg, Victor, "Imperium Maius in the Roman Republic," *The American Journal of Philology* 74.2 (1953), pp. 113–36.

Ellen, Eric (ed.), *Piracy at Sea* (Paris: International Maritime Bureau, 1989).

Euripides, *Hypsipyla*, ed. G. Italie (Berlin: A. Ebering, 1923).

Evans, Alona E. and John F. Murphy (eds.), *Legal Aspects of International Terrorism* (Lexington: Lexington Books, 1978).

Fairman, Charles, "A Note on Re Piracy Jure Gentium," *The American Journal of International Law* 29.3 (1935), pp. 509–12.

Fenn, Percy Thomas, "Justinian and the Freedom of the Sea," *The American Journal of International Law* 19 (1923), pp. 716–29.

Fenves, Peter David, *Late Kant: Towards Another Law of the Earth* (London: Routledge, 2003).

Ferone, Claudio, Lesteia, *Forme di predazione nell'egeo in età classica* (Naples: G. Procaccini, 1997).

Ferrary, Jean-Louis, "Recherches sur la législation de Saturninus et de Glaucia," *Mélanges d'archéologie de l'École française de Rome* 89.1 (1977), pp. 619–60.

Ferrer i Mallol, María Teresa, "Productes de commerç catalano–portuguès segons una reclamació per pirateria," *Miscellània de Textos Medievals* 6 (1992), pp. 137–63.

Finch, George A., "Piracy in the Mediterranean," *The American Journal of International Law* 31.4 (1937), pp. 659–65.

Fisher, Godfrey, *Barbary Legend: War, Trade and Piracy in North Africa, 1415–1830* (Oxford: Clarendon Press, 1957).

Fleischmann, Max (ed.), "Der Lusitania Fall im Urteile von Deutschen Gelehrten," *Zeitschrift für Völkerrecht* 9 (1916), pp. 135–237.

Foerster, Wendelin and Johann Trost (eds.), *Wistasse Le Moine. Altfranzösischer Abenteuerroman des XIII. Jahrhunderts nach der einzigen Pariser Handschrift* (Halle: Niemeyer, 1891).

Fokas, Terence, "The Barbary Coast Revisited: The Resurgence of International Maritime Piracy," *USF Maritime Legal Journal* 9.1 (1996–1997), pp. 427–60.

Franciosi, Gennaro, "Res nullius e occupatio," *Atti dell'accademia di scienze morali e politiche di Napoli* 75 (1964), pp. 237–52.

Freitas, Seraphin de, *De Iusto Iperii Lusitanorum Imperio Asiatico Adversus Grotii Mare Liberum* (Valladolid, 1625).

Freund, Julien, "Der Partisan oder der kriegerische Friede," in Helmut Quaritsch (ed.), *Complexio Oppositorum: Über Carl Schmitt* (Berlin: Duncker & Humblot, 1988), pp. 387–91.

Fulton, Thomas Wemyss, *The Sovereignty of the Sea, an Historical Account of the Claims of England to the Dominion of the British Seas, and of the Evolution of the Territorial Waters: With Special Reference to the Rights of Fishing and the Naval Salute* (Edinburgh and London: William Blackwood and Sons, 1911).

Gabbert, Janice J., "Piracy in the Early Hellenistic Period: A Career Open to Talents," *Greece and Rome* 33 (1986), pp. 156–63.

Gabrielson, Vincent, "Economic Activity, Maritime Trade and Piracy in the Hellenistic Aegean," *Revue des études anciennes* 103.1-2 (2001), pp. 219–40.

Galiani, Fernando, *De' doveri de' principi neutrali verso i pirncipi guerreggianti, e di questi verso i neutrali* (Naples, 1782).

Galligani, Rodomontes, "*Cicero Infesissimus Antoni Hosti,*" *Latinitas* 44.2 (1996), pp. 115–38.

Garibian, Sévane, "Souveraineté et légalité en droit pénal international: Le concept de crime contre l'humanité dans le discours des juges à Nuremberg," in M. and R. Roth Henzelin (eds.), *Le droit pénal à l'épreuve de l'internationalisation* (Paris; Bruxelles; Genève: LGDJ, Georg, Bruylant, 2002).

———, "Génocide arménien et conceptualization du crime contre l'humanité: De l'intervention pour cause d'humanité à l'intervention pour violation des lois de l'humanité," *Revue d'Histoire de la Shoah* 177–178 (2003), pp. 274–94.

Garlan, Yvon, "Étude d'histoire militaire et diplomatique II: Sur le règlement des droits de représailles," *Bulletin de correspondence hellénique* 89 (1965), pp. 332–48.

———, *La guerre dans l'antiquité* (Paris: Fernand Nathan, 1972).

———, "Signification historique de la piraterie grecque," *Dialogues d'histoire ancienne* 4 (1978), pp. 1–16.

———, "War, Piracy and Slavery in the Greek World," in M.I. Finley (ed.), *Classical Slavery* (London: Frank Cass, 1987), pp. 7–21.

———, *Guerre et économie en Grèce ancienne* (Paris: La Découverte, 1989).

Garmon, Tina, "International Law of the Sea: Reconciling the Law of Piracy and Terrorism in the Wake of September 11th," *Tulane Maritime Law Journal* 27 (2002), pp. 257–75.

Garner, James Wilford, *International Law and the World War*, 2 vols. (London: Longmans, Green and Co., 1920).

Gasché, Rodolphe, "The Partisan and the Philosopher," *New Centennial Review* 4.3 (2004), pp. 9–34.

Gauthier, Philippe, *Symbola: Les étrangers et la justice dans les cités grecques*, Annales de l'est, mémoire, 42 (Nancy: Université de Nancy II, 1972).

———, "Notes sur l'étranger et l'hospitalité en Grèce et à Rome," *Ancient Society* 4 (1973), pp. 1–21.

———, "Les saisies licites aux dépens des étrangers dans les cités grecques," *Revue historique de droit français et étranger* 60 (1982), pp. 553–76.

Gebert, Hugo, *Die völkerrechtliche Denationalisierung der Piraterie* (Kiel: Schmidt & Klaunig, 1914).

Genet, Raoul, "La qualification de 'pirates' et le dilemme de la guerre civile," *Revue internationale française du droit des gens* 3 (1937), pp. 13–25.

———, "The Charge of Piracy in the Spanish Civil War," *The American Journal of International Law* 32.2 (1938), pp. 253–63.

Gentili, Alberico, *De Jure Belli Libri Tres* (Hanau: Apud Haeredes Guilielmi Antonii, 1612).

———, *Hispanicae Advocationis Libri Duo.* (Amsterdam: Johannes Ravenstein, 1661).

———, *The Two Books of the Pleas of a Spanish Advocate of Alberico Gentili, Jurisconsult,* trans. Frank Frost Abbott (Washington, D.C.: Carnegie Endowment for International Peace, 1921).

———, *Three Books on the Law of War,* trans. John C. Rolfe (Washington, D.C.: Carnegie Endowment for International Peace, 1933).

Gernet, Louis, *Anthropologie de la Grèce antique* (Paris: François Maspero, 1968).

———, *Recherches sur le développement de la pensée juridique et morale en Grèce* (Paris: Albin Michel, 2001).

Gidel, Gilbert, *Le droit international public de la mer* (Chateauroux: Les Établissements Mellottée, 1932–1934).

Giovannini, Adalberto and Grzybek, Erhard, "La *lex de piratis persequendis*," *Museum Helveticum* 35 (1978), pp. 33–47.

Girerd, Patrick, "De l'utilité du concept de 'piraterie?'," *Annuaire de droit maritime et océanique* 22 (2004), pp. 77–105.

Giulli, Marina Cristina, Laura de Angelis and Luisa Chiappa Mauri, "I Congresso Internazionale di Storia Mediterranena (Palma De Mallorca, 17–22 Dicembre 1973)," *Nuova rivista storica* 58 (1974), p. 191.

Glare, P. G. W. (ed.), *Oxford Latin Dictionary* (Oxford: Clarendon Press, 1983).

Glass, Charles, "The New Piracy," *London Review of Books* 25.24 (2003).

Glowka, Wayne. "Yachtjacking, Boatnapping, or Getting Seajacked by Ship-Jackers," *American Speech* 62.2 (1987), pp. 181–82.

Goodwin, Joshua Michael, "Universal Jurisdiction and the Pirate: Time for an Old Couple to Part," *Vanderbilt Journal of Transnational Law* 39 (2006), pp. 963–1011.

Gottschalk, Jack A., and Brian P. Flanagan, *Jolly Roger with an Uzi: The Rise and Threat of Modern Piracy* (Annapolis, MD: US Naval Institute Press, 2000), pp.

85–94.

Gosse, Philip, *The History of Piracy* (London: Longmans, Green & Co., 1932).

Graven, Jean, *Les crimes contre l'humanité*, Receuil De Cours, Académie De Droit International De La Haye, vol. 76 (Paris: Recueil Sirey, 1950).

Green, L. C., "The *Santa Maria*: Rebels or Pirates," *British Yearbook of International Law* 37 (1961), pp. 496–505.

———, "Terrorism and the Law of the Sea," in Yoram and Mala Tabori Dinstein (eds.), *International Law at a Time of Perplexity: Essays in Honor of Shabtai Rosenne* (Dordrecht: Martinus Nijhoff, 1989), pp. 249–71.

Greenberg, Karen J. (ed.), *The Torture Debate in America* (Cambridge: Cambridge University Press, 2005).

Greenberg, Karen J. and Joshua L. Dratel (eds.), *The Torture Papers: The Road to Abu Ghraib* (Cambridge: Cambridge University Press, 2005).

Grewe, Wilhelm G., *Epochen der Völkerrechtsgeschichte* (Baden-Baden: Nomos Verlagsgesellschaft, 1984).

Griffith, Guy Thompson, *The Mercenaries of the Hellenistic World*, 2nd ed. (Cambridge: Cambridge University Press, 1968).

Groningen, B. A. van (ed.), *Aristote: Le second livre de l'Économique* (Leiden: A. W. Sijthoff, 1933).

Grotius, Hugo, *De Jure Belli Ac Pacis Libri Tres, in Quibus Jus Naturae & Gentium, Item Juris Publici Praecipua Explicantur* (Washington, D.C.: Carnegie Endowment for International Peace, 1946).

———, *The Freedom of the Seas, or the Right Which Belongs to the Dutch to Take Part in the East Indian Trade*, ed. James Brown Scott, Carnegie Endowment for International Peace, Division of International Law (New York: Oxford University Press, 1916).

———, *The Law of War and Peace, in Three Books, Wherein Are Set Forth the Law of Nature and of Nations Also the Principles of Public Law*, trans. Francis W. Kelsey (Washington, Cheyette: Carnegie Endowment for International Peace, 1925).

Guiral-Hadziiosif, Jacqueline, "Course et piraterie à Valence de 1410 à 1430," *Anuario de estudios medieavles* 10 (1980), pp. 759–65.

———, *Valence, port méditerranéen au XVe Siècle* (Paris: Publications de la Sorbonne, 1986).

Habermas, Jürgen, "Kants Idee des ewigen Friedens—aus dem historischen Abstand von 200 Jahren," *Kritische Justiz* 28 (1995), pp. 293–319.

245

Haggenmacher, Peter, *Grotius et la doctrine de la guerre juste* (Paris: Presses universitaires de France, 1983).

Halberstam, Malvina, "Terrorism on the High Seas: The Achille Lauro, Piracy and the Imo Convention on Maritime Safety," *The American Journal of International Law* 82.2 (1988), pp. 269–310.

Hall, William Edward, *A Treatise on International Law*, 8th ed. (Oxford: Clarendon Press, 1924).

Halldórsson, Ólafur (ed.), *Foeringa Saga* (Reykjavík: Stofnun Árna Magnússonar á Íslandi, 1987).

Hamilton, H. C., Esq., and W. Falconer (eds.), *The Geography of Strabo*, 8 vols. (Cambridge, MA: Harvard University Press, 1923).

Hassall, Mark, Michael Crawford, and Joyce Reynolds, "Rome and the Eastern Provinces at the End of the Second Century BC: The so-called Piracy Law and a New Inscription from Cnidos," *The Journal Roman Studies* 64 (1974), pp. 195–220.

Hatzenberger, Antoine, "Haïdoucs, Bou Regreg, Bolos: Des sociétés contre l'état," *Critique* 631 (2000), pp. 989–1003.

Haussoullier, Bernard, *Traité entre Delphes et Pellana: Étude de droit grec* (Paris: Champion, 1917).

Hautefeuille, Laurent Basile, *Histoire des origines, des progrès et des variations du droit maritime international*, 2nd ed. (Paris: Guillaumin & Compagnie, 1869).

Heers, Jacques, *Les barbaresques: La course et la guerre en Méditteranée, XIVe–XVIe siècle* (Paris: Perrin, 2001).

Hellegouarc'h, Joseph, *Le vocabulaire latin des relations et des partis politiques sous la république* (Paris: Les Belles Lettres, 1963).

Hertslet, Edward, *The Map of Europe by Treaty*, 4 vols. (London: Butterworths, 1875).

Higgens, A. Pearce, "Le régime juridique des navires de commerce en haute mer en temps de paix," *Académie de droit international, Recueil de Cours,* vol. 30 (1929), pp. 5–77.

Hilka, Alfons, *Der altfranzösische Prosa-Alexander-Roman nach der Berliner Bilderhandschrift, nebst dem lateinischen Original der Historia de Preliis* (Halle: Niemeyer, 1920).

Hill, Thomas E., "Humanity as an End in Itself," *Ethics* 91.1 (1980), pp. 84–99.

Holleaux, Maurice, "The Romans in Illyria," in F. E. Adcock, S. A. Cook, and M. P. Charlesworth (eds.), *The Cambridge Ancient History, Vol. 7: The Hellenistic*

Monarchies and the Rise of Rome (Cambridge, UK: Cambridge University Press, 1928), pp. 822–57.

———, *Études d'épigraphe et d'histoire grecques: Rome, la Macédoine et l'orient grec, première partie*, vol. 4 (Paris: Librairie d'Amérique et d'Orient Adrien-Maisonneuve, 1952).

Huber, Wolfgang, "Feindschaft und Feindesliebe: Notizen zum Problem des 'Feindes' in der Theologie," *Zeitschrift für evangelische Ethik* 26.2 (1982), pp. 128–58.

ICC International Maritime Bureau, *Piracy and Armed Robbery Against Ships: Annual Report — 2006*.

———, *Piracy and Armed Robbery Against Ships: Annual Report — 2007*.

Jackson, Alastar H., "Privateers in the Ancient Greek World," in M. R. D. Foot (ed.), *War and Society: Historical Studies in Honour and Memory of J. R. Western, 1928–1971* (London: Paul Elek, 1973), pp. 214–53.

———, "War and Raids for Booty in the World of Odysseus," in John Rich and Graham Shipley (eds.), *War and Society in the Greek World* (London: Routledge, 1993), pp. 64–76.

Jacobson, Peter M., "From Piracy in the High Seas to Piracy in the High Skies: A Study of Aircraft Highjacking," *Cornell International Law Journal* 5 (1972), pp. 161–87.

Jaeger, Gérard A. (ed.), *Vues sur la piraterie: Des origines à nos jours* (Paris: Jules Tallandier, 1992).

———, *Pirates, filibustiers et corsairs: Histoire et légendes d'une société d'exception* (Avignon: Aubanel, 1987).

Jal, P., "*Bellum Civile... Bellum Externum* dans la Rome de la fin de la république et au début de l'empire," *Les études classiques* 30 (1962), pp. 257–67.

———, "Le 'Soldat' des guerres civiles à Rome à la fin de la république et au début de l'empire," *Pallas* 11 (1962–1964), pp. 7–27.

———, "*Hostis (Publicus)* dans la littérature latine de la fin de la république," *Revue des études anciennes* 65 (1963), pp. 53–79.

Jameson, Shelach, "Pompey's Imperium in 67: Some Constitutional Fictions," *Historia* 19 (1970), pp. 539–60.

Jardé, Auguste, *La formation du peuple grec* (Paris: La Renaissance du Livre, 1923).

Jashemski, Wilhelmina Mary Feemster, *The Origins and History of the Pro-Consular and the Propraetorian Imperium to 3 BC* (Chicago: University of Chicago

Press, 1950).

Jeannel, J., *La piraterie* (Paris: Librairie Nouvelle de Droit et de Jurisprudence, 1903).

Johnson, D. H. N., "Piracy in Modern International Law," *Transactions of the Grotius Society* 43 (1957), pp. 63–85.

Jurovics, Y., "Les controverses sur la question de la qualification du trrorisme: Crime de droit commun, crime de guerre ou crime contre l'humanité?" in Christakis K. Bannlier, O. Corten, and B. Delcourt (eds.), *Le droit international face au terrorisme* (Paris: Pedone, 2002), pp. 95–105.

Kant, Immanuel, *Werke: Akademie Textsausgabe*, 9 vols. (Berlin: De Gruyter, 1968).

———, *Groundwork of the Metaphysics of Morals*, trans. H. J. Paton (New York: Harper & Row, 1964).

———, *The Metaphysics of Morals*, trans. Mary Gregor (Cambridge, UK: Cambridge University Press, 1991).

———, "Perpetual Peace: A Philosophical Sketch," in H. S. Reiss (ed.), *Kant: Political Writings* (Cambridge, UK: Cambridge University Press, 1991).

Karabélias, E., "Le roman de Cariton d'Aphrodisias et le droit: Renversements de situation et exploitation des ambiguïtés juridiques," in G. Nenci and G. Thür (eds.), *Symposium* (Cologne and Vienna: Böhlau, 1988), pp. 369–96.

Kaser, Max, "Der Römische Eigentumsbegriff," in Hans Dölle (ed.), *Deutsche Landesreferate zum VI. internationalen Kongreß für Rechtsvergleichung in Hamburg 1962* (Berlin: Walter De Gruyter, 1962), pp. 19–38.

———, "The Concept of Roman Ownership," *Tydskrif vir hedendaagse Romeins-Hollandse Reg.* 27 (1964), pp. 5–19.

Katele, Irene B., "Piracy and the Venetian State: The Dilemma of Maritime Defense in the Fourteenth Century," *Speculum* 63.4 (1988), pp. 865–89.

Kelsey, Harry, *Sir Francis Drake: The Queen's Pirate* (New Haven, CT: Yale University Press, 2000).

Kiesel, Helmuth (ed.), *Briefe 1930–1983: Ernst Jünger, Carl Schmitt* (Stuttgart: Klett-Cotta, 1999).

Klingenberg, George, "*Maris Proprium* in D. 47, 10, 14," *The Legal History Review* 72.1–2 (2004), pp. 37–60.

Kohler, Josef and Max Fleischmann, "Der Lusitania-Fall im Urteil von Deutschen Gelehrten," *Zeitschrift für Völkerrecht* 9 (1915), pp. 133–273.

Koselleck, Reinhart, *Vergangenen Zukunft: Zur Semantik geschlichtlicher Zeiten* (Frankfurt: Suhrkamp, 1979).

————, *Futures Past: On the Semantics of Historical Time*, trans. Keith Tribe (Cambridge, MA: The MIT Press, 1985).

Krüger, Johannes, *Zum Begriffe "Herrenlos" im bürgerlichen Gesetzbuch* (Leipzig: Robert Noske, 1905).

Laclau, Ernesto, "On 'Real' and 'Absolute' Enemies," *The New Centennial Review* 5.1 (2005), pp. 1–12.

Lampredi, Giovanni Maria, *Del commercio dei popoli neutrali in tempo di guerra*, 2 vols. (Milan: G. Silvestri, 1831).

Landau, Sidney I., "More on *Skyjack* and *Skyjacker*," *American Speech* 47.3/4 (1972), p. 307.

Langewiesche, William, *The Outlaw Sea: A World of Freedom, Chaos and Crime* (New York: North Point Press, 2004).

Last, Hugh, "*Imperium Maius*: A Note," *The Journal of Roman Studies* 37.1/2 (1947), pp. 157–64.

Latte, Kurt, "Συλᾶν," in *Kleine Schriften zu Religion, Recht, Literatur und Sprache der Griechen und Römer*, ed. Olof Gigon, Wolfgang Buchwald and Wolfgang Kunkel (Munich: Beck, 1968), pp. 416–19.

Lécrivain, Charles-Albert, "Le droit de se faire justice soi-même et les représailles dans les relations internationales de la Grèce," *Mémoires de l'académie des sciences de Toulouse* 9 (1897), pp. 277–90.

Lehr, Peter, *Violence at Sea: Piracy in the Age of Global Terrorism* (London: Routledge, 2006).

Lesky, Albin, *Geschichte der griechischen Literatur*, 3rd ed. (Bern and Munich, 1971).

Lewis, Walker, "John Quincy Adams and the Baltimore 'Pirates,'" *American Bar Association Journal* 67 (1981), pp. 1011–14.

Libero, Loretana de, "'*Ut eosdem quos populos romanus amicos atque hostes habeant:*' Die Freund-Feind-Klausel in den Beziehungen Roms zu griechischen und italienischen Staaten," *Historia* (1997), pp. 270–305.

Liddell, George and Robert Scott, *A Greek-English Lexicon*, 9th ed. (Oxford, UK: Clarendon Press, 1996).

Lintott, Andrew W., "Notes on the Roman Law Inscribed at Delphi and Cnidos," *Zeitschrift für Papyrologie und Epigraphik* 20 (1976), pp. 65–82.

Lo Basso, Luca, *In traccia de' legni nemici: Corsari europei nel mediterraneo del settecento* (Ventimiglia: Philobiblon, 2002).

Loader, W. R., "Pompey's Command under the Lex Gabinia," *The Classical Review* 54.3 (1940), pp. 134–36.

Lucian, *Lucian: Phalaris. Hippias or the Bath. Dionysus. Heracles. Amber or the Swans. The Fly. Nigrinus. Demonax. The Hall. My Native Land. Octogenarians. A True Story. Slander. the Consonants at Law. The Carousel (Symposium) or the Lapiths*, vol. 1, trans. M. A. Harmon, 8 vols. (Cambridge, MA: Harvard University Press, 1913).

Lydon, James G., *Pirates, Privateers, and Profits* (Upper Saddle, NJ: Gregg Press, 1970).

MacDonald, Briam, "Ahisteia and Lhizomai in Thucydides and in *IG* I (3rd ed.) 41, 67 and 75," *The American Journal of Philology* 105.1 (1984), pp. 77–84.

Macedo, Stephen (ed.), *Universal Jurisdiction: National Courts and the Prosecution of Serious Crimes under International Law* (Philadelphia: University of Pennsylvania Press, 2003).

Mackay, P. A., "Klephtika: The Tradition of the Tales of Banditry in Apuleius," *Greece and Rome*, 10.2 (1963), pp. 147–52.

MacMullen, R., "The Roman Concept Robber-Pretender," *Revue internationale des droits de l'antiquité* 10 (1963), pp. 221–25.

Magdelain, André, "Remarques sur la perduellio," *Historia* 22 (1973), pp. 405–22.

Maier, Anneliese, *Kants Qualitätskategorien*, Kant-Studien 65 (Pan-Verlag, Kurt Metzner: Berlin, 1930).

Malkin, H. W., "The Washington Conference (November 12, 1921 – February 6, 1922)," *British Yearbook of International Law* 3 (1922–1923), pp. 179–82.

———, "The Inner History of the Declaration of Paris," *British Yearbook of International Law* 8 (1927), pp. 1–44.

———, *Corsarios castellanos y vascos en el mediterráneo medieval* (Barcelona: Consejo Superior de Investigaciones Científicas, Institución Milá y Fontanals, Departamento de Estudios Medievales, 2000).

Maroi, Fulvio, "Sulla condizione giuridica del mare e delle sue rive in diritto romano," *Rivista italiana per le scienze* 62 (1919), pp. 151–70.

Maróti, Egon, "Die Rolle der Seeräuber unter den Anhänger des Sextus Pompeius," in H. Diesner et al. (eds.), *Sozialökonomische verhältnisse im alten Orient und klassischen Altertum* (Berlin: Akademie-Verlag, 1961).

————, "Ho Koinos Polemos," *Klio* 40 (1962), pp. 124–27.

————, "Der Sklavenmarkt auf Delos und die Piraterie," *Helikon* 9–10 (1969–70), pp. 24–42.

————, "Die Rolle der Seeräuber in der Zeit des Mithridatischen Krieges," in Luigi de Rosa (ed.), *Ricerche storiche ed economiche in memora di Corrado Barbagallo*, vol. 1 (Naples, 1970), pp. 479–93.

————, "On the Problem of M. Antonius Creticus' *Imperium Infinitum*," *Acta Antiqua Academiae Scientiarum Hungaricae* 19.1–2 (1971), pp. 259–72.

Martens, Baron Charles de, *Causes célèbres du droit des gens*, 5 vols., 2nd ed. (Leipzig: F. A. Brockhaus, 1858–1861).

Mas Latrie, René de. *Du droit de marque, ou droit de représailles au Moyen-Âge* (Paris: A. Franck, 1883).

Mattingly, Garett, "No Peace Beyond What Line?" *Transactions of the Royal Historical Society* 5.13 (1963), pp. 145–62.

Mattingly, H. B., "M. Anotonius, C. Verres and the Sack of Delos by the Pirates," in M. J. Fontana (ed.), *Philias Charin: Miscellanea di studi classici in onore di Eugenio Manni*, vol. 4 (Rome: Bretschneider, 1980), pp. 1489–515.

Mayer, Jane, *The Dark Side: The Inside Story of How the War on Terror Turned into a War on American Ideals* (New York: Doubleday, 2008).

McLeod, Grant, "Wild and Tame Animals and Birds in Roman Law," in Peter Birks (ed.), *New Perspectives in the Roman Law of Property*, pp. 169–76.

McWhinney, Edward (ed.), *Aerial Piracy and International Law* (Dobbs Ferry, NY: Oceana Publications, 1971).

Melville, Herman, *Billy Budd, Sailor and Other Stories*, ed. Frederick Busch (New York: Penguin, 1986).

Menchaca, Fernando Vásquez de, *Illustrium Controversiarum Aliorumque usu Frequentium Libri Tres* (Venice, 1564).

Menefee, Samuel Pyeatt, "Adding Blight to Existing Conventions by Developing National Laws Concerned with the Investigation and Prosecution of Ship Hijackers in National Waters," *Singapore Journal of International and Comparative Law* 3 (1999), pp. 545–54.

Merlin-Chazelas, Anne, "Ordonnance inédite de François Ier pour la repression de la piraterie," *Bulletin philologique et historique (jusqu'à 1610) du comité des travaux historiques et scientifiques* (1966), vol. 1, pp. 87–93.

Merrien, Jean, *Histoire des corsaires* (Saint-Malo: L'Ancre de Marine, 1992).

Mieli, A., "'Res Publica,' 'Res Communis Omnium,' 'Res Nullius': Grozio e le fonti romane sul diritto del mare," *Index* 26 (1998), pp. 383–87.

Miglio, Gianfranco, Moreno Morani, Pier Paolo Portinaro and Alessandro Vitale, *Amicus (Inimicus) Hostis: Le radici concettuali della conflittualita privata e della conflittualita politica* (Milano: Giuffre, 1992).

Milan, Alessandro, "Ricerche sul *Latrocinium* in Livio I: *Latro* nelle fonti preaugustee," *Atti dell'Istituto veneto di scienze, lettere ed arti, Classe di scienze morali e lettere* 138 (1979–1980), pp. 171–97.

Milner, Jean–Claude, *Les penchants criminels de l'Europe démocratique* (Paris: Verdier, 2003).

Molinié, Georges, *Chariton, le roman de Chairéas et Callirhoé*, 2nd ed. (Paris: Les Belles Lettres, 1989).

Mollat, Michel, "Guerre de course et piraterie à la fin du Moyen Âge: Aspects économiques et sociaux, position de problèmes," *Hansische Geschichtsblätter* 90 (1972), pp. 1–14.

———, "De la piraterie sauvage à la course réglementée (XIVe–XVe siècle)," *Mélanges de l'École française de Rome* 87 (1975), pp. 7–25.

———, "Essai d'orientation pour l'étude de la guerre de la course et la piraterie (XIIIe–XVe siècles)," *Annuario de estudios medievales* 10 (1980), pp. 743–49.

———, (ed.), *Course et piraterie: Études présentées à la commission internationale d'histoire maritime à l'occasion de son XVe colloque international pendant le XIVe congrès international des sciences historiques*, 3 vols. (San Francisco: Institut de Recherche et d'Histoire des Textes, Centre National de Recherche Scientifique, 1975).

Molloy, Charles, *De Iure Maritimo Et Navali, or, a Treatise of Affaires Maritime and of Commerce in Three Books* (London: Printed for Thomas Passinger, 1682).

Mommsen, Theodor, *Römisches Staatsrecht*, 2 vols., 3rd ed. (Leipzig: S. Hirzel, 1877).

Monaco, Lucia, *Persecutio Piratarum: Battaglie ambigue e svolte costituzionali nella Roma repubblicana* (Naples: Casa Editrice Dott. Eugenio Jovene, 1996).

Mousseigne, Édouard (ed.), *Eustache le Moine, pirate boulonnais du XIIIe siècle* (Paris: La Voix du Nord, 1986).

Müller, Alexander, *Die Piraterie im Völkerrecht unter besonderer Berücksichtigung des Entwurfes der Völkerbundeskommission und der Regierungsäußerungen* (Grünberg: Hch. Ritter, 1929).

Muller, Samuel, *Mare Clausum, Bijdrage Tot de Geschiedenis der Rivaliteit van*

Engeland en Nederland in de Zeventiende Eeuw (Amsterdam: F. Muller, 1872).

Münkler, Herfried, *Über den Krieg: Stationen der Kriegsgeschichte im Spiegel ihrer theoretischen Reflexion* (Weilerswist: Velbrück Wissenschaft, 2002).

Nederman, Cary J., "A Duty to Kill: John of Salisbury's Theory of Tyrannicide," *The Review of Politics* 50.3 (1988), pp. 365–89.

Neff, Stephen C., *War and the Law of Nations: A General History* (Cambridge, UK: Cambridge University Press, 2005).

Neocleous, Mark, "Off the Map: On Violence and Cartography," *European Journal of Social Theory* 6.4 (2003), pp. 409–25.

Nippel, Wilfried, "'Krieg als Erscheinungsform der Feindschaft' (28–37)," in Reinhard Mehring (ed.), *Carl Schmitt, Der Begriff des Politischen: Ein Kooperativer Kommentar* (Berlin: Akademie Verlag, 2003), pp. 61–70.

Nörr, Dieter, *Aspekte des römischen Volkerrechts: Die Bronzetafel von Alcántara* (Munich: Verlag der Bayerischen Akademie der Wissenschaften, 1989).

November, Celine Y., "Aircraft Piracy: The Hague Hijacking Convention," *The International Lawyer* 6.3 (1972), pp. 642–56.

Nowag, Werner, *Raub und Beute in der archaischen Zeit der Griechen* (Frankfurt am Main: Haag/Herchen, 1983).

Noyes, John E, "An Introduction to the International Law on Piracy," *International Law Journal* 105 (1990–1991), pp. 105–21.

Nys, Ernest, *Les origines du droit international* (Bruxelles: A. Castaigne, 1894).

———, "Une bataille de livres: Épisode de l'histoire littéraire du droit international," in *Études de droit international et de politique* (Paris: A. Fontemoing, 1901), pp. 261–72.

———, *Le droit international: Les principes, les théories, les faits*, vol. 2 (Paris: Albert Fontemoign, 1905).

Oppenheim, Lassa, *International Law: A Treatise*, ed. H. Lauterpacht, 8th ed. (London: Longmans, 1955).

Ormerod, Henry A., *Piracy in the Ancient World: An Essay on Mediterranean History* (Liverpool: Liverpool University Press, 1924).

Pampaloni, Muzio, "Sulla condizione giuridica delle rive del mare in diritto romano e odierno: Contributo alla teoria delle 'res communes omnium'," *Bullettino dell'Istituto di diritto romano* 4 (1891), pp. 197–246.

Paradisi, Bruno, "International Law and Social Structure in the Middle Ages," *The Indian Year Book of International Affairs* 2 (1964), pp. 148–73.

Paris, Alexander of, *Le roman d'Alexandre*, ed. E. C. Armstrong et al., trans. Laurence Harf-Lancner (Paris: Le Livre de Poche, 1994).

Parritt, Brian A. H. (ed.), *Violence at Sea: A Review of Terrorism, Acts of War and Piracy, and Countermeasures to Prevent Terrorism* (Paris: ICC Publishing, 1986).

Parry, Milman, "The Traditional Metaphor in Homer," *Classical Philology* 28.1 (1933), pp. 30–43.

Pella, Vespasian, "La répression de la piraterie," *Recueuil des cours de l'Académie de droit international de La Haye* V (1926), pp. 145–275.

Pérotin-Dumon, Anne, "The Pirate and the Emperor: Power and the Law of the Sea, 1450–1850," in James Tracy (ed.), *The Political Economy of Merchant Empires* (Cambridge, UK: Cambridge University Press, 1991), pp. 196–227.

Perruso, Richard, "The Development of the Doctrine of *Res Communes* in Medieval and Early Modern Europe," *The Legal History Review* 1–2 (2002), pp. 69–93.

Perry, B. E., "Chariton and His Romance from a Literary-Historical Point of View," *American Journal of Philology* 51 (1930), pp. 93–134.

Pertusi, Agostino (ed.), *Venezia e il Levante fino al secolo XV* (Florence: Olschki, 1973).

Phillimore, Robert, *Commentaries Upon International Law*, 3 vols. (Philadelphia: T. J. W. Johnson, Law Booksellers, 1854–1867).

Phillipson, Coleman, *The International Law and Custom of Ancient Greece*, 2 vols. (London: Macmillan, 1911).

Philonenko, Alexis, *Essais sur la philosophie de la guerre* (Paris: Vrin, 1976).

Piggott, Francis, *The Declaration of Paris, 1856: A Study* (London: University of London, 1919).

Poe, Edgar Allan, *The Narrative of Arthur Gordon Pym of Nantucket*, ed. Richard Kopley (New York: Penguin, 1994).

Pohl, Hartel, *Die römische Politik und die Piraterie im östlichen Mittelmeer vom 3. bis zum 1. Jh. V. Chr.*, Untersuchungen zur antiken Literatur und Geschichte, vol. 42 (Berlin: de Gruyter, 1993).

Pontavice, E. du., "La piraterie aérienne: Notion et effets," *Revue générale de l'air et de l'espace* 32.3 (1969), pp. 276–339.

Potter, Pitman B., *The Freedom of the Seas in History, Law, and Politics* (New York: Longmans, Green & Co., 1924).

Powell, Frederick York, trans., *The Tale of Thrond of Gate: Commonly called*

Færeyinga saga (London: D. Nutt, 1896).

Premerstein, A. von,"Vom Werden und Wesen des Prizipats," *Abhandlung der Bayerischen Akademie der Wissenschaften, n.s.* 15 (1937).

Pritchard, James Bennett (ed.), *Ancient Near Eastern Texts Relating to the Old Testament* (Princeton, NJ: Princeton University Press, 1955).

Pritchett, W. Kendrick, *The Greek State at War*, part 5 (Berkeley: University of California Press, 1991).

Prodi, Paolo, *Il Giuramento politico nella soria costituzionale dell'occidente* (Bologna: Il Mulino, 1992).

Pufendorf, Samuel, *De Jure Naturae Et Gentium Libri Octo* (London: Sumtibus Adami Junghans iprimebat Vitus Haberegger, 1672).

————, *Of the Law of Nature and Nations, Eight Books, Written in Latin by the Baron Pufendorf, Counsellour of State to His Late Swedish Majesty, and to the Late King of Prussia*, 3rd ed., trans. Basil Kennet (London: R. Sare et al., 1717).

Putzulu, Evandro, "Pirati e corsari nei mari della Sardegna durante la prima metà del secolo XV," in *IV Congreso de historia de la corona d'Aragón: Actas Y Communicaciones*, vol. 1 (Palma de Mallorca, 1959), pp. 155–79.

Querrien, "Le rivage de la mer ou la difficulté d'être légiste," *Études et documents du Conseil d'État* (1973), pp. 75–87.

Radin, Max, "The Roman Law of Delphi and the Lex Gabinia," *The Classical Journal* 23.9 (1928), pp. 678–82.

Raffles, Sir Stanford, "The Maritime Code of the Malays," *Royal Asiatic Society of Great Britain and Ireland; Malayan Branch* (1879), pp. 62–84.

Ramraj, Victor V., Michael Hor, and Kent Roach (eds.), *Global Anti-Terrorism and Policy* (Cambridge, UK: Cambridge University Press, 2005).

Rankin, Hugh F., *The Golden Age of Piracy* (Williamsburg, VA: Colonial Williamsburg, 1969).

Reardon, B.P., "Theme, Structure and Narrative in Chariton," *Yale Classical Studies* 27 (1982), pp. 1–27.

————, (ed.) *Collected Ancient Greek Novels* (Berkeley: University of California Press, 1989).

Rediker, Marcus, *Between the Devil and the Deep Blue Sea: Merchant Seamen, Pirates and the Anglo-American Maritime World 1700–1750* (Cambridge: Cambridge University Press, 1987).

————, *Villains of All Nations: Atlantic Pirates in the Golden Age* (Boston: Beacon

Press, 2004).

Requemora, Sylvie and Sophie Linon-Chipon (eds.), *Les tyrans de la mer: Pirates, corsaires et filibustiers* (Paris: Presses de l'université de Paris-Sorbonne/ CELAT, 2002).

Richardson, J. S., "*Imperium Romanum*: Empire and the Language of Power," *The Journal of Roman Studies* 81 (1991), pp. 1–9.

Rigaud, Philippe, "Pirates et corsaires sur le bas-Rhône: IXe–XXe siècles," in Michel Vergé–Franceschi (ed.), *Guerre et commerce en Méditerranée IXe–XXe siècles* (Paris: Éditons Veyrier, 1991), pp. 37–57.

———, (ed.) *Pirates et corsaires dans les mers de la Provence, XVe–XVIe siècles: Letras de la costiera* (Paris: Éditions de la CTHS, 2006).

Rigsby, Kent, *Asylia: Territorial Inviolability in the Hellenistic World* (Berkeley: University of California Press, 1996).

Ritchie, Robert C., *Captain Kidd and the War and the War against the Pirates* (Cambridge, MA: Harvard University Press, 1986).

Robbe, Ubaldo, *La differenza sostantiale fra 'res nullius' e 'res nullius in bonis' e la distinzione delle 'res' pseudo-marcianea "che non ha capo nè coda,"* vol. 1 (Milan: A. Giuffrè Editore, 1979).

Røksund, Arne, *The Jeune École: The Strategy of the Weak* (Leiden: Brill, 2007).

Röling, V. A., "The Nuremberg and the Tokyo Trials in Retrospect," in M. Chérif Bassiouni and Ved P. Nanda (eds.), *A Treatise on International Criminal Law* (Springfield, IL: Thomas, 1973), pp. 590–608.

Röling, V. A. and Antonio Cassese, *The Tokyo Trial and Beyond: Reflections of a Peacemonger* (Cambridge, UK: Polity Press, 1993).

Ronzitti, Natalino (ed.), *Maritime Terrorism and International Law* (Dordrecht: Martinus Nijhoff, 1990).

Roques, Mario (ed.), *Aucassin et Nicolette: Chantefable du XIIIe siècle*, 2nd ed. (Paris: Champion, 1982).

Roscoe, E. S., "Mediaeval Piracy and the Lords High Admiral of England," *Law Magazine and Review* 24.155 (1898–1899), pp. 144–55.

Rosenzweig, Franz, "Globus: Studien zur weltgeschichtlichen Raumlehre," in Reinhold and Annemarie Mayer (eds.), *Der Mensch Und Sein Werk, Gesammelte Schriften*, vol. 3: *Zweitstromland, Kleinerer Schriften Zu Glauben Und Denken* (Dordrecht, 1984), pp. 313–68.

Ross, David J., *Studies in the Alexander Romance* (London: Pindar Press, 1985).

Rougé, J., "Le droit de naufrage et ses limitations en Méditerranée avant l'établissement de La domination de Rome," in André Debord (ed.), *Mélanges d'archéologie et d'histoire offerts à André Piganio*, vol. 3 (Paris: S.E.V.P.E.N., 1986), pp. 1467–79.

Rouse, Richard H. and Mary Rouse, "John of Salisbury and the Doctrine of Tyrannicide," *Speculum* 42.4 (1967), pp. 693–709.

Roxburgh, Ronald, "Submarines at the Washington Conference," *British Yearbook of International Law* 3 (1922–1923), pp. 150–58.

Rubin, Alfred P., "Terrorism and Piracy: A Legal View," *Studies in Conflict and Terrorism* 3.1–2 (1980), pp. 117–30.

———, "The Law of Piracy," *Denver Journal of International Law and Piracy* 15.2–3 (1987), pp. 173–233.

———, *The Law of Piracy*, 2nd ed. (Irvington-on-Hudson, NY: Transnational Publishers, 1998).

Ruíz-Montero, C., "Una observación para la cronología de Caritón de Afrodisias," *Estudios classicos* 24 (1980), pp. 63–69.

Runyan, Timothy J., "The Rolls of Oleron and the Admiralty Court in Fourteenth Century England," *The American Journal of Legal History* 19.2 (1975), pp. 95–111.

Rutter, Owen, *The Pirate Wind: Tales of Sea-Robbers of Malaya* (London: Hutchinson & Co., 1930).

Saenz Morales, Manuel, "A Textual Corruption in Chariton 1.7.1 and the Operational Base of the Pirate Theron," *Mnemosyne* 45.6 (2002), pp. 731–35.

Sallust, *The Jugurthine War. The Conspiracy of Catiline*, trans. S. A. Handford (London: Penguin Classics, 1964).

Saxoferrato, Bartolus of, *Apostilla Domini Bartoli De Saxoferato Super Secunda Parte Digesti Novi* (Milan: Johannes Antoni de Donato, 1486).

Schickel, Joachim, *Gespräche mit Carl Schmitt* (Berlin: Merve, 1983).

Schindler, Dietrich and Jiří Toman, *The Laws of Armed Conflicts: A Collection of Conventions, Resolutions, and Other Documents*, 3rd ed. (Dorchecht: Nijhoff, 2004).

Schlesinger, Eilhard, *Die griechische Asylie* (Göttingen: W. F. Kaestner, 1933).

Schlikker, Gerhard, *Die völkerrechtliche Lehre von der Piraterie und den ihr gleichgestellten Verbrechen* (Borna-Leipzig: Robert Noske, 1907).

Schmitt, Carl, "Der Führer schützt das Recht: Zur Reichstagsrede Adolf Hitlers vom 13. Juli, 1934," *Deutsche Juristen-Zeitung* 39 (1934), pp. 945–50.

———, "Il concetto della pirateria," *La vita italiana* 26 (1938), pp. 189–94.

———, "Die deutsche Rechtswissenschaft im Kampf gegen den jüdischen Geist," *Deutsche Juristen–Zeitung* 40.20 (1936), pp. 1193–199.

———, *Positionen und Begriffe im Kampf mit Wiemar* (Berlin: Duncker & Humblot, 1994).

———, *Staat, Großraum, Nomos: Arbeiten aus den Jahren 1916–1969*, ed. Günther Maschke (Berlin: Duncker & Humblot, 1995).

———, *Theorie des Partisanen: Zwischenbemerkung zum Begriff des Politischen*, 4th ed. (Berlin: Duncker & Humblot, 1995).

———, *Der Nomos der Erde im Völkerrecht des Jus Publicum Europaeum*, 4th ed. (Berlin: Duncker & Humblot, 1997).

———, *Land und Meer: Eine weltgeschichtliche Betrachtung*, 4th ed. (Stuttgart: Klett-Cotta, 2001).

———, "The Theory of the Partisan: A Commentary/Remark on the Concept of the Political," trans. A. C. Goodson, *The New Centennial Review* 4.3 (2004), pp. 1–78.

———, *Frieden oder Pazifismus? Arbeiten zum Völkerrecht und zur Internationalen Politik, 1924–1978*, ed. Günther Maschke (Berlin: Duncker & Humblot, 2005).

Schmitz, Heinz-Gerd, "Kants Lehre von *hostis iniustus* und Carl Schmitts Kritik dieser Konzeption," *Archiv für Rechts-und Sozialphilosophie* 89.3 (2003), pp. 399–417.

Schoenborn, W., "La nature juridique du territoire," *Recueil des cours de l'Académie de Droit International de La Haye* 30.V (1929), pp. 81–189.

Schwartz, Saundra, "The Trial Scene in the Greek Novels and in Acts," in T. Penner and C. Stichelle (eds.), *Contextualizing Acts: Lukan Narrative and Graeco-Roman Discourse* (Atlanta: Society of Biblical Literature Symposium Series, 2003), pp. 105–37.

Schwelb, Egon, "Crimes against Humanity," *British Yearbook of International Law* 23 (1946), pp. 178–226.

Scott, James Brown, *The Catholic Conception of International Law: Francisco De Vitoria, Founder of the Modern Law of Nations, Francisco Suárez, Founder of the Modern Philosophy of Law in General and in Particular of the Law of Nations, a Critical Examination and a Justified Appreciation* (Washington, D.C.: Georgetown University Press, 1934).

Selden, John, *Mare Clausum, Seu De Dominio Maris Libri Duo* (London: Will.

Stensbeii pro Richardo Meighen, 1636).

————, *Of the Dominion, or, Ownership of the Sea, Two Books*, trans. Marchimont Nedham (London: William Du Gard, 1652).

Semmes, Raphael, *Memories of Service Afloat During the War Between the States* (Baltimore, MD: Kelly, Piet & Co., 1869).

Semple, Ellen Churchill, "Pirate Coasts of the Mediterranean," *Geographical Review* 2.2 (1916), pp. 134–51.

Seneca the Elder, *Declamations*, 2 vols., trans. M. Winterbottom (Cambridge: Harvard University Press, 1974).

Senior, C. M., *A Nation of Pirates: English Piracy in Its Heyday* (New York: Crane, Russak & Company, 1976.)

Sestier, Jules M., *La piraterie dans l'antiquité* (Paris: A. Marescq Aîné, 1880).

Shaw, Brent D., "Bandits in the Roman Empire," *Past and Present* 105 (1984), pp. 3–52.

Siber, Heinrich, *Das Führeramt des August*, Abhandlung der philologisch-historischen Klasse der sächsischen Akademie der Wissenschaften, vol. 44 (Leipzig: S. Hirzel, 1940).

Simbula, Pinuccia Franca, "Îles, corsaires et pirates dans la Méditerranée médiévale," *Médiévales* 47 (2004), pp. 17–30.

Sorel, Jean-Marc, "Existe-t-il une définition universelle du terrorisme?" in T. Christakis, K. Bannlier, O. Corten, and B. Delcourt (eds.), *Le droit international face au terrorisme* (Ed. Paris: Pédone, 2002), pp. 35–68.

Stark, Francis Raymond, "The Abolition of Privateering and the Declaration of Paris," *Studies in History, Economics and Public Law* 8.3 (1897), pp. 222–383.

Stehr, Michael, *Piraterie und Terror auf See: Nicht-staaliche Gewalt auf dem Weltmeeren 1990 bis 2004* (Berlin: Verlag Dr. Köster, 2004).

Steinmayr, Gabriele, "Sviluppi semantici della base *latro* in Grecia e in Roma," *Atti e memorie dell'Academia di Verona* (1955–1956), pp. 151–63.

Stiel, Paul, *Der Tatbestand der Piraterie nach geltendem Völkerrecht unter vergleichender Berücksichtigung der Landesgesetzgebungen*, Staats-Und Völkerrechtliche Abhandlungen, vol. 2 (Leipzig: Duncker & Humblot, 1905).

Stoerk, F. *Nouveau recueil général de traités*, vol. 26 (Leipzig: Librairie Dieterich, 1902).

Stoneman, Richard, *The Greek Alexander Romance* (London: Penguin Books, 1991).

Selections from Three Works of Francisco Suárez, S. J.: De Legibus, ac Deo legislatore 1612; Defensio fidei catholicae, et apostolicae adversus anglicanae sectae errors, 1613; De triplici virtute theologica, fide, spe, et charitate, 1612, trans. Gwladys L. Williams, Ammi Brown and John Waldron, rev. Henry Davis, S. J. and an introduction by James Brown Scott (Oxford, UK: Clarendon Press, 1944), 2 vols.

Summers, Walter C., "Notes on the *Controversiae* of the Elder Seneca," *The Classical Quarterly* 5.1 (1911), pp. 17–23.

Sundberg, Jacon W. F., "Piracy: Air and Sea," *De Paul Law Review* 20 (1971), pp. 337–435.

Syme, Ronald, "Observations on the Province of Cilicia," in W. M. Calder and Josef Keil (eds.), *Anatolian Studies Presented to W. H. Buckler* (Manchester: Manchester University Press, 1939), pp. 299–322.

Szanto, E., "Asylia," in Georg Wissowa (ed.), *Paulys Real-Encyclopädie der Classischen Altertumswissenschaft*, vol. 4 (Stuttgart: Mtezler, 1896), pp. 1879–81.

Tassel, Yves, "Terrorisme, piraterie et guerre sous le rapport de l'assurance maritime," *Annuaire de droit maritime et océanique* 23.5 (2005), pp. 86–94.

Taverner, Ferran Valls i (ed.), *Consolat de mar*, 3 vols. (Barcelona: Editorial Barcino, 1930–1933).

Tenenti, Alberto, "I corsari in mediterraneo all'inizio del cinquecento," *Rivista Storica Italiana* 72 (1960), pp. 234–87.

———, *Venezia e i corsari, 1680–1615* (Bari: Laterza, 1961).

———, "Venezia e la pirateria nel levante: 1300 c. – 1460 c.," in Agostino Pertusi (ed.), *Venezia e il Levante fino al secolo XV* (Florence: Olschki, 1973), pp. 705–71.

Thomas, Yan, "*Imago Naturae*: Note sur l'institutionnalité de la nature à Rome," *Théologie et droit dans la science politique de l'état moderne: Actes de la table ronde organisée par l'École française de Rome avec le concours du CNRS, 12–14 Novembre 1987* (Rome: École française de Rome, 1991), pp. 201–27.

———, "*Fictio Legis*: L'empire de la fiction romaine et ses limites médiévales," *Droit* 21 (1995), pp. 17–64.

———, "Le sujet de droit, la personne et la nature: Sur la critique contemporaine du sujet de droit," *Le débat* 100 (1998), pp. 85–107.

Thomas, Yan and Olivier Cayla, *Du droit de ne pas naître: À propos de l'affaire Perruche* (Paris: Gallimard, 2002).

Thomson, Janice E., *Mercenaries, Pirates, and Sovereigns: Extraterritorial Violence in Early Modern Europe* (Princeton, NJ: Princeton University Press, 1994).

Thucydides, *The Pelaponnesan War: The Complete Hobbes Translation*, ed. David Grene (Chicago: University of Chicago Press, 1989).

Timbal, Pierre-Clément, "Les Lettres de marque dans le droit de la France Médiévale," *Recueils de la société Jean Bodin* 10.2 (1958), pp. 109–38.

Touret, Corinne, *La piraterie au vingtième siècle: Piraterie maritime et aérienne* (Paris: Éditions Montchrestien, 1998).

Turner, Robert F., "State Responsibility and the War on Terror: The Legacy of Thomas Jefferson and the Barbary Pirates," *Chicago Journal of International Law* 4.1 (2003), pp. 121–40.

Triepel, H. (ed.), *Nouveau recueil general de traités*, vol. 3 (Leipzig: Librairie Dieterich).

Twiss, Sir Trevor (ed.), *Monumenta Juridica* (London: Longman & Co., 1873).

Unali, Anna, *Mariners, Pirates i corsaris catalans a l'època medieval*, trans. Maria Teresa Ferrer i Mallol and Maria Antònia Oliver (Barcelona: Edicions de la Magrana, 1986).

Various, *Modern Germany in Relation to the Great War, by Various German Authors*, trans. William Wallce Whitelock (New York: Mitchell Kennerly, 1916).

———, *Thesaurus Linguae Latinae, editus issu et auctoritate consili ab academiis societatibusque diversarum nationalum electi*, 10 vols. (Lepzig: Teubner, 1981).

Vattel, Emerich de, *Le droit des gens, ou Principes de la loi naturelle, appliqués à la conduite et aux affaires des nations et des souverains* (Amsterdam: E. van Harreveld, 1758).

———, *The Law of Nations, or the Principles of Natural Law Applied to the Conduct and to the Affairs of Nations and of Sovereigns*, trans. Charles G. Fenwick (Washington, D.C.: Carnegie Instutution of Washington, 1916).

Vernant, Jean-Pierre (ed.), *Problèmes de la guerre en Grèce ancienne* (Paris and The Hague: Mouton, 1968).

Verne, Jules, *Vingt mille lieues sous les mers*, ed. Jacques Noiray (Paris: Folio Gallimard, 2005).

Versnel, H. S., *Triumphus: An Inquiry into the Origin, Development and Meaning of the Roman Triumph* (Leiden: Brill, 1970).

Villar, Roger, *Piracy Today: Robbery and Violence at Sea since 1980* (Portsmouth: Carmichael and Sweet, 1985).

Villon, François, *Oeuvres*, ed. Auguste Lognon and Lucien Foulet (Paris:

Champion, 1992).

Vitoria, Francisco de, *Political Writings*, ed. Anthony Pagden and Jeremy Lawrence (Cambridge, UK: Cambridge University Press, 1991).

Vitoria, Francisco de, *De Iure Belli*, ed. Carlo Galli (Bari: Laterza, 2005).

Voci, Pasquale, *Piccolo manuale di diritto romano* (Milano: Giuffrè, 1979).

Walker, Wyndham L., "Territorial Waters: The Canon Shot Rule," *British Yearbook of International Law* 22 (1945), pp. 210–31.

Walther, Henri, *L'affaire du "Lotus"; ou, De l'abordage hauturier en droit pénal international* (Paris: Les Éditions Internationales, 1928).

Walzer, Michael (ed.), *Regicide and Revolution: Speeches at the Trial of Louis XVI* (New York: Columbia University Press, 1993).

Ward, A. M., "Caesar and the Pirates," *American Journal of Ancient History* 2 (1977), pp. 27–36.

Watson, Alan, *The Law of Property in the Later Roman Republic* (Oxford, UK: Clarendon Press, 1968).

———, *International Law in Archaic Rome* (Baltimore: The Johns Hopkins University Press, 1993).

Watteville, Jacques de, *La piraterie aérienne: Étude de droit international et de droit suisse* (Lausanne: Imprimerie Vaudoise, 1978).

Weber, Max, *Gesammelte politische Schriften*, 5 vols., ed. Johannes Winckelmann (Tübingen: Mohr, 1988).

Welwood, William, *An Abridgement of All Sea-Lawes, Gathered Forth of All Writings and Monuments, Which Are to Be Found among Any People or Nation Upon the Coasts of the Greate Ocean and Mediterranean Sea: And Specially Ordered and Disposed for the Use and Benefit of All Beneuolent Sea-Farers, within His Maiesties Dominions of Great Britanne, Ireland, and the Adiacent Isles Thereof* (London: T. Man, 1613).

———, *De Dominio Maris, Iuribusque ad Dominium Praecipe Spectantibus Assertio Brevis* (Cosmpoli: G. Fonti-Filiusus, 1615).

Westlake, H. D., "Seaborne Raids in Periclean Strategy," *Classical Quarterly* 39.3–4 (1945), pp. 75–84.

Whatley, B. A., "Historical Sketch of the Law of Piracy," *Law Magazine and Review* 3 (1874), pp. 536–55.

Wilcken, Ulrich, "Zur Entwicklung der römischen Diktatur," *Abhandlungen der Preusssischen Akademie* 11 (1940), pp. 3–32.

Wilhelm, A., "Die lokrische Mädcheninschrift," *Jahreshefte der österreichischen archäologischen Instututs in Wien* 14 (1911), pp. 163–256.

Wilke, Christiane, "A Particular Universality: Universal Jurisdiction for Crimes against Humanity in Domestic Courts," *Constellations* 12.1 (2005), pp. 83–102.

Wilson, George Grafton, "The Submarine and Place of Safety," *The American Journal of International Law* 35.3 (1941), pp. 496–97.

Winstedt, R., and P. E. Josselin de Jong, "The Maritime Laws of Malaca," *Journal of the Malayan Branch of the Royal Asiatic Society, Singapore* 29.3 (1956), pp. 22–59.

Wolf, John B., *The Barbary Coast: Algiers under the Turks* (New York: Norton, 1979).

Wolff, Christian, *The Law of Nations Treated According to a Scientific Method*, trans. Joseph H. Drake (Washington, D.C.: Carnegie Endowment for International Peace, 1934).

———, *Jus Gentium Methodo Scientifica Pertractatum, in Quo Jus Gentium Naturale Ab Eo, Quod Voluntarii, Pactitii Et Consuetudinarii Est, Accurate Distinguitur* (1749), in Jean École et al. (eds.), *Gesammelte Werke*, vol. 25 (Hildesheim, New York: Georg Olms, 1962).

Wortley, B. A., *"Pirata Non Mutat Dominium,"* *British Yearbook of International Law* 24 (1947), pp. 258–72.

Wynn, William, *The Life of Sir Leoline Jenkins, Judge of the High-Court of Admiralty...Ambassador and Plenipotentiary for the General Peace at Cologn and Nimegue...And a Compleat Series of Letters,...Never before Published*, 2 vols. (London: Joseph Downing; William Taylor; William and John Innys; and John Osborn, 1724).

Ziebarth, Erich, *Beiträge zur Geschichte des Seeraubs und Seehandels im alten Griechenland* (Hamburg: De Gruyter, 1929).

Ziegler, Karl-Heinz, "Pirata communis hostis omnium," in Manfred Harder and Georg Thielmann (eds.), *De Iustitia et Iure: Fesgabe für Ulrich von Lübtow* (Berlin: Duncker & Humblot, 1980), pp. 93–103.

Zimmermann, Franz, "Kallirhoes Verkauf durch Theron: Ein juristisch-philologische Betrachtung zu Chariton," in Johannes Irmscher (ed.), *Aus der byzantinischen Arbeit der Deutschen Demokratischen Republik* (Berlin: Akademie-Verlag, 1957), pp. 72–81.

Zink, Michel (ed.), *Le roman d'Apollonius de Tyr* (Paris: Librairie Générale

Française, 2006).

Ziskind, Jonathan, "The International Legal Status of the Sea in Antiquity," *Acta Orientalia* 35 (1973), pp. 35–49.

———, "International Law and Ancient Sources: Grotius and Selden," *The Review of Politics* 35.4 (1973), pp. 537–59.

Zitelmann, Ernst, "The War and International Law," trans. Mitchell Kennerly, *Modern Germany in Relation to the Great War, by Various German Authors* (New York, 1916), pp. 584–614.

Zouche, Richard, *Iuris et Iudicii Fecialis, Sive, Iuris Inter Gentes, et Quaestionum de Eodem Explicatio, Qua Quae ad Pacem et Bellum Inter Diversos Principes, aut Populos Spectant, ex Praecipuis Historico-Jure-Peritis, Exhibetur* (Oxford, UK: T. Robinson, 1650).

———, *An Exposition of Fecial Law and Procedure, or of Law between Nations, and Questions Concerning the Same*, trans. J.L. Brierly (Washington, D.C.: Carnegie Endowment for International Peace, 1911).

Index

Zone Books series design by Bruce Mau
Typesetting by Meighan Gale
Printed and bound by Maple-Vail on Sebago acid-free paper